CENTER
STREET

LARGE
PRINT

Also by Scott McEwen

American Sniper (with Chris Kyle)
Sniper Elite
Target America

Also by Rich Miniter

Leading from behind
Mastermind
Disinformation
Shadow War
Losing bin Laden
The Myth of Market Share

EYES
ON
TARGET

INSIDE STORIES FROM
THE BROTHERHOOD
OF THE U.S. NAVY SEALS

SCOTT McEWEN *and*
RICHARD MINITER

CENTER STREET

LARGE ■ **PRINT**

Center Street
Hachette Book Group
237 Park Avenue
New York, NY 10017

www.CenterStreet.com

Printed in the United States of America

RRD-C

First edition: March 2014
10 9 8 7 6 5 4 3 2 1

Center Street is a division of Hachette Book Group, Inc.
The Center Street name and logo are trademarks of Hachette Book Group, Inc.

The Hachette Speakers Bureau provides a wide range of authors for speaking events. To find out more, go to www.HachetteSpeakersBureau.com or call (866) 376-6591.

The publisher is not responsible for websites (or their content) that are not owned by the publisher.

Library of Congress Cataloging-in-Publication Data

Miniter, Richard.
  Eyes on target : inside stories from the brotherhood of the U.S. Navy SEALs / Richard Miniter and Scott McEwen. — First edition.
        pages cm
  Includes bibliographical references.
  ISBN 978-1-4555-7569-5 (hardcover) — ISBN 978-1-4555-4966-5 (large print hardcover) — ISBN 978-1-4555-7568-8 (ebook) — ISBN 978-1-4789-5240-4 (audiobook)   1. United States. Navy. SEALs—History.   2. United States. Navy—Commando troops—History.   3. Benghazi Consulate Attack, Banghazi, Libya, 2012.   4. Special operations (Military science)—United States—History—21st century.   I. McEwen, Scott.   II. Title.   III. Title: Inside stories from the brotherhood of the U.S. Navy SEALs.

  VG87.M57 2014
  359.9'84—dc23
                                                          2013047350

To the brotherhood of Navy SEALs who have devoted their lives to the defense of this nation. All gave some, some gave all.

Contents

Introduction ix

CHAPTER 1 The Froggy Origins of the
Navy SEALs 1

CHAPTER 2 The Violent Birth of SEAL Team Six 27

CHAPTER 3 From Pirates to Professionals 58

CHAPTER 4 Drago's War 73

CHAPTER 5 Afghanistan: Operation Red Wings 93

CHAPTER 6 Fallujah: The Perfect Op That
Led to Prosecutions 115

CHAPTER 7 Benghazi, Libya: SEALs Alone 142

CHAPTER 8 Benghazi 911: When SEALs Answer
the Call 168

CHAPTER 9 The Rescue That Wasn't 192

CHAPTER 10 Benghazi Timeline 237

CHAPTER 11 The Teams: Why the Unique
Culture of the SEALs Matters 259

CONTENTS

APPENDIX   Interim Progress Report   281

Notes   329

Glossary   345

Bibliography   351

Acknowledgments   357

Introduction

The skinny guy on the bar stool was a minute away from being mauled.

It was already getting late in the dimly lit bar in Lakeside, California, a place where tattooed men buy beer for a dollar and drink from the bottle. It was a favorite of bikers and recent parolees, morose cowboys, and sailors waiting to be discharged. It had seen its share of bar fights.

As Don Zub, who had served in the Navy SEALs, downed another shot, his eye zoomed in on the skinny guy's T-shirt. He spotted a small black raven insignia. A semisecret symbol of the SEALs. It was like a Crip eyeing a Blood.

The only thing that SEALs hate more than terrorists is "fake SEALs"—civilians, or even other service members, who pretend to be a part of their sacred brotherhood. Fake SEALs can get their ribs broken, their noses smashed, and, if the bouncers are not quick-footed enough, their windpipes flattened.

Zub's temperature was already rising. One of us— Scott McEwen—had seen it happen before, and now he was watching it again.

If the short, skinny guy and his brunette girlfriend knew what was coming, they didn't let on. They pretended not to see Zub's bulging eyes or hear the menace in his voice. "I think I recognize that shirt. Where did you get it?"

The skinny guy hardly looked up. "I got it from the owner of the bar."

The Raven is a Virginia Beach bar—and more than a bar, it is a symbol. A SEAL bar where male outsiders aren't welcome. A secret cave where SEALs commune.

The brunette said nothing. She had seen this kind of thing before.

"Oh yeah?" said Zub, doubt creeping into his voice. "Where is it located?"

The skinny guy's voice was still carefully casual. "Virginia Beach."

Zub wasn't backing down. To the bartender or any passersby, this might have seemed like an ordinary conversation. But it wasn't. It was a verbal dogfight. One wrong answer and fists would fly. "How do you know the owner?"

"I used to work with him."

"*Where* did you work with him?"

"In the military."

"How long did you work with him?"

"Fifteen years. I used to babysit his kids."

Zub was more certain than ever that he had spotted a fake SEAL. His fingers were balling into fists. "I used to work with the same guys as him."

The skinny guy said nothing. What was there to say?

Zub pressed. "What kind of work did you do together?"

"I really don't want to talk about it."

Zub pulled out a new Spyderco knife, flipped it open, and locked the blade. It flashed in the overhead light.

The skinny guy pretended not to notice the knife. At one time, it was a standard-issue tactical blade among the SEALs, who used it to cut away parachute cords and underwater entanglements. It, too, was a kind of totem.

Zub reached over and slammed the blade into the bar.

The knifepoint landed between the brunette's small hands and stayed there, planted into the wood of the bar. The knife was a challenge. No one moved. The brunette did not even move her hands. She had seen this kind of thing before.

McEwen had noticed both the skinny guy's non-reaction and the brunette's careful nonchalance. Urgently, he turned to face his SEAL friend. "Don, he's real. The chick's real. Back off!"

Zub looked at him and then eyeballed the skinny guy.

Then the skinny guy spoke. "My name is Johnny Walker. I was a Plank Owner in SEAL Team Six with Dick Marcinko."

Marcinko founded SEAL Team Six, perhaps the world's best-known elite fighting unit, and Marcinko frequented the Raven, the legendary bar in Virginia Beach that was a longtime SEAL hangout. It was the kind of bar where no one called the cops. A Plank Owner is a founding member of the U.S. Navy SEAL unit. It meant that Walker was handpicked by the founder of SEAL Team Six and had hung out at Marcinko's favorite bar. And he literally got the coveted T-shirt. He was, therefore, SEAL royalty.

Zub gave his name and announced that he was a member of SEAL Team One, sometimes called "No Fun One." He had served from 1975 to 1979 on the West Coast. Walker had joined "the teams"—as the SEALs call themselves—later and had served on the East Coast.

The tension rushed away, like steam streaming from a pinhole in a pipe.

Zub bought drinks, and the men swapped stories. Two Navy SEALs had met and challenged each other and the bonds of brotherhood were established.

* * *

This was one of the greeting rituals of the world's smallest and strangest fraternities, the U.S. Navy SEALs. If you are a member, it doesn't matter where or when you served. You can show up uninvited at the funerals of the youngest or oldest veterans and be hailed as a brother by total strangers. You can phone another SEAL whom you've never met and be taken for a drink. You might show up to mow the lawn of a widow whose husband died before you served. The bonds are strong partly because the group is so small. There have been fewer than three thousand U.S. Navy SEALs in the history of the world and about half of them are still alive. They all know, or know of, each other. The SEALs call themselves a "brotherhood," and they actually are one.

The brotherhood is forged by one of the most demanding selection processes on Earth—Basic Underwater Demolition/SEAL, known universally as "BUD/S." Even being selected for BUD/S means running a gauntlet of approvals inside the U.S. Navy. Once a sailor, Marine, or other service member is cleared to attend BUD/S, the climb to becoming a SEAL gets steeper and harder. Chuck Pfarrer, who was a member of SEAL Team Six, recalls his first day at BUD/S. A humorless Navy officer stepped to the podium in a small concrete room at a SEAL base in Coronado, California. He told the men to look left and look right. Each man did. In the next few weeks, the officer said, "almost two-thirds of you are going to quit." The high washout rate was expected. He said it without regret, as a simple cold fact. He was daring the men to meet the highest standards and expecting that only a few of them would.

The training was demanding enough to persuade many hard men to ring the bell to quit. "I've seen Olympic-quality athletes wash out," Pfarrer said.

The Navy is happy to see them go. What defines a SEAL is his unwillingness to ever, ever give up. It requires extraordinary will in all three aspects of human existence: body, mind, and spirit. Very, very few men are dominant in all three.

A Navy corpsman, who supervises the medical care for SEALs during BUD/S, told us: "Injuries that I would usually send someone to the hospital for, in BUD/S I just patch up. Those guys don't want to quit."

Still, some are forced to—regardless of their determination or ability to succeed. Broken legs, smashed arms, cuts requiring more than a dozen stitches...

Medical reasons can knock as many as one of every five applicants out of BUD/S. Usually, men given medical leave are begging the corpsman to put a little tape over their cracked ribs and assuring the medical officer that they are fine...as the stretcher carries them off.

Those who survive and graduate from BUD/S realize two truths: they are now members of a small, exclusive group; and they are part of a larger, profoundly important tradition. Their class numbers and names are painted on a wall at Coronado, alongside the class numbers and names of the men who came before them.

Still, BUD/S graduates are not yet SEALs. Another training program, SEAL Qualification Training, known invariably as "SQT," transforms the BUD/S graduate into a SEAL. Some call it "BUD/S on paper." In that months-long course, students learn Navy history, ballistics math, ocean currents, enemy ideologies, and other useful subjects. After months of training and written tests, the men who survive receive the distinctive pin known officially as "the trident" and unofficially as "the Budweiser"—a brass-plated pin of an eagle with an anchor and Neptune's trident in its claw. Like Masai warriors, SEALs have brutal rites of passage. The informal part of the SEAL initiation process usually involves pounding the metal pin into the new

SEAL's bare chest. The wound and the blood are part of the rite. No one complains as the blood trickles and drips off his pectoral muscles. It is a moment of joy and pain, fused paradoxically together, like the mixed nature of victory in combat. It is a feeling SEALs will experience throughout their careers.

Still, the process is not over. SEALs are constantly under observation by chief petty officers, whose watchful evaluations are merciless. Months after SQT and specialized schooling, new SEALs may be shifted to an operational unit and still treated as rookies because they have not yet endured hours of combat. Sometimes they are called "fresh meat." Every conversation, every training evolution, every "down range" operation is a test. SEALs are endlessly examining themselves and their comrades, hunting for dangerous weaknesses.

At each stage, the ideal of brotherhood is forged, hammered, tempered, and sharpened.

* * *

For almost forty years, their unique ethos was unwritten, passed along by gruff instructions from chief petty officers and the molds of men who came before. When it wasn't said, it was shown. It was the sum of things that were quietly praised and the body of things noisily ridiculed. SEALs have a vivid and vicious sense of humor; sharp words are meant to point out a path. The sensitive and the weak are weeded out early. "If you can't take it," one SEAL said, "get the fuck out."

By 2005, the backgrounds of SEAL officers had changed. More officers were graduates of the U.S. Naval Academy at Annapolis and fewer were "mustangs," officers who had come up through the ranks. It began to seem natural that the SEALs would have a written credo, much like a corporation's vision statement or the U.S. Army Rangers' written creed. (SEALs and Rangers sometimes operate together.)

Mark Devine, a SEAL officer, was part of the team (composed of both officers and enlisted men) who helped put the unwritten ethos in black-letter type. It was a long, soul-searching process, debated in dull conference rooms and late-night bars. Akin to the operating ethos of the teams, it was a product of many heads, the sum of many experiences. In the end, the code summarizes SEAL culture as carefully, specifically, and expertly as a mission plan.

The SEAL Code

- Loyalty to Country, Team, and Teammate
- Serve with Honor and Integrity On and Off the Battlefield

- Ready to Lead, Ready to Follow, Never Quit
- Take Responsibility for your Actions and the Actions of your Teammates
- Excel as Warriors through Discipline and Innovation
- Train for War, Fight to Win, Defeat our Nation's Enemies
- Earn your Trident every day

United States Navy SEAL—The SEAL Creed

In times of war or uncertainty there is a special breed of warrior ready to answer our Nation's call. A common man with uncommon desire to succeed.

Forged by adversity, he stands alongside America's finest special operations forces to serve his country, the American people, and protect their way of life.

I am that man.

My Trident is a symbol of honor and heritage. Bestowed upon me by the heroes that have gone before, it embodies the trust of those I have sworn to protect. By wearing the Trident I accept the responsibility of my chosen profession and way of life. It is a privilege that I must earn every day.

My loyalty to Country and Team is beyond reproach. I humbly serve as a guardian to my fel-

low Americans always ready to defend those who are unable to defend themselves. I do not advertise the nature of my work, nor seek recognition for my actions. I voluntarily accept the inherent hazards of my profession, placing the welfare and security of others before my own.

I serve with honor on and off the battlefield. The ability to control my emotions and my actions, regardless of circumstance, sets me apart from other men.

Uncompromising integrity is my standard. My character and honor are steadfast. My word is my bond.

We expect to lead and be led. In the absence of orders I will take charge, lead my teammates, and accomplish the mission. I lead by example in all situations.

I will never quit. I persevere and thrive on adversity. My Nation expects me to be physically harder and mentally stronger than my enemies. If knocked down, I will get back up, every time. I will draw on every remaining ounce of strength to protect my teammates and to accomplish our mission. I am never out of the fight.

We demand discipline. We expect innovation. The lives of my teammates and the success of our *mission depend on me—my technical skill, tactical proficiency, and attention to detail. My training is never complete.*

We train for war and fight to win. I stand ready to bring the full spectrum of combat power to bear in order to achieve my mission and the goals established by my country. The execution of my duties will be swift and violent when required yet guided by the very principles that I serve to defend.

Brave men have fought and died building the proud tradition and feared reputation that I am bound to uphold. In the worst of conditions, the legacy of my teammates steadies my resolve and silently guides my every deed. I will not fail.

In short, SEALs are supposed to be superheroes out of the old American playbook: physically fit, morally sound, and humbly quiet about their achievements. SEALs must follow orders and, in the absence of orders, improvise to save the lives of their teammates or accomplish their mission. A SEAL is an ordinary man who emerges, trains to an extraordinary standard, serves his country, and anonymously returns to civilian life. He aspires to be an unknown hero, whose record serves to inspire the next generation of SEALs, in a perpetually renewed tradition.

This is their culture and this is the story they tell themselves about themselves. And it is true.

But it is not the whole story of their unique culture, which is both precious and strangely fragile. As we shall see in the course of this book, politics and bureaucracy—the twin curses of the SEALs' many successes—threaten to destroy what is unique about this elite unit.

A culture is never the product of abstract reasoning; it is a living, organic thing that forms and grows through experience, some of it sweet, more of it bitter. Cutting out parts that seem unreasonable to outsiders is always a dangerous undertaking. Is the "unnecessary" organ an appendix or a lung? The risk of operating on a living culture is that one can't tell the difference between a vital organ or an unneeded appendage, until after the operation, when the patient may be killed or crippled.

Nevertheless, SEAL culture is now facing several traumatic operations. These operations include unfounded prosecutions, oversight by those who have limited knowledge of special operations, and an overall attempt to impose political correctness on their ranks.

* * *

This is the first book to treat the U.S. Navy SEALs, whose storied history reaches back more than forty years and whose origins stretch back to World War II, as a character in its own right. Its exemplary individuals make up parts of an unusual and a unique whole. The teams, as the SEALs call themselves, have the arc of a single character: illustrious parents, daring birth, growing pains in its adolescent years, finding itself in the early twenties, and now, after a span of remarkable achievements, a crossroads. A midlife crisis.

By tracing the life of the SEALs as a unit, we aim to define its distinctive culture and to warn the nation against trying to tamper with it too drastically. The war on terror is increasingly a special-forces war—a battle of covert operatives dropped into hostile territories to kill or capture those who would dearly love to inflict another September 11 on the United States. The SEALs are the tip of the spear. If you dull its edge, it may not function. America and her allies would lose a key asset in its ability to wage the war on terror.

* * *

There is no predictable prototype for a Navy SEAL, even though the U.S. Navy has spent millions of dollars in research studies to find a formula. It costs the Navy more than one million dollars (measured in man-hours and equipment) to train a potential SEAL. If the Navy could discover which essential attributes enable a man to succeed in its demanding program, it could reduce the failure rate and save money. But it can't. There is no formula.

SEALs hail from all backgrounds. Some tower over six feet, but many are average sized. Some spent their childhoods in cold waters off the Northeastern and Northwestern United States; others had never seen the ocean until basic training. A few come from illustrious military families, many more from families who previously served only due to a draft. Some were award-winning athletes in high school or college; others had never worn a team jersey until they joined the Navy. Some had served in the U.S. Navy or the Marine Corps; others came straight from civilian life. Some were the sons of millionaires; others subsisted on food stamps. Some were straight-A students; others barely graduated from high school. Many were native born; yet some of the most distinguished were born overseas. There are SEALs of every race and many of mixed race. The only thing that the successful graduates of BUD/S and SQT have in common is an unwillingness to quit when their bodies were spent, their brains exhausted, and the odds seemed insuperable. What makes a SEAL is not genetics, background, education, or even aptitude—it is a quality of character that the men themselves are not sure that they possess until they demonstrate it. There is no formula for this.

* * *

Once you spend some time with the SEALs, as we have, their internal inconsistencies become obvious.

They have covert identities and can be very tight-lipped. Ask a SEAL who doesn't know you, what he does for a living, and he is likely to say that he is "in the military" or "in the Navy" and leave it at that. Yet, once they are among their teammates, they can be very free with their opinions—mercilessly taunting a fellow SEAL who failed in a training evolution or boasting about stealing a girl away from an ordinary mortal. They have little patience for any of their own who miss the standard by even an inch. One SEAL, who took three attempts in order to pass BUD/S, was called a "turd" because he was slow in training or took longer to prepare his gear. Later he was called a "shit bird" because he frequently had driving accidents with a SEAL minisub off of Hawaii. He later won a Navy Cross and other honors. These blunt assessments are common among SEALs. They have no time for "happy talk" or "blowing sunshine up your ass." SEALs are brutal, because small errors cost lives in training and combat.

Even SEAL officers are brutally and bluntly evaluated by enlisted men. One SEAL officer, whose name is omitted because he is still on active duty, was described to us by a fellow teammate. "He really was a detriment, to be frank. He was so stupid and he was not a top performer," said Carl Higbie, a SEAL Team Ten member. "He could shoot straight, yeah, but his reasoning skills were not to the caliber of a Navy SEAL." These kinds of comments are not rare among SEALs, if the men believe a teammate does not measure up.

SEALs are competitive and praise each other in quantitative terms. They will talk about their teammates in terms of body weight or body-fat percentage. They boast about who can bench the most, swim the longest, or shoot the straightest. Cars, stereo, and computer equipment are constant sources of competition among them. And, among SEALs of a certain age, so are girls. SEALs are always keeping score.

They are not politically correct, and enlisted SEALs are often puzzled by the entire notion that certain words or phrases are off limits. If a man has proven himself, words should be harmless to him. If he has not, he has bigger problems than words.

The constant joking and taunting nature of SEAL banter excludes any kind of politically correct restrictions, especially when officers aren't around. When they do run into political correctness, which is common on civilian college campuses, they tend to refer to it as "bullshit." SEAL officers often try to keep the comments of their men in bounds—a constant struggle. Still, the officers realize the dangers of being zealous in policing speech. SEAL teams are not political coalitions and every man must be free to express a view in order for missions to succeed.

Tattoos are as common among SEALs as they are among South Sea Islanders. But sometimes they lead to trouble. After a stint in the U.S. Army's 101st Airborne Division, Denny Chalker joined the Navy and was admitted to BUD/S. There instructors spotted his tattoo on his arm ("God is my jump master") and they used it in place of his name. "Instead of 'Chalker' being called out, it was "Where is 'God is my jump master'?"[1]

Many will admit to being adrenaline junkies. To relax, they race motorcycles, surf big waves, ski black diamond trails, or scale icy mountains. Brandon Webb, a former SEAL Team Three member and SEAL Head Sniper instructor, bought a thirty-five-year-old Soviet Yak-52 trainer aircraft. It is old, poorly built, and has few flight instruments. It had crashed before. He would often hold mock dogfights with former SEALs in other aircraft. When Webb showed a Hollywood producer a picture of his plane, the man asked: "You actually go up in that?"

* * *

Though most SEALs are not Irish, many of their rituals revolve around fighting, drinking, and death.

Bar fights are common. At one time, so were fights on duty. In the 1970s, when a dispute started, someone would say: "Take it behind the conex box," Zub recalls.

The conex box was a shipping container at Coronado that was too high and too long for officers to see around or over. It was a black hole where SEALs would go to fight SEALs. The routine was always the same. Two men would go behind the box and emerge, a few minutes later, bloody, dirty, and sandy. No one would join them to watch, and no one would ever talk about it. "There was no bragging. It was just kept real quiet," Zub said.

But it settled things.

Another SEAL, Ryan Job, put it this way: "Despite what your momma told you, violence does solve problems." (After being shot in the face in Ramadi, Iraq, Job died on an operating table in Phoenix, Arizona.)

Today, fights still occur, but they are much more

likely to happen off base. On-duty fights can now lead to dismissal from the SEAL teams or even courts-martial.

SEALs drink at reunions, graduations, and deaths, and after work. It remains an informal weeding-out process. "There are team guys and then there are guys in the teams," Zub said. There are guys with a strong sense of brotherhood, but there are some who merely do their jobs.

Commander Dick Marcinko, the founder of SEAL Team Six, was legendary for drinking with the enlisted men under his command. After a hard training evolution in the waters off Virginia Beach, he would invite his men to a dive bar. (Later, he bought a nearby bar, the iconic bar called the Raven.) They would stay until closing time and sometimes beyond.

Zub first met Marcinko in 1982, when a Navy buddy introduced them in a San Diego bar named El Capitan.

Marcinko didn't act like any naval officer that Zub had ever seen before. While other Navy men could be hard drinkers and admirers of female bodies, Marcinko took it to a whole new level. He bragged about out-drinking men and bedding women. He pulled out what Zub remembers as a "wad of money," and he gave Zub and his two former Navy buddies a few hundred bucks each. As the drinking progressed, Marcinko revealed that he was wearing a small-caliber pistol on each ankle and two knives hidden on his body. Then he fanned out a stack of fake identification cards. "It was wild," said Zub.

They went on a tour of bars on Shelter Island and strip clubs that ended at dawn.

In the 1970s and 1980s, after-work drinking sessions would either strengthen the bonds among men or mark out the man who could not be a team player. Swimming in alcohol together, for building trust among the SEALs, was once as important as swimming in water together. Drinking wasn't just accepted, it was encouraged. "Alcohol is a truth serum. You've got a problem with somebody, you keep it under your hat. You get drinking, the hat comes off," Zub said. Those drinking sessions would settle disputes and reestablish equilibrium.

In those days, SEALs seemed safest in rough seas and most at risk when the water was small, flat, and cubed. Drinking caused divorces, DUIs, and even deaths.

Now drinking is much more carefully done. Just as attitudes about drinking have changed in American society, so have they shifted among the SEALs. Today a single DUI offense usually leads to dismissal from the SEAL teams. In 2010, Virginia Beach police stopped a new SEAL. The legal blood-alcohol limit was 0.08 at the time. The SEAL, who submitted to a Breathalyzer, was measured at 0.09. He had been in the teams for only a few weeks, and he knew that the ticket would cost him his career. "You don't have to do this," he pleaded. He briefly explained the training and the sacrifice that got him to that point and the fact that he had only two beers in an hour. The cop, as he recalls, was heartless. "Yes, I do." He was exiled from the teams as soon as the officer-in-charge learned of his offense. He spent the rest of his time in the Navy aboard ship and left the service bitterly disappointed.

Once it was a badge of honor to have alcohol stashed in your locker or to sneak a drink on base. Today, even drinking in war zones is forbidden. SEALs still drink—it remains a vital part of their culture—but they do so off duty and off base, and they make sure that their girlfriend or a taxi driver takes them home. Not getting caught is also a key part of the SEAL way.

* * *

SEALs are often treated as the bastard stepchildren of the Navy. Deployed outside the United States, they often grow long, shaggy beards and wander around base in flip-flops and cutoffs. David B. Rutherford, a SEAL Team One combat medic, remembers walking into a chow hall outside of Kandahar, Afghanistan, in 2002. A full-bird colonel started shouting at Rutherford and his teammates to shave and wear appropriate desert "digital" camouflage uniforms—or go somewhere else.

Rutherford was returning from "an op" in the mountains that had lasted for seven months, directing air strikes against al Qaeda and Taliban fighters. "I don't even know the gross ordnance dropped. I lost track at five hundred thousand pounds" in the first few months. The flip-flops and the beards were essential for blending with their local allies and, therefore, not becoming a target for enemy snipers.

He just shook his head in disbelief at the colonel. "The ridiculousness that pollutes DoD [Department of Defense]," he says he thought.

Later, "Big Navy," what SEALs call the rest of the navy, managed to get his beard and take away his ability to operate in Afghanistan. A senior Navy officer was arriving to inspect SEAL Team One. His Master Chief told him the rank "deserved a show of respect." He was told to shave and wear a clean and complete uniform. It hurt his "operational readiness," he said, but he understood. "It is challenging to find the fusion between Big Army/Navy and SoF [Special Operations Forces]," he said.

SEALs pay a high price for their high performance. "We are the ultimate war fighters and dysfunctional human beings," Rutherford said. "It's two sides of the same coin."

He explains that many SEALs struggle to define themselves after they leave the teams. No one asks, he said, "What happens to the operator after the op?" He compared leaving the teams to leaving the MS-13 gang. "The commitment level and the violence level are similar," he said. Of course, SEALs aren't criminals. But their adjustment to civilian life can be hard and that posttraumatic stress syndrome is a genuine cost of battle.

SEALs also have a strange relationship with sleep. Two-man sniper teams will often hole up in a "hide" for two days, without food and with little water. One is always at the gun while the other sleeps. On a C-130 in Iraq, SEALs will lace their arms in the cargo netting to form a human hammock or simply lay flat on a shipping container. Within minutes after takeoff, they all will be asleep. On long flights, only the pilots will stay awake. SEALs will awaken only to pee in a bucket at the back of the plane and immediately return to sleep. It is known as "sleep discipline," the ability to stay alert when needed and to fall sleep within minutes.

SEALs don't usually learn languages like Green Berets and other special forces do; they often operate without words in any language. When sweeping buildings in Iraq, some SEALs operated alongside the Polish counterterrorist forces known as GROM. The Poles spoke very little English, and the SEALs spoke no Polish. Hand signals and eye movements allowed the teams to operate fluidly, shooting insurgents without speaking to each other.

Unlike other members of the Navy, SEALs are usually excellent shots. They drill constantly to maintain their accuracy and rate of fire. Marcinko told us that SEALs would routinely use some 3,500 rounds of ammunition per week in target practice. (By contrast, the average big city police department uses fifty rounds every year per officer in its qualification tests.) SEALs would use even more ammunition in "kill house" exercises, plywood buildings packed with obstacles and dummies that spring up in surprising places. SEALs would have a fraction of a second to decide if each dummy represented a civilian or a target and to place their rounds accurately. Their timing and accuracy was constantly evaluated. One of the key attributes of any SEAL is the rapid categorization—immediately classifying someone as a "threat or no threat," explains Ryan Zinke, a former SEAL Team Six assault element leader.

As a result, SEALs are likely the best close-quarters combat fighters in the world.

Over time, the missions of the SEALs would have them farther away from the waters from which the frogmen sprung. Today, in Afghanistan, a SEAL jokes that the only water near him is in his CamelBak, a plastic pouch with a long, strawlike drinking tube that is worn on the back. The frogs now operate far from the sea.

Like the samurai of a bygone age, SEALs often have personal relationships with their knives and firearms. Some still carry a Spyderco, but many prefer the 5½-inch Benchmade brand knife. It is a third hand, used for cutting line, slicing open food pouches, and sometimes silently dispatching a foe.

Few of the weapons used by SEALs are standard issue. A modified M-4 carbine is common, although the modifications are as individual as the SEALs themselves. Shotguns are often used for clearing rooms, especially pump-action Remington 870s. A SIG Sauer .45-caliber pistol, as a backup weapon, is considered a necessity. "Nothing has the stopping power of a forty-five," one SEAL told us. It replaced the M1911

A1, which didn't tend to survive saltwater conditions. The Beretta 92-F, named after SEAL Chuck Fellers, is another favorite.

SEALs often have extensive gun collections in their homes. Firearms are the tools of the trade, but they seem to also have a totemic value among SEALs. Most gun collections are measured in dozens and many in the hundreds.

An extraordinary pain threshold is assumed among SEALs—as is the ability to govern their emotions, especially fear. After one training evolution, one SEAL told another: "You're bleeding." With some surprise and some interest, the other said: "Oh yeah? From where?"

His comrade pointed to the blood running down his leg.

When other SEALs are told this story by one of us, they shrug. So?

Most telling is the SEALs' relationship with the bell during BUD/S. Ring the bell and you're out of the teams immediately. Officially, it is known as "Dropped by Request," or DOR.

The bell is always with them during basic training. At meals. At the obstacle course. In the exercise yard, known as "the grinder." On long beach runs, they haul it in a truck bed. At sea, it is in a nearby boat. It is always within reach, for a man ready to signal that he has had enough, that he is done.

When the men are running with heavy logs on their shoulders or struggling in the surf with hypothermia, the instructors taunt them: "Just ring the bell. There are doughnuts and hot coffee waiting."

"The reason that the bell exists is because when you're in battle, there is no bell," one SEAL instructor told us. "And we want to know who needs [that bell] and who doesn't."

The SEALs are composed entirely of men who saw the bell, heard its mournful clang, and refused to ring it. They refused to give up.

In the almost fifty-year existence of the U.S. Navy SEALs, not one has surrendered or been taken captive. The bell, in their mythology and in their lives, has done its job.

This is no accident. It is the result of a long history of fortunate accidents in the evolution of the SEALs. It is a culture made by the hammers of hard experience.

Their story begins on a dark beach, ill lit by moonlight.

EYES
ON
TARGET

CHAPTER 1

The Froggy Origins
of the Navy SEALs

Fort Pierce sits on a serpentine, sandy barrier island, several hours north of Palm Beach, Florida. Aside from a chain-linked fence around a string of Navy bunkers and buildings and a small town with a five-and-dime store and a few bars, it was uninhabited and alone. On a night in the winter of 1942, viewed from the sea, it was a desolate strip of palm trees washed by the cold Atlantic waves—much as the Spanish explorers might have seen it centuries earlier. No lights appeared on shore and the moon revealed no landmarks.

Swimming with the tide, men with blackened faces and air tanks on their backs swam up to the empty beach. They were met with large concrete Xs and barbed wire, painted to blend into the night.

Without a word, the frogmen began their work, cutting through obstacles.

The halo of a flashlight beam soon found them. The voice of an officer carried over the crash of the waves: "Chief, your men will have to try that again."

The exercise of the U.S. Navy's first Underwater Demolition Teams had been going on for weeks. The men, known as frogmen, were training to clear beach obstacles and to attach limpet mines to enemy vessels.

Less than a year before, the Japanese had attacked the U.S. Navy, Marine Corps, and Army bases at Pearl Harbor, Hawaii, violently shoving America into World War II. The early Sunday morning surprise attack, when most men were asleep or at services, came in two waves, with a total of some 350 Japanese bombers, fighters, and other attack aircraft. Some 2,403 Americans (including civilians) died in the December 7, 1941, attack, which sank or capsized four battleships, sank three cruisers, and three destroyers (the cruisers and destroyers were later raised and re-built), along with a number of minesweepers and auxiliary craft. Four other battleships were so severely damaged that they would not be put to sea until the following year. Of the 402 American aircraft stationed in Hawaii on that day, 169 were destroyed and another 159 crippled, many of them on the ground, according to U.S.

Navy records. The Japanese lost only 29 planes and no ships. It was the biggest defeat in American naval history.

* * *

Meanwhile, the navy was already developing new techniques for amphibious landings. The slaughter of British forces attempting to land on hostile beaches in Turkey during the Gallipoli campaign in World War I had concentrated the minds of senior officers. They knew that any future war would mean masses of men on the beach under withering fire.

Five months before the Japanese attacks, the Navy tasked 2nd Lt. Lloyd E. Peddicord to research the need for Navy swimmers to assess the reefs, fortifications, and other obstacles to landing sailors and Marines. These reconnaissance teams needed to move undetected in enemy waters and collect the kind of intelligence that could be gathered only by skilled observers at sea level. Aerial surveillance provides only a top-down view, not a beach-level view, of enemy entrenchments, Peddicord warned. (Later, in 1943, he would prove tragically correct. Marines were sent to seize the Japanese-held island of Tarawa. Photographs from spotter planes indicated that the reefs were deep enough to pass easily under the Marine landing craft. But those photographs were taken near high-tide. At low-tide, the reefs became speed bumps, trapping the craft hundreds of yards offshore under murderous machine-gun fire. The Marines who managed to escape the trapped crafts plunged into waist-deep water and waded without cover over hundreds of yards as defenseless targets of Japanese gunners. The death toll was high.)

Peddicord's report was already working its way upstream when the Japanese surprise attack on December 7, 1941, quickened the Navy's interest in new capabilities. By August 1942, Peddicord was operating a training facility at Little Creek, Virginia. Peddicord called the new unit the Navy Scouts and Raiders. Decades later, Little Creek would be one of the homes of the U.S. Navy SEALs.

At the same time, the U.S. Army and Navy opened a joint Amphibious Scout and Raider School at Fort Pierce, Florida. From the start, those extraordinary men were hard to handle. Some narrowly escaped court-martial when they kidnapped an admiral in Miami as a Christmas party prank.

One of Peddicord's first recruits was a professional football player with the Cleveland Rams, named Phil H. Bucklew. He joined the navy the day after the Pearl Harbor attacks. In the years ahead, he would be hailed as "the father of Naval Special Warfare" and, therefore, the "godfather of the SEALs."

Tall and dark-haired, he also had the habits of a scholar (and would earn his PhD at Columbia University after the war).

Bucklew's career traced the origins of naval special warfare. He swam into an enemy harbor in North Africa in November 1942 to cut the antisubmarine nets and surveil the airfield for an Allied assault as part of Operation Torch. The summer of 1943 found Bucklew in a small boat off of Sicily, the large Italian island then held by the Nazis. Through binoculars, he gathered vital intelligence on Nazi beach defenses, which proved essential for Allied landings in July 1943. His reports saved lives and surged the chances of victory.

It was Bucklew's role in the D-Day invasions of Normandy, France, that made him a legend in the history of naval special warfare. Six months before the largest amphibious landing in human history, Bucklew and another Navy scout dived off a small boat a half mile off the coast of France and swam through the cold and treacherous waters of the Atlantic. It was a January night in 1944. The Nazi pillboxes and fortifications loomed over him as he dug sand from the beach on that moonless night. He packed the sand into a small kit bag and swam back out toward a darkened boat.

The wet sand was precious cargo.

Back in England, allied planners tested the sand to see if it would bear the weight of tanks and other allied tracked vehicles. It could. That same beach was soon code-named Omaha, and it was the scene of some of the bloodiest fighting of the Normandy invasion.

On another dark night, Bucklew and his swim buddy again left the comfort of a small boat to swim to the rocky French coast. Nazi patrols were a constant danger. They hid for hours on the exposed beach to collect sand samples and study the Nazi troop movements. They learned the patrol schedules and noted the numbers of soldiers and the type of guns that they carried. This, too, provided vital intelligence for the D-Day landings.

On D-Day itself, Bucklew and his small boat were back supporting the first wave of tank assaults on Omaha Beach, the very shore he had reconnoitered less than six months before. His boat was probed by Nazi machine-gun fire and raked by waves of stormy seas. Landing craft exploded around him, under seemingly endless artillery fire. As the enemy shells made geysers of water all around him, he reached into the bloody seas to haul soldiers aboard, saving many from drowning.

* * *

After the war, Bucklew left the Navy, married his sweetheart, and adopted the quiet life of a graduate student at Columbia University in New York. Like many veterans, he longed for a semblance of prewar normalcy. Too old and too worn out to play professional football, he learned that many of the prewar teams had vanished.

Soon, the call of the sea roared in his ears. When he returned to the Navy in 1948, he saw action in Korea and other parts of Asia.

Later, as mandatory retirement neared in 1962, the phone rang. He was asked to command a new unit that was just being approved by President John F. Kennedy, called Naval Special Warfare Group One. In addition to two Underwater Demolition Teams and a Boat Support Unit, which were each familiar to him, the command included something entirely new—SEAL Team One.

* * *

John F. Kennedy's shortened presidency set in motion a lot in a few years: the challenge to land the first men on the moon, the tax cuts that triggered the enormous 1960s economic boom, and the creation of the U.S. Navy SEALs.

The SEAL name stood for Sea, Air, Land. The young president imagined a mobile commando force that could stalk, hunt, and kill in any terrain on Earth, operating from the ships, submarines, and aircraft of the U.S. Navy.

Kennedy had been a naval officer during World War II, commanding a small, fast PT boat in the Pacific. He had seen combat against the brutal Japanese Navy and nearly died when his PT 109 had been sunk in a firefight. He and his crew survived through escape and evasion in the jungles of enemy-held Asia. And, like many Democrats and Republicans of his era, he understood the threat of Soviet Communism and the dire stakes in the escalating Vietnam War.

So he signed off on the creation of a new type of frogman, the SEALs, in 1962. It would not be long before the SEALs were deployed as Bucklew once was: at night, on enemy shores.

* * *

Captain Bucklew didn't like what he saw in South Vietnam in 1964. The North Vietnamese Army and its irregular guerilla arm, the Vietcong, were freely landing on beaches in the South, moving ashore men and materiel. The South Vietnamese army would arrive too late, or not at all, and the allied navy was ill equipped and poorly led. America's ally couldn't stop the movement of North Vietnamese fighters on land or sea.

If America didn't act quickly, its ally would succumb to Communist invasion. Its democratically elected leaders, village elders, and schoolteachers would be killed or sent to political "reeducation" camps, Hmong and Chinese minorities would be persecuted or killed, and its entire population enslaved. Food and schooling, when it was provided at all, would be doled out on a political basis. And America's pledge to her ally would be shown to be worthless—frightening other allies from relying on the United States. (Indeed, all of these things would come to pass in 1975.) None of these things had to be explicitly said by Bucklew; the risks were well known.

Bucklew recommended a complete blockade of the coastline by the U.S. Navy, a suggestion that his superiors had expected.

The rest of the now-famous "Bucklew report" was more controversial. He recommended that special operations teams—including his SEAL team—be used to patrol and ambush the Communist invaders along the Mekong and Bassac rivers that flowed into the western interior of South Vietnam from Cambodia. These winding rivers were packed with shallow-draft boats, sampans, and junks, which carried fish and rice to the markets on its muddy banks. They were also ideal for smuggling insurgents and automatic weapons. From the air, enemy movements would be hidden among the native boats. Only on the ground or in the shallow water could the invaders be stopped.

The Navy was comfortable with its traditional blue-water role, patrolling and fighting in deep ocean waters. Sending naval forces far from the sight of its oceangoing vessels struck many as novel and strange. Wasn't that what Marines were for?

The U.S. Navy quickly chased the North Vietnamese from the South China Sea, and the enemy moved to the unguarded rivers, exactly as Bucklew had predicted.

So the SEALs would follow them into the small, jungle-shaded rivers. No longer seen as a force to clear beach obstacles for large-scale naval invasions, the SEALs went far beyond the blue waters of the traditional Navy to the brown and muddy waters of counterinsurgency in the jungles of Vietnam and Cambodia. There, in the mosquito-infested jungles where Vietcong hid behind rain-dripping fronds, the SEALs came into their own.

* * *

One of them was Michael Thornton.

Thornton was a new member of SEAL Team One when he arrived in Southeast Asia on January 1, 1970. As he stepped off the plane, the heat rushed on him like the opening of an oven door.

Within days, he was deployed up-country, moving in small inflatable boats and lying in wait, among tall weeds, for enemy troop movements to cross his gun barrel. For the next two years, as the American public thought the war in Vietnam was winding down, he and his teammates were ambushing North Vietnamese Army regulars. (The infamous Vietcong guerilla fighters had ceased to exist as a separate fighting unit following their utter defeat during the 1968 Tet Offensive.) The enemy was highly trained (often by Soviet advisors), disciplined, and bold. And the Communists could stage ambushes of their own—providing Thornton with his share of close calls.

Thornton, under the command of Lt. Thomas R. Norris, along with three men from the South Vietnamese Special Forces (known as the LDNN), was given a mission that would define his career and illustrate the bold new role of the SEALs.

Norris was already a legend among the SEALs. From a forward operating base (FOB) in northern South Vietnam, he led a five-man team to locate a downed pilot on April 10, 1972. Throughout the night, his team carefully moved through terrain crowded with North Vietnamese forces. At dawn, he found the pilot hiding in the jungle and led him safely back to the base. The Communists announced their displeasure with massive mortar and rocket attacks on the small, sandbagged base. Only round-the-clock air support kept the remote outpost from being overrun by the determined enemy.

Norris knew that the North Vietnamese were searching for the copilot. The next day, he led two more patrols into the wilderness owned by the enemy. No joy. The copilot remained missing, and Norris and his men were lucky to escape with their lives.

On April 12, he decided to try again. He disguised himself as a Vietnamese fisherman and, along with a brave South Vietnamese soldier, pushed out on an old sampan, a native wooden boat. Maneuvering the boat throughout the night, he finally found the wounded pilot. But the North Vietnamese had moved in along the riverbank. He covered the pilot in bamboo and weeds and moved the boat back into the muddy creek. With sheer bravado, he eased the boat past North Vietnamese patrols. As the trio climbed out of the sampan, less than two thousand yards from the FOB, Norris heard the telltale bark of a Soviet-made machine gun. He hit the deck as bullets savaged the foliage above. They were trapped. Concealed in vegetation, he gamely called in an air strike near his own position. Seconds after the explosions rocked the jungle, Norris, the pilot, and the South Vietnamese soldier scrambled to reach the FOB. The smoke and debris gave them some momentary cover. But it wouldn't last. They had to run for their lives and cross nearly a half mile of jungle before Charlie raised his head and resumed firing.

With the crack of enemy rifle fire overhead, they made it. Norris would later be awarded the Medal of Honor for his bravery that day.

Five months later, Norris was outlining a mission that would take him back to the same territory where he nearly lost his life. This time, he wanted to take Thornton with him.

Norris traced his finger on a map showing the North Vietnamese's Cua Viet River Base, on the jagged coastline of South Vietnam's Quảng Trị Province. It was October 31, 1972, and, Thornton knew, this Halloween mission was likely to be one of the last SEAL operations in Southeast Asia. The numbers of SEALs left in country had dwindled from hundreds in 1966 to roughly a dozen in 1972.

The mission was simple and dangerous: capture

North Vietnamese prisoners and gather intelligence from a spot of jungly marsh only a few miles from the border of North Vietnam. Though they would be landing in South Vietnam, the area was entirely in Communist hands. The North Vietnamese were numerous, their patrols were constant, and they were well armed with machine guns and Soviet-made rocket launchers. Artillery and tanks could be nearby.

They would have to move without sign or scent. If they were discovered, the lucky ones would die quickly. Capture by the North Vietnamese meant torture and disappearance into nightmarish prison camps. At this stage of the war, no prisoners had ever been released from North Vietnam, and very few had escaped. The risks were sky-high, and the SEALs were told that they could bow out. None did.

*　*　*

A weather-beaten Chinese-style junk took them up the hostile coast. The men stayed out of sight of Communist patrol planes. The thud of the diesel outboard and the whine of flimsy sails carried them ever northward as the sun crawled across the hot sky.

After sunset, the team reached its objective. In the humid darkness, they inflated a small boat and put it over the side of the junk. The SEALs and the South

Vietnamese commandos carefully transferred their guns and equipment into the bobbing boat and then lowered themselves aboard.

The distant coastline was a dark tangle of trees. As they paddled toward it, they did not know if enemy lookouts had spotted them.

Still more than a mile out, the men attached their gear to their web vests and climbed over the side. They swam with their full load out, through the waves and currents of the inky-dark sea.

They crept ashore under the tropical stars, which, this far from electrical light, were numerous and bright—like sugar spilled on a black tablecloth. They would have to be careful to avoid detection. They communicated only in hand signals.

They could hear North Vietnamese soldiers talking and see them moving around campfires, drinking tea, and making jokes. They crept slowly through the underbrush, pausing often to avoid creating a pattern of sound.

First light found them deep in the jungle, with Norris poring over the map. The commander quickly realized that the ocean currents had taken them too far north. They were actually in North Vietnam. There was no hope of rescue there.

Norris decided to creep back toward the coast.

Once near the beach, they could use a compass to wend their way south. With luck, they would avoid Communist patrols and make it into the water.

But their luck had run out.

A North Vietnamese force of more than fifty soldiers soon spotted the commandos. They fired on them instantly, with AK-47s, their 7.62-millimeter rounds slicing through palm trunks.

Thornton and the other men were outnumbered in hostile terrain. They returned fire, running and gunning, stopping only to reload. The moving battle raged for more than five hours as the SEALs fought to get to the coast.

Soon, the enemy was close enough to hurl grenades. An explosion stunned Thornton, and shrapnel cut through his leg. His camo pants were soaked with his own blood. Still, he had to keep moving or he would die. He knelt down to take aim at his attackers.

One of the South Vietnamese commandos crawled over to Thornton. The situation had gotten worse. Norris had been shot in the head, and Thornton was told, he was dead.

Now Thornton had to make a decision. Norris was at least five football fields to his rear and most likely dead. Still, the SEAL mantra—"Leave no man behind"—echoed in Thornton's head.

Despite his wounds, he made his way over the rough ground, taking fire from enemy soldiers.

He found Norris in a puddle of his own blood. As Thornton tried to move him, Norris moved. He was alive. Barely.

Thornton picked him up and staggered toward the beach.

Another explosion knocked the two men down. It was artillery fire, likely from an American cruiser offshore.

Thornton struggled to get up again and pulled Norris onto his back.

Again, they made for the shore. Bullets screamed past the lumbering duo. The shots were getting closer.

Thornton winced. A North Vietnamese bullet had smashed through his leg, pumping out more of his own blood. Now he was wounded in both legs.

Yet Thornton kept going. Somehow.

In the surf, he found a wounded South Vietnamese commando. Another teammate. Thornton dragged both men into the ocean. He fought against the rising tide as bullets splashed around him.

With a burning sun overhead, Thornton would have to keep himself and two other men floating and breathing. It wasn't easy. All three men had potentially mortal wounds, and their open, bleeding wounds sapped their energy to fight the merciless waves and the ruthless sun. Given the amount of blood in the tropical water, shark attack was a definite possibility.

It would take two hours of paddling in the open ocean before help arrived. Sailors, aboard the same junk that had dropped them off the night before, helped haul them aboard. Remarkably, all three men lived.

The story, like the best SEAL stories, has a coda.

Almost exactly a year later, Thornton was ordered to report to Washington to receive the Medal of Honor, the nation's highest decoration. He had one request. He wanted Norris, who was in the midst of a three-year battery of operations to restore him from his head injury, to join him at the White House ceremony. Norris was a few miles north of the White House at Bethesda Naval Hospital, but the doctors firmly said no. It was too risky to move their patient.

Thornton paid his old commander a visit in his hospital room. He sat by his bedside, swapping stories. When the night shift came on, Thornton calmly lowered Norris into a nearby wheelchair and wheeled him out of the hospital. No one stopped to question them. Thorton had just kidnapped the man he saved.

The following afternoon, on October 15, 1973, Thornton and Norris were side by side in the White

House. As President Richard Nixon put the blue sash holding the gold medal around Thornton's neck, the president asked: "Is there anything I can do for you?"

"Sir," Thornton said, "if you could break this medal in half, the other half belongs to the man beside me."[1]

He meant Norris.

Thornton would later get his wish, although his medal was never broken in half. Norris was awarded the Medal of Honor by President Gerald R. Ford on March 6, 1976, for rescuing the two downed pilots in 1972.

Thornton was asked many times: why did he do it? He always gave an answer similar to the one he gave the Norfolk *Virginian Pilot* newspaper: "We loved, and we gave, and we understood each other—that's what SEAL teams are about....We would have given our lives for each other."

Thornton's case remains the only time in the twentieth century that one Medal of Honor winner saved another.

* * *

A Medal of Honor winner can always get a meeting. In 1979, Norris went to see FBI director William H. Webster.

Norris hoped to persuade the FBI director to let

him join the Bureau, despite his war injuries. Webster was a tough-minded man, a former federal judge who stared down several mafia dons in his New York court-room. His refusal to knuckle under the pressure from the mob and its lawyers brought him to prominence and led President Jimmy Carter to appoint him to run the FBI. Webster considered the risks: the potential news story saying a decorated SEAL was unfit for the FBI versus putting a man in the line of fire who might not be capable of performing his duties. At length, Webster told him that if he passed all the tests, like any other FBI special agent, the Bureau would accept him. It was a tough but fair decision.

Norris passed the tests and would go on to serve twenty years as a special agent. A building is named for Norris at the SEAL base in Coronado.

* * *

With the end of the Vietnam War, Thornton was sent to be a senior instructor at the SEAL training base at Coronado, an island in San Diego Bay. This is where BUD/S happens.

The world's most fearsome training program begins in a small compound of two-story buildings ringed by chain-link fence. It borders the famous Victorian-style Hotel Del Coronado. From its stately porches, guests can casually sip their cappuccinos while watching SEALs struggle in the surf below. The ease of civilian life is clearly visible to the salt-and-sand-starched SEALs as they struggle to attach a line to wet rocks or run in the sand with heavy logs on their shoulders.

Don Zub attended BUD/S in 1975, as part of class 91. This was where he met Thornton.

In Zub's day there was a significant cultural divide in the SEALs between the Vietnam veterans, like Thornton, and the "new guys." During the war, civilian society pivoted away from the traditional ideals of self-sacrifice, patience, and forbearance, values essential for military service. Self-discipline eased into a "let it all hang out" attitude. Many SEALs of Thornton's generation found the changes unnerving. The riots, assassinations, and bombings, prompted by calls for a radical new society, only confirmed their suspicions. So the veteran instructors beat out any vestige of this thinking in their recruits. When they said "the only easy day was yesterday," it was initially meant as a challenge to the drift of American society. At the receiving end, the recruits didn't like it much. "There was some tension," Zub admits.

Virtually all of the instructors were Vietnam veterans, like Thornton. They were hard men who had been hardened by war. "They saw a lot of their brothers die," Zub said. "They did stuff that they couldn't get away with today. They were very professional, at the extreme end of professional. The deadly end."

Their professionalism and their hardness showed itself in unusual ways. One day Zub and several other SEALs were taking cold showers to condition themselves for training in the cold waters of the Pacific. One instructor ripped open the shower curtain and kicked Zub in the balls. He doubled over in pain. The instructor barked: "If I kicked you in the balls ten times, would the eleventh time feel any different?"

The instructor's point was that shivering in a cold shower would not prepare you for the rigors of cold-water training. The way he illustrated that lesson, which would be a criminal offense today, was never forgotten.

* * *

The Emerson rig is a bubble-rebreather made in France. The specially made device lets U.S. Navy SEALs dive up to thirty-two feet underwater and swim undetected beneath the waves. But the device requires considerable training to avoid drowning. Zub and his fellow SEALs began a series of training sessions—called "evolutions"—with the Emerson rig in 1976. They practiced in a pool, then in a nearby bay. Then they practiced using it in the bay at night. Each practice drill was more taxing than the last. Finally, in May 1976, the day came to use the Emerson rig in the ever-dangerous ocean.

SEAL Team One stood on the beach on Coronado Island that morning, watching the wild eight-foot waves roar against the rocks and feeling the wind lash their faces. "There is no way that we are diving today," Zub told his teammates.

They were silent. Would their instructors actually send them into the stormy seas? Would their Vietnam-hardened instructors be that crazy? Everyone wondered, but no one dared to ask.

The suspense didn't last long. The men were lined up in groups of two, swim buddies side by side. (SEALs in training are always divided into teams of two, called "swim buddies.") The water was cold. The currents were unpredictable, strong and strange.

Zub and his swim buddy survived through strategy: they put extra lead weights in the pockets of their rebreathing vests. The weight drove them deeper into the water and kept them out of the wild waves raging above them. But it came at a price. They had to work hard to stop from sinking to a depth of thirty-two feet, which would kill them. Anything higher than ten feet, where the waves would smash them onto knife-edged rocks, might also kill them. They were trying to swim a path between perils.

Not every pair of SEALs followed Zub's strategy. Others took their chances in the waves. The gamble didn't pay off for all of them.

When Zub crawled out of the surf, he could see the instructors anxiously running up and down the beach. Worry was written on their faces.

One of the unweighted SEALs had separated from his swim buddy and was caught in a claw of angry waves. His body washed onto the shore, helpless and motionless, like driftwood.

Zub saw one of the instructors repeatedly perform CPR. But it was no use. The man was dead.

That night at dinner, the SEALs were quiet. But their instructors were not. Each instructor, including Thornton, stood behind a table of SEALs, whispering over and over the dead man's name. "They were rubbing it in that he had died," Zub said.

Each sailor knew the dead man well. They had trained with him, ate with him, slept near him. Some had met his parents, who came from a tough section of East Los Angeles. The men were taking the loss hard, and the instructors were making it harder.

The instructors were teaching a brutal but necessary lesson: In training and in combat, your team-mates will die. You had better get used to it. The instructors themselves had seen their friends die in the fast-moving waters, dark jungles, and sun-cooked rice paddies of South Vietnam. They knew that if the trainees could not accept the human cost of combat, they would be useless as fighting men.

And they also knew that SEALs find it easier to accept the possibility of losing their own lives than the risk of losing teammates. It was the loss of friends and teammates that they would have to learn how to handle.

What was the purpose? Zub sums it up: "What doesn't kill you will make you stronger." But, still, Zub didn't like it very much.

Yet Thornton's hardened imprint was passed onto Zub and the others. It helped make them SEALs.

* * *

In Zub's days there was an incredible rivalry between the SEALs based on the East Coast and those based on the West Coast. Each had a nasty nickname for the teams of the other coast. It was "East Coast pukes" versus "Hollywood SEALs." Over the years, the nicknames have faded and the rivalry reduced. But it remains.

The intense rivalry was there because there was no war and no mission to unite the brotherhood.

But that was about to change. A self-described "rogue warrior" and a bearded mullah were about to utterly change the Navy SEALs.

CHAPTER 2

The Violent Birth
of SEAL Team Six

"You get a mission and they say: 'What's the probability of success?' Who gives a shit? If I win, I win. If I lose, I'm dead. Take your statistics and jam it. It's my ass on the line, not yours."

—Lt. Cmdr. Richard Marcinko,
founder of SEAL Team Six

In a windowless room in the E-ring of the Pentagon, Lt. Cmdr. Richard Marcinko was in charge of briefing the Chief of Naval operations on intelligence and terrorism. Yet nothing prepared him for the news coming across the television monitors on November 4, 1979.

An armed mob, mostly masked or hooded, had surged into the U.S. embassy compound in Tehran, Iran's capital city, and taken some fifty-two American diplomats and U.S. Marines hostage, including the Acting Ambassador, Bruce Laingen. A national nightmare had begun.

* * *

The attackers had gathered during dawn prayers at a nearby university, and by bus, taxi, and private car, they had filtered to Ferdowsi Avenue, outside the U.S. embassy in Tehran.

By 6:30 a.m. there were more than three hundred members of a front group calling itself Muslim Student Followers of the Imam's Line. The "imam" in the group's name was Ayatollah Ruhollah Khomeini, the bearded religious dictator who, months earlier, had overthrown the democratic pro-American government that had replaced the Shah, Mohammad Reza Pahlavi. Khomeini had destroyed Iran's embryonic democracy and now he wanted to humiliate and vanquish America. In his sermons, he said that it was Allah's will.

The militants' plan was designed to use America's virtues against her. Women college students would take the lead because, they believed, U.S. Marines were less likely to stop them, let alone frisk them. Thus, the student who cut the chain on the U.S. embassy's front gates was a woman with bolt cutters hidden under her chador, a flowing Islamic robe meant to signal modesty and submission. Boldly, she snapped through the chains, and the front gates creaked open. She led hundreds of veiled women through gates.

Hundreds of "students" poured through, each with printed signs on lanyards around their necks. The signs, in English, read: "Don't be afraid. We just want to set-in." The printer had a poor translator. They meant "sit-in," a popular 1970s protest strategy. The term was designed to be reassuring and familiar, and to put the mob in the same context as American civil rights and antiwar protestors. They didn't mean any harm, the women leaders said in good English, they just wanted to protest American policies and go home. They were lying.

Behind the wall of women came bearded young men, first with clubs and then with guns.

* * *

By the time Marcinko saw the television images, the Iranian radicals were besieging the main building. Dozens of Americans were surrounded by hundreds of armed radicals.

29

The embassy grounds were nearly a city block long and included four major buildings, in the style of Eisenhower-era public high schools, as well as a swimming pool, tennis courts, and a computer facility. The upper windows offered a view of the sunburned brick slums and white wastes of the Dasht-e Kavir salt desert. Every one, inside and outside, knew it was just a matter of time before the radicals got in.

As the radicals tugged at the bars over the windows and repeatedly rammed the front doors, inside the chancery, diplomats began to realize that it was not another protest—the embassy had been briefly invaded months earlier in February 1979—but something more sinister. The diplomats began to burn sensitive intelligence files. Others made desperate phone calls to high-ranking Iranian officials and to Washington. In both capitals, the officials who actually answered the phone said that they were powerless to help.

Marcinko sat in on several secure high-level briefings that day. Each new development disturbed him. The U.S. Marines at the front gates were ordered not to load their weapons, so they fled. Phone calls to Tehran's chief of police went unreturned. A police patrol, located near the embassy motor pool, refused to help—they knew that the radicals had more political clout in the new revolutionary government than they did. The prime minister was refusing to take calls from the acting U.S. ambassador or from Washington. The entire might of the Iranian government seemed to be behind the embassy takeover.

Marcinko listened as all of the short-term diplomatic options died away.

Then he followed the admirals, the generals, and other senior officers into a room with a television screen. It showed live images from Tehran. At first, he just saw a mob of nearly one thousand people pushing and shoving. Then he saw the Americans being shoved along. They had been beaten and bruised and blindfolded.

They were hostages now.

Fifty-two American civilians, many on their first overseas assignment, were now at the mercy of zealots who believed that they were subhuman unbelievers. The radicals believed that these Americans should be used as impersonally as chess pieces, a game that the Persians had invented many centuries earlier.

The Carter administration, Marcinko was told, was using every mechanism of international law to free the hostages. He knew it was hopeless. Invading embassies as well as kidnapping and torturing diplomats were red-letter violations of international law, the norms of every civilized nation. If the Iranian revolutionaries were willing to do that, no treaty fine print would awe them.

Silently Marcinko waited. In time, he believed, President Carter would ask for a covert military option. The former SEAL commando hoped to be a part of that mission somehow, someway. He would get his wish.

After all, Marcinko thought, in the bitter winter of 1979, the president and the nation faced a fundamental choice: Kill the hostage takers or let the hostages die.

For him, that wouldn't be a hard call.

*   *   *

Richard Marcinko was born on Thanksgiving Day, 1940, in a coal-mining town in Carbon County, Pennsylvania. His family were Czechs who had crossed the ocean to coax coal from the Pennsylvania rock in humid, dark tunnels. Aboveground they said little and drank much. "Life was simple and life was hard," he said.

During Marcinko's high school years, his parents split up. His mother worked as a Sears department store clerk, and she moved the shattered family into public housing. Meanwhile, his father rented a room over a bar called Yusko's. There were few happy endings in Carbon County.

Young Marcinko was falling apart, too. By 1958, Marcinko—a class cutter and serial seducer—had dropped out of high school. He had to do something, he knew, or his life would spiral down to meaninglessness. He didn't want to end up on skid row or in jail. When President Dwight Eisenhower sent the U.S. Marines to Lebanon in 1958, he was inspired and tried to enlist. The Marine recruiter told him to finish high school first. Marcinko didn't want to do that. He was afraid the fighting would end before he got to Lebanon. A few months later, in September 1958, he decided to try the U.S. Navy. The recruiter tested and accepted him.

After basic training at the U.S. Navy's Great Lakes facility, Marcinko studied to become a radioman and accepted a temporary assignment to a Naval base at Quonset Point, Rhode Island. There, he saw a movie that changed his life.

It was called *The Frogmen*, starring Richard Widmark and Dana Andrews. It dramatically told the story of the U.S. Navy's Underwater Demolition Teams (UDTs) fighting the Japanese in World War II. He had heard his calling and seen his future. He wanted to be "Demolition Dick, Shark Man of the Navy."

But how could an ordinary radioman get into this elite team?

* * *

As he completed radio school in Norfolk, Virginia, he learned that the home of the UDT was nearby. He applied, passed the tests, and was accepted. His future seemed bright and assured.

It was a false victory. Shortly after his acceptance, Marcinko got into a fistfight with another sailor and broke his hand. The injury (and perhaps its cause) disqualified him. He had to go back to "Big Navy" and a life as an enlisted flunky. He hated it.

He filed paperwork, pleaded with officers, and did his job. He waited impatiently for years. Finally, in 1961, he received orders to go UDT training.

His immediate superior signed his transfer to UDT training just to get rid of him. "Sea duty would be too easy for you, Marcinko. I'm going to send you where they'll knock all of this aggressive shit right out of you."

Marcinko didn't care why he was going, only where. He was finally on his way to the place where Shark Men are made.

* * *

Marcinko arrived at the Navy base at Little Creek, Virginia, on June 21, 1961. He was an official member of UDT class 26. If he failed, he would be sent back to the regular Navy—a punishing alternative, in his estimation.

Marcinko's chances were not great. Only one out of every five students made it to graduation day. All around him, Marcinko watched as hard, experienced men—former U.S. Army Green Berets and Rangers—failed or quit. But Marcinko was determined. He knew that he would likely never get another chance. He worked through fear, physical injury, harsh verbal abuse, deep, ice-cold waters, and the ever-present nagging gnaw of fatigue. The more the tape in his head screamed *Quit!* the more Marcinko fought back. He made it. He graduated and joined the U.S. Navy elite Underwater Demolition Teams. (The forerunners of the SEALs were merged into this elite unit. UDTs would be phased out in 1983.)

He soon distinguished himself as a hard-working, hard-drinking enlisted man. He was considered a "true frog"—a classic UDT man. Soon, several officers and senior enlisted men suggested that Marcinko apply for Officer Candidate School. Could a high school dropout be an officer? At first, he resisted the idea. The goal seemed too far away, too improbable. Yet by December 1965, he graduated from Officer Candidate School in Newport, Rhode Island. He was close to where his dream began and farther along than he ever thought he would get. He was commissioned as an ensign and assigned to a destroyer.

Still, he wanted to become a SEAL. He pulled every string he could to get himself assigned to SEAL Team Two in Virginia Beach. By June 1966, with the Vietnam War devouring SEALs, Marcinko was back at Gate Five of the SEAL base at Little Creek. He was home.

But not for long. After Christmas 1966, he was sent to Vietnam.

* * *

Thirteen kilometers west of Tra Noc, South Vietnam, Marcinko was leading a pair of SEAL Tactical Assault Boats (STABs) to ambush Vietcong in the spring of 1967. The night air was wet and phosphorescent fish jumped in the wake of their small boats.

They surprised the Communists on a small river island. The SEALs' opening salvo raised a hornet's nest of well-organized opposition. Return fire was fast and accurate. AK-47 rounds sliced through the night air, sending up geysers of river water and punching small holes in boat hulls.

The firefight was intense. The Vietcong were combat veterans: they were dug in, and they knew their deadly business.

After two hours of heavy fire—tracer rounds arcing to and from concealed jungle positions—Marcinko radioed for an air strike.

On duty was an AC-47, known as "Puff the Magic Dragon" for its lethal firepower that made enemies disappear. Its four Vulcan Gatling guns raked the enemy island. Leaves and dirt jumped into the air as the aircraft poured more than six thousand rounds per minute into the enemy stronghold.

After a few minutes, the aircraft fire stopped—leaving only the rumble of the SEALs' boat engines. Total victory.

At least it seemed that way until Marcinko returned to base. A junior officer told Marcinko that he had violated protocol by calling in an air strike. Marcinko told him off. The next day, the commanding officer listed the rules he had broken. He had gone into combat without clearance, then called in an air strike without clearance.

These were prerogatives of much more senior officers, not Marcinko himself. (Today SEAL officers can radio in air strikes, but forty years ago in Vietnam, air strikes were seen precisely as Napoleon saw artillery—a strategic decision to be made from a desk, not the field.)

Marcinko's insubordination was the start of a

pattern. He was brilliant at securing hard-won battle-field victories and equally brilliant at enraging senior officers above him.

In his mind: he cared about combat, they cared about careers.

In theirs: Marcinko threatened the entire chain of command.

It was a conflict that would dog Marcinko through-out his life—and it is a conflict that remains a part of the DNA of the U.S. Navy SEALs.

* * *

Marcinko's first big authorized mission began on the night of May 18, 1967. The U.S. Navy would ulti-mately call it "the most successful SEAL operation in the Mekong Delta."[1]

During the Tet Offensive in 1968, Marcinko led his platoon in an operation in the town called Chau Doc. Disguised Vietcong had hitchhiked and walked into the town as revelers were preparing for South Vietnam's New Year, known as "Tet."

It was a surprise attack. Once in position, they pulled out their weapons from their knapsacks and suitcases and started slaughtering civilians. They were organized, expertly led, and totally committed to their murderous mission.

American nurses and schoolteachers fled to the city's church and hospital. It was their Alamo, a temporary sanctuary that would fall if the cavalry didn't arrive.

Marcinko's platoon was sent to rescue them.

Chau Doc, a picturesque village a few days earlier, was now an apocalyptic ruin and open-air human slaughterhouse. Braving machine-gun blasts and mortar attacks, Marcinko led his team along stone walls sprayed with Communist graffiti. Tongues of flame licked up the wood-frame tiny French–style homes, and the wind blew oatmeal-colored ash onto the SEALs. Murdered civilians lay in groups. Whole families had been slain together. Dogs were shot dead at the ends of their leashes.

Marcinko kept his men moving and firing. They knew the stakes. If they failed to break through to the trapped Americans, those well-meaning nurses and schoolteachers would be executed as had so many Vietnamese civilians.

Leading from the front, Marcinko ran toward the church bell tower. He and his platoon arrived in time. They gathered up the survivors and led them to safety. For his bravery under fire, Marcinko earned his first Bronze Star.

Ultimately, Marcinko would win four Bronze

stars in Vietnam, as well as a Vietnamese Cross of Gallantry.

*   *   *

After two tours in Vietnam and a two-year stateside staff assignment, Marcinko was promoted to lieutenant commander and assigned to the office of the Naval Attaché in Cambodia in 1973. There he led covert operations against Communist rebels on the muddy rivers of Cambodia.[2] His command of French grew strong enough to lead Cambodia's *phoc*, or amphibious fighters, on nighttime raids. He delighted in jungle ambushes. War isn't hell for all men; Marcinko truly loved it, and he missed it when it was over.

But as he climbed the career ladder, he got farther and farther away from combat. By 1979, Marcinko was one of two Navy representatives for a Joint Chiefs of Staff task force known as the Terrorist Action Team (TAT). Thus, he had a front row seat to the biggest foreign policy calamity of the 1970s—the Iranian hostage crisis. Perhaps, in this national tragedy, there was an opportunity for him.

*   *   *

The crisis in Iran had been building for decades.

Ruhollah Mostafavi Musavi Khomeini—known

in the West simply as Ayatollah Khomeini—believed that democracy was irredeemably flawed because it allowed people to vote to make or unmake laws. Law, he said, should not be determined by elections—just as right and wrong cannot be decided by a popularity contest. Instead, clerics like him should rule and their law determined by the Koran and centuries-old scholarly interpretations. Since the Koran doesn't mention jet planes or birth control, those matters would have to be decided by the clerics' interpretations. Khomeini's interpretations could not be questioned, even by other clerics. He wanted to be as infallible as the Pope and as tyrannical as Joseph Stalin.

After years in exile in Iraq and France, Khomeini triumphantly returned to Iran on February 1, 1979. The Shah had fled almost a month before and a transitional democratic government was in place. Seduced by the alliance of Communists and Islamists against a middle-class democracy, a *New Yorker* writer traveled with Khomeini and wrote a laudatory article about how revolutionary the ayatollah promised to be. (Every rebel is a reformer when he is out of power.) In reality, Khomieni's first goal was to overthrow the elected government. The ayatollah soon became the most brutal dictator in Iran's bloody history. It would take years before the *New Yorker* and the European left conceded that it was wrong about the bearded ayatollah.

Within a week of Khomeini's return, violent demonstrations and bombings rocked the country. (Theaters and discos were popular targets.) Khomeini soon seized power.

While in exile in France, Khomeini said he supported the Universal Declaration of Human Rights. "We would like to act according to the Universal Declaration of Human Rights. We would like to be free." The Western press took the ayatollah at his word, without ever reading any of his books or tracts—which explicitly promised a religious dictatorship. Amazingly, *Time* magazine named Khomeini Person of the Year for 1979.[3]

Once in power, Khomeini took a hard line against dissent, warning political rivals: "I repeat for the last time: abstain from holding meetings, from blathering, from public protests. Otherwise I will break your teeth."[4]

Khomeini introduced Sharia law, enforced by the Revolutionary Guards, a group akin to Hitler's Brownshirts or Mao's Red Guards. Women were required to cover their hair, and men were forbidden from wearing shorts. Men and women were banned from sunbathing in the same area. Alcohol was banned. Western movies were barred. The broadcasting of any music, other than religious singing without musical instrumentals, was forbidden. These bans, and the punishments they carried with them, would last for the remainder of Khomeini's life.

* * *

Next came the dress rehearsal for the embassy takeover.

On February 14, 1979, armed gunmen stormed the U.S. embassy in Tehran and took 102 Americans hostage. While not directly attributed to his forces, the takeover had taken place within two weeks of Khomeini's return to Iran. In events eerily similar to the recent invasions of U.S. embassies in Cairo and Benghazi, the U.S. embassy in Teheran was overrun by hundreds of militants, who climbed the walls and breached the gate. A Marine contingent of just nineteen guards opened fire into the air, as ordered, in an attempt to protect the compound. They failed.

The U.S. ambassador, William Sullivan, ordered the destruction of all classified material and then, reluctantly, instructed the Marines to surrender. Amid wafting tear gas, embassy employees were led outside with their hands above their heads to be paraded for the Iranian press corps. Khomeini had won.

Several hours later, Ebrahim Yazdi, deputy prime minister of the revolutionary government, arrived at the embassy and "convinced" the attackers to disperse.

One Iranian employee of the U.S. embassy was dead, and a U.S. Marine was wounded. The embassy invaders were not punished under Iranian law, as the revolutionary government initially promised.

Other than a White House statement documenting President Carter's "disappointment," the Carter administration did virtually nothing in response to the takeover of the embassy. Evacuations of American personnel, including thousands of oil-field technicians, accelerated.

What no one in the Carter administration considered was the possibility that the February embassy invasion was a dress rehearsal for a bigger attack. Ten months later, the attack came. The second attack would result in fifty-two Americans being held for 444 days.

Seemingly helpless to free the hostages through negotiation, the Carter administration ultimately instructed the military to draw up plans for a rescue mission.

* * *

Marcinko joined the planning for a secret mission to rescue the American hostages. Different options were debated: blockading the Iranian oilfields, mining its harbors, aerial bombardment, and a rescue attempt. The rescue mission was code-named Operation Eagle Claw.

U.S. Army Maj. Gen. James B. Vaught was appointed Joint Task Force commander. Vaught turned to America's special forces leaders including: Col. Charles A. Beckwith (founder of the Army's new Delta counterterrorist group), Col. James H. Kyle (longtime U.S. Air special operator), and Lt. Col. Edward Seiffert (an experienced Marine night-vision flyer). From the beginning, the idea that all the services should have a "piece of the action" plagued the operation, producing poisonous compromises.

Operation Eagle Claw called for three C-130 planes to ferry an assault force of some 120 troops from the island of Masirah, off the coast of Oman, to Iran. The troops were to land approximately two hundred miles southeast of Tehran at a desolate, uninhabited location code-named Desert One. The C-130s were to be accompanied by three EC-130s, which are refueling airplanes. After landing in the desert, the planes were to wait for eight RH-53 helicopters from the USS *Nimitz*, an aircraft carrier located in the Gulf of Oman.

The choppers were to arrive at Desert One within

thirty minutes of the landing of the C-130s. The choppers would then load the assault troops, refuel, and drop the troops at a remote oasis some sixty-five miles from Tehran, where they would rendezvous with agents coming from Tehran. After dark, the agents would escort six drivers and six translators to Tehran, retrieve trucks that had been acquired in the outskirts of Iran's capital, and return to the oasis. The assault team would then climb into the trucks and drive into Tehran.

Once in Tehran, the assault team would make two rescues, one at the embassy and the other at another location where an additional three hostages were being held. Once they had the hostages aboard, the assault team would then head to a soccer field in Tehran, await helicopters, and airlift all personnel to Manzariyeh, where an Army Ranger Team would be holding the airport until the helicopters arrived. The rescued hostages and assault team were then supposed to board onto military aircraft and be flown out of the country. All remaining material used in the operation was to be blown up at the airfield.

It was a complicated plan with many moving parts. It didn't take long for those parts to grind into each other.

* * *

After five months of planning and training, Operation Eagle Claw began on April 24, 1980. The first C-130 crossed into Iranian airspace and reduced its altitude to less than five hundred feet to evade enemy radars. As planned, at approximately halfway to the rendezvous point, the commander received a radio message indicating that the eight helicopters had lifted off from the USS *Nimitz*.

After successfully landing the C-130 at Desert One, team members began unloading equipment. Then, the unexpected struck.

As the Ranger team and Delta operators set up a security perimeter around the site, an Iranian city bus arrived. The bus was fired upon and it halted.

Forty-five Iranians were then detained. Shortly thereafter, a fuel truck (likely smugglers) appeared on the road. It refused to stop. Delta launched an M72 LAW (a 66-millimeter "light antitank weapon") at the truck, scoring a direct hit, and immediately creating a huge fireball. To make matters even worse, a small pickup truck appeared next, picked up the driver of the burning truck and fled the scene at what can only be assumed was the highest speed achievable by the pickup.

Cover for the entire mission was blown.

Killing a busload of Iranians would not have bothered

Marcinko: "We're helping 'em out. We're the extended arm of the Iranian law. Same thing with the curfew violator with the pickup truck…"

Despite the complications, the U.S. ground commander decided not to scrub the mission. The element of surprise was now gone. A second C-130 landed shortly after the first. The light from the burning tanker truck actually served as a landing beacon for the aircraft.

At first, the helicopter part of the mission was running according to plan. Then, some two hours into the mission, a red warning light flashed inside one helicopter cockpit, indicating a main rotor blade spar crack. While a false reading for this was relatively common on the RH-53Ds, the crew landed the chopper and decided to abandon it after inspecting the rotor blades. Another chopper landed and picked up the crew. The rescue team was now down to seven helicopters on a mission that they had planned required a minimum of six.

Then they met the haboob.

The haboob is a dense dust storm that moves across the horizon like a black curtain on a stage. It is fast and reduces visibility, turning noon into midnight.

As the helicopters moved deeper into Iranian airspace, pilots saw what they thought was a fog bank several miles ahead. As they neared it, they realized it was not harmless fog but a dangerous sandstorm. As the RH-53s flew deeper into the dirty skies, they suffered near hurricane force winds. Visibility dropped to less than seventy-five feet. And, unlike today, those helicopters did not have a GPS (Global Positioning System) or advanced avionics. They were flying blind over hostile territory.

Back at the Pentagon, Marcinko followed the action through a secure radio transmission. Marcinko told us: "The one we missed, in Murphy's Law, is the porosity or the density of when you have a sandstorm. So what happened, probably just as much a feature of the problem with the helicopter was there was a sandstorm and it clogged the filters. No one thought about changing filters to that degree to stop the flying, so you end up that you have a helicopter that's not functioning up to par, plus the back blast, so it just turns to shit in a hurry. But my gut feeling is this is blown, so go. You know?"

One of the helicopter's pilots was forced to return to the aircraft carrier. Maintaining radio silence, the crew of the helicopter was unable to alert Kyle (the ground commander) or Seiffert (the helicopter mission commander) that the mission had lost another chopper.

The mission was now down to its minimum number of helicopters needed for the rescue operation.

Six helicopters from the original eight successfully landed at Desert One. However, one of the helicopters that made it (designated Bluebeard 2) had a hydraulic system failure. After observing the condition of the chopper, Seiffert made the decision that the chopper was a no-go. Now the force was left with five helicopters to accomplish the mission, and most difficult portion of the mission was still ahead of them.

Colonel Beckwith was forced to abort the remainder of the mission, as six helicopters had been the agreed-upon minimum needed for the operation. In reality, five may have sufficed, but the commanders in Washington knew the operation was below its bare minimum of required aircraft. Kyle radioed Vaught and reluctantly recommended scrubbing the mission. Conscious of the political fallout of overruling his military commanders, President Carter approved the request within minutes.

With the rescue mission canceled, the worst was yet to come. As the force prepared to depart, one of the helicopters (Bluebeard 3) moved closer to the EC-130s to refuel. In the dust and spray from the rotor wash, the crew of the refueling helicopter got too close to the refueling plane. Its rotor blade smashed into the plane's side, setting off a fireball.

The explosion killed eight men and destroyed both aircraft. Marcinko still thought that the mission should go forward, but no one consulted him on the matter. "There was the explosion when the helicopter went into the C-130. My gut wrenched. And I thought: 'All right, so somebody probably knows we're here. Let's just accelerate and go.'"

The ground commander released the Iranian civilians, who had been detained from the bus, loaded the C-130s, and evacuated. The remaining helicopters were abandoned on the ground. Unfortunately, the helicopters had not been sufficiently sanitized. Classified material, including the names of the Iranians working for the Americans, fell into the hands of the Revolutionary Guard. Those Iranians were soon hunted and killed. The rescue mission was a perfect failure in every dimension.

* * *

The Defense Department would spend months drawing hard lessons from this bitter tutorial.

One concerned training. Component training for the rescue operation took place in scattered locations across the United States, including Hurlburt Field, Florida, for the Air Force; Yuma, Arizona, and Twenty-Nine Palms, California, for the Marines; and Fort Bragg, North Carolina, for Delta Force.[5] Rarely did participants see members from other services. They did not train together. There was no "full up" dress rehearsal. In fact, problems that surfaced during training tended to reappear during the actual mission. However, crewmen seemed satisfied that their individual parts would work as expected. They were confident of success. But no one saw the big picture.

While there would appear to have been many failures that contributed to the catastrophe called Eagle Claw, many blamed the real problem on the inability of the different branches of the military to communicate, particularly the inability to communicate between the Navy helicopters and the Army's Delta Force. The planning process for this mission was deliberately kept compartmentalized and secretive. No outside group of senior officers could review the finished plan for a reality check.

The Special Operations community would never intentionally repeat this string of unforced errors.

The press dubbed the deadly disaster Desert One, and its name remains shorthand for bureaucratic disaster to this day. Something would have to change dramatically.

The hostages, when they were freed during President Ronald Reagan's January 1981 inauguration after 444 days of captivity, would have agreed with

Marcinko's bold approach. At a U.S. military hospital, reporters asked one former hostage if he would ever like to return to Iran. "Yeah, in a B-52."[6]

And that gave Marcinko an idea.

* * *

Across the military branches—Army, Navy, Marines, and Air Force—senior officers realized that America could not suffer another Desert One. The military was still recovering from low public approval in the aftermath of the Vietnam War. Congress, run by Democrats who had opposed the Vietnam War in its final years, had refused to raise military pay while inflation raged. As a result, nearly one-third of enlisted soldiers and Marines were receiving welfare checks to supplement their pay in 1979. Some senators talked about abolishing the Marine Corps or merging the U.S. Air Force back into the army. The military was in crisis.

Something had to be done. And, for senior officers, that something meant memos and plans. Phone-book-sized plans circulated. Most were proposals to create a cross-branch counterterrorism force, led by the U.S. Army.

In the wake of Eagle Claw, Marcinko was asked to review the U.S. Army's white paper for the commander of naval operations.

* * *

In the early drafts of the proposal, the Army simply wanted a small group of Navy divers to work for them. Marcinko disagreed. "The Army paper asked for roughly thirty SEALs. They wanted 'em down at Fort Bragg, which is good, but you don't get much maritime environment at Fort Bragg [it is landlocked]. They get a canteen on their hip and a couple of lakes and a river. But, so I upgraded [the SEAL unit] from a detachment to a command, then I explained it to the CNO [Chief of Naval Operations], and I said, 'Look, we have no control of this. It's theirs. We're going to have to join forces [with the army], and they'll turn green.' Going back to that time frame, special operations was Army, and it was just a sheer force of numbers when you go into planning. Who had the most experience? Army generals. Not Navy admirals. We didn't have admirals in the SEALs yet and so, you know you have that green machine that was going to get the gooder missions."

Marcinko saw his chance. He spent nights and weeks drafting and redrafting a memo of his own. He wanted to ensure that the SEALs would be an important part of special operations. He even dreamed that the SEALs would fight terrorists and rescue hostages on their own. "I changed it into a command and I guess that's where it started ruffling, really ruffling feathers."

Marcinko's new SEAL unit was code-named Mob-6; it later became SEAL Team Six. Now, Marcinko thought, if he could only find a way to command the new team he had created.

*   *   *

SEAL Team Six would have different equipment and a different mentality from anything else in the U.S. military.

For equipment, Marcinko said it was "trial and error."

"We started in Boston whalers, moved to A1 rigid hulls to cigarette boats."

It was the cultural difference that really set the SEALs apart.

Marcinko then explained how it was that the SEALs became the "pirates" who would end up characterizing SEAL Team Six by the end of his command. Marcinko took advantage of the foresight of Adm. Elmo Zumwalt. The SEALs needed an antiterrorist team that did not fit the mold or the look of the military; they needed to look like civilians in order to blend in and maintain covert identities. "When he [Admiral Zumwalt] became commander of naval operations [CNO], a series of messages came out that were called Z-grams, but they went to the fleet and he had authorized longer hair," Marcinko said. "It was just an upheaval of traditional Navy blue and gold." Marcinko used these "Z-grams" to allow the SEALs to grow long hair and wear earrings.

Explaining why he believed the spec ops were looked down upon by Big Navy, Marcinko said, "In 1980 you're still talking about division warfare. You know, special operations were expendables. There's that riffraff that's out there that does whatever the hell they do, drag their knuckles in the dirt, you know, chew on betel nut, or whatever it is, and basically a pain in the ass." In short, Big Navy and Big Army dismissed the U.S. Navy SEALs as exotic expendables.

The prejudice against the SEALs by larger, traditional military commanders soon shifted, Marcinko observed. "You know that the philosophical change since Desert One, and the formulation of J-SOC [Joint Special Operations Command] and SOCOM [Special Operations Command], created an immense difference. If you look at the deployment in Iraq and Afghanistan for examples, and now you have the old mentality and the old way the plans were written was that the special operations were in support of the divisions." Now large divisions support small special operations.

Beyond beards and earrings, Marcinko forged a unique SEAL Team Six culture: officers were required to learn every skill mastered by the men under their command. Ideas from below were welcomed, not dismissed. He required every man to be able to perform every task, including the most physically demanding jobs. Marcinko outlined his unique selection criteria for men who wanted to join SEAL Team Six: "Their level of responsibility and criticality of what they perform requires a certain, a higher degree of maturity and experience. In my language, everybody had to go over the rail—that means everybody had to board ships, and that's how it started and there wasn't the dog team and there wasn't the DoD team, we all go over the rail and the other is just the sideshow."

In the end Marcinko had done his job. He had formed and trained a unique, hardened group of war fighters. They did not look like your typical military types, with tightly shaved hair and polished boots. They looked like surfers and bikers, with machine guns. Instead, he had put together a team of pirates who were each willing, in all conditions, to take the knife in his teeth and go over the rail.

CHAPTER 3

From Pirates to Professionals

Lt. Ryan Zinke drove through the security checkpoint at the secretive base of SEAL Team Six, near Virginia Beach, in the spring of 1990. Not knowing what to expect, he appeared in his starched Navy dress whites. That was a mistake.

He had been selected to join SEAL Team Six—the team within the teams. It has a demanding selection process, both formal and informal. At six foot two and 220 pounds, Zinke had proven himself as an athlete, a scholar, and a SEAL. He lettered all four years in a Pacific 10 football program, graduated from the University of Oregon (Eugene) with honors and passed BUD/S on his first attempt, class 136. After earning his trident, he was assigned to SEAL Team One in

Coronado, California, where he led counterinsurgency and contingency operations in the Persian Gulf and the Pacific theater of operations. He had jumped from airplanes and dived into cold oceans far from home. He was about to learn that all of that meant little to SEAL Team Six.

At first, he couldn't even find the office of the commanding officer. Unlike other naval bases, there were no signs pointing the way. He stopped in at a few buildings, but the sailors inside couldn't tell him exactly where the command was. They simply didn't know. That was strange.

As a SEAL, he knew that he could never give up. He had to keep hunting. He would stop at every building and question every uniform, if necessary.

Finally, he spotted what looked like an ammunition bunker. The door opened and two men emerged, in a hurry. They looked like outlaw bikers. Beards, long hair, earrings, tattoos. He wondered how the pair got past base security. Then, he noticed the second man was carrying a belt-fed M-60 machine gun. Before Zinke could decide whether he should report the men to the shore patrol, the two Vikings mounted a Harley-Davidson motorcycle and rode off toward a gun range on the horizon. If they were Navy men, why weren't they using official naval bunker trucks?

He had never seen that before on a U.S. Navy base.

He decided to go inside the bunker, if only to ask for directions.

Inside, he found a team room, a meeting and staging area for SEAL teams. The dirty white drop-ceiling tiles had collapsed from the weight of empty beer cans secreted up there. He had never seen that before in the U.S. Navy, either.

He had found SEAL Team Six.

The men and even the officers were wearing civilian clothes. Many looked like bikers. Their appearance was designed to allow them to blend in among civilians during covert operations in the most dangerous parts of the world. Still Zinke was shocked. In his bright whites and short hair, he was a typical squared-away naval officer—and his appearance made him an oddball. The very thing that made him normal in the Navy made him abnormal in the U.S. Navy's SEAL Team Six. It was the first of many shocks. He had joined the pirates, and the swashbuckling was about to begin.

* * *

Zinke quickly realized that the culture of the SEAL Team Six was unique. It was daring and bold but also wild and raw. It was a lion, ruthlessly effective at hunting and killing, but also a beast that answered only to itself.

The typical military hierarchy was upside down. The senior enlisted guys had come in under Lt. Cmdr. Richard Marcinko and, to an extent far greater than in any other corner of the U.S. Navy, the senior enlisted men ran the day-to-day operations. Zinke soon realized it would be unwise for an officer to buck the senior enlisted men who were technically under him. Zinke knew he must win the respect of the enlisted men under him or he would be sidelined as an officer. In the rest of the Navy, the reverse was true.

"The ship was run by Fred Fritsch, the senior enlisted man, and, if you crossed Fred, you were out. That was it. And in that organization, a master chief versus a lieutenant, the young Lieutenant Zinke would lose. It was part of the process. I knew my limit, and made sure I knew how to run a mission."

The facilities were unusual by U.S. Navy standards. In Big Navy, a ruthless campaign was underway to eliminate alcohol on base. Among the SEALs, alcohol was as common as diving masks or spare magazines. Every team room had a bar. The men didn't drink on duty, but they drank enthusiastically on base as soon as the "beer lamp" was lit. "You never drank and shot, but you certainly drank....I mean these guys were hard men. They would train hard, they would go out and they would drink hard, they would play hard, everything they did was hard."

Even though Marcinko was no longer there, SEAL Team Six was still basically an operation living under rules he laid down. "Things were pretty wild. And wild, I mean that guys were hard, we're moving fast, there probably wasn't as much accountability," Zinke said. "You know, it was called a 'porthole to Hell' for officers."

Even the officer corps at SEAL Team Six was different. Most of the officers were "mustangs," meaning that they were enlisted men who had worked their way up through the ranks, as opposed to officers who received Commissions straight out of the Naval Academy at Annapolis. In Big Navy, the SEALs' dismissive term for the regular navy, officers were rarely mustangs. SEAL Team Six seemed like a world turned upside down.

There were two major reasons for the high concentration of mustangs among the SEALs. Marcinko, the founder of SEAL Team Six, was a mustang, and he preferred other mustangs. That preference cut a cultural groove that took decades to overcome.

Also, many officers actively avoided being sent to the SEAL teams. Being an officer in the SEALs wasn't considered a solid career move at the time. Few SEAL officers rose to captain and, at this point, none had become an admiral. And the SEALs were seen as a hard bunch to command. Why kill your career to take on a thankless command that would inevitably take you into cold waters, parachute jumps, and shoot-outs with terrorists? Wasn't drinking coffee on the warm bridge of a Navy cruiser a better move?

The transition was hard on Zinke. He wasn't a mustang. Plus, he was a college man and therefore suspect. He had to earn his men's respect in a way that simply wouldn't apply in Big Navy. His rank and his uniform meant little. He had to impress the pirates of SEAL Team Six with his work ethic and his ability to get the job done, or he wasn't going to make it.

* * *

Zinke worked overtime to acclimate to SEAL Team Six. He had to become a pirate like the rest of the men. He spent nights on inflatable boats, bouncing over the waves while the radio antenna whipped him in the back. He excelled at physical exercise. He never complained. And he started ignoring naval regulations on grooming and haircuts.

"I called them 'Last of the Mohicans.' At my wedding, I had a ponytail. So did everyone around me."

He knew that when he had earned a nickname (they called him "Z"), he was in. He bonded with enlisted men. "You know, I was very tight with the SEAL teams, and the guys, and one could probably argue too tight, but also, I defended them. I was extremely loyal to the guys, and they were very loyal to me."

The unusual culture had its advantages. It was more flexible and more forgiving than Big Navy. "The SEAL culture was fundamentally different in the 1980s and 1990s. As far as the bond between the officer and the enlisted, it was a little tighter. I think that mistakes were made, you were held accountable, but your career could recover. The commander would look at you and punish you, but the punishment wasn't a shot-in-the-head dismissal."

Long before the bloodletting of constant combat began in 2001, an internal bloodletting began in the SEAL teams. A triumphant training exercise had an unexpected traumatic effect. Zinke would be an eyewitness to a turning point in SEAL history.

* * *

Zinke was on the scene when the world changed for the SEALs.

In 1991, SEAL Team Six was divided into Red

Team, Gold Team, and Blue Team, which was the most piratical of the pirates. Blue Team was called upon to demonstrate its ability to board fast-moving ships from small inflatable boats. Until they demonstrated it, the feat was considered impossible.

Using small inflatable boats with big outboard engines, the SEALs banged over the waves and approached a wall of metal several stories high—the smooth side of a U.S. Navy cruiser. Using grappling hooks and cables, they quickly scaled the slippery side of the ship. It was hard work. The inflatable boats were moving and so was the cruiser. And waves washed the hull of the ship, trying to pry off the SEALs climbing up the wet walls. Then they bounded onto the pitching deck and fanned out to dominate the crew hatches.

Through the glass of the bridge windows, senior officers watched the SEALs through binoculars. Next to Navy captains and admirals stood Zinke, the SEAL officer serving as liaison to the brass.

At first, the officers were impressed by the prowess of the SEALs—the quick and silent boarding of the ship, the rapid domination of control points of the vessel.

Then one SEAL removed his diving mask. His earring flashed in the sunlight. They watched as he shook wet hair free, exposing his long ponytail.

The officers sucked in their breath through their teeth and put down their binoculars.

Admiral Lopez, a three-star, was the senior officer on the bridge. Zinke heard Lopez say: "My Navy, these guys are in my Navy?"

"That was, I think, the last straw," Zinke said. "Right after that, came what I called the 'great bloodletting.'"

Big Navy didn't want Naval Special Warfare to be too special. It wanted the SEALs to look and act more like sailors. It wasn't just long hair, shaggy beards, and diamond earrings that would go. It was a degree of the informality and the power of the senior enlisted. The pirates would have to become professionals.

* * *

The housecleaning began with Adm. Eric Thor Olson, who took command of Seal Team Six in 1994.

Before his retirement, Admiral Olson would not only be credited with the re-creation of the world's ultimate fighting force, but he would rise higher in the ranks than any other SEAL—all the way to four-star admiral, the Navy's highest rank. He would also earn the title "Bullfrog" as the longest-serving Navy SEAL still on duty. Before retirement, he served thirty-eight years.

The admiral had impeccable SEAL credentials, making him the ideal agent of cultural change. Olson graduated from the U.S. Naval Academy in 1973 and qualified as a SEAL in 1974, graduating in BUD/S in class 76. He served in several operational capacities with the SEALs, ultimately commanding at every level, including the Underwater Demolition Team, Seal Delivery Vehicle Team, Seal Special Boat Squadron, and SEAL Team Six. He also served as a SEAL instructor, strategy and development officer, and joint special operations officer. Olson won the Silver Star for his bravery during the Battle of Mogadishu, where the Navy found that he "demonstrated a complete disregard for his own personal safety in the accomplishment of his mission." Known as both a gentleman and a frogman, Olson was arguably the perfect choice to accomplish the task he was given: to reinvent the SEALs as sailors, not buccaneers.

When Olson assumed command of Naval Special Warfare Command (which commands all SEAL teams) in 1999, he immediately started reshaping the SEALs. His cultural influence continued to be felt when he rose to commander of all special operations (SOCOM) in 2007. He retired from the Navy in 2011, when he relinquished command of SOCOM to Admiral William H. McRaven. It marked the first time that command of SOCOM shifted from one SEAL officer to another. (SOCOM includes Army, Navy, Marine, and Air Force components.)

So Olson had the chops to win the respect of the SEALs. But it was his personality—the opposite of Marcinko's—that surprised them. Zinke said, "He was quiet."

"He's not the bull in the room. And when you look at the personalities between Dick Marcinko and Eric Olson, it's a big difference. One is bravado and in your face, and the other one is quiet, very thoughtful. I think the teams followed Olson's lead and his personality. I think Olson had a profound influence on the change of culture of the teams, probably more than anyone else," he said.

It wasn't an easy evolution, several SEALs said.

Olson made several changes immediately. All SEALs under his command would be in uniform while on duty without exception. Regulation haircuts were once again required. Earrings were banned.

And the way Olson communicated the new policies was different, too. "I remember when his new policies came in, he didn't go down to the team rooms and explain it. He made a video, which we all watched. This was a very tough group, that was very senior enlisted driven, and these were hard, hard men.

They were kind of, they had their ways and in order to change the culture, you know, it was hard."

The SEALs did not like it. But the video format itself was a message. These policy changes were not subject to a back-and-forth discussion, like in the Marcinko days. Instead it was a command.

Olson made it clear to the men of the SEAL teams that they had to change or they had to leave. Many did. The old guard that had served enough time to earn a pension quickly retired. Others stuck it out until they made their twenty years, qualified for a pension, and then they, too, left. Some even departed before they could secure a pension. The cultural shift was too much of a shock. Within four years, most of the old guard—officers and enlisted—were gone. Tens of millions of dollars' worth of training and experience left with them. It was a real loss, though few dared say so.

"I think they looked at what the future was going to be and didn't want any part of it," Zinke said.

A new SEAL team culture emerged, one that won the confidence of Big Navy's admirals. It was clean-cut and by the book. It was more like the U.S. Army's elite Delta Force. It narrowed the cultural gap between regular and irregular (special) forces.

* * *

By the end of his second stint with Team Six, Zinke began to see the well-oiled machine that Six had become. In 2004, Zinke was assigned as deputy and acting commander, Combined Joint Special Operations Task Force—Arabian Peninsula in support of Operation Iraqi Freedom, where he led a force of special operations personnel in Iraq in the conduct of 360 combat patrols, 48 Direct Action missions, and hundreds of sensitive operations. He was responsible for killing or capturing 72 known enemies, insurgents, and terrorists. By the end of 2006, he was awarded two Bronze Stars for combat.

However much the technology had changed, Zinke noticed that the attitudes of SEALs had been transformed. "I can't overemphasize enough the ability of them to make the decision, and it's tied to their trigger finger. If you're not compliant, there's ways of making you comply, but if you're a threat in that environment, you will die in a hurry," Zinke said.

In the mind of every SEAL in a covert operation, Zinke explained, is a rapid calculation beyond words. "They're only engaging what goes through their mind, which is threat/nonthreat." It doesn't really matter who has a gun. The decision is: is that target presenting himself as a threat? SEALs call this "threat/no threat." It is a nearly instantaneous categorization of people that they encounter during operations. Honing this ability takes thousands of hours of training, in the "Kill House" training sites and in firefights far from home. It is imperative to the survival of the man and those working with him.

Zinke cited the Osama bin Laden raid as an example of the lightning fast "threat/no threat" calculation: "I think they honestly were looking at what they were trained to do and I don't think you can deviate from that, because that's what they do every time: does he have a weapon?" That is really the only consideration. "I think he [Osama bin Laden] presented himself as a threat and they took the shot. I don't think they even thought about it."

He pointed out that there were others in the bin Laden compound who were not shot, Zinke added: "The other guys along the way, if also presented as a threat, and they would have been killed." The fact that civilians were not killed during a high-adrenaline operation is a testament to SEAL training, he said.

Like many within the teams, Zinke thinks too much media coverage—from the *New Yorker* magazine to a Hollywood film—is a kind of poisoned gift, a necklace with a sharp, rusty edge. "I think you know very well the SEALs have been glamorized recently. But, I think people oftentimes forget how hard, and ultimately 'blue collar tough' the job is when you're involved in day-to-day training. You're not jumping out of airplanes every day. There's a certain grind to it, and you have to be dedicated to be good. It's a lot of time away from your family, the divorce rate is really high. The number of days deployed remains well over two hundred, I'm sure. That's the job that we forget."

The SEAL community is very tight, and there's a lot of sadness within it. "There's sadness over how many SEALs we've lost, of how many only sons that we've lost," Zinke said, with no attempt to mask his pain. "It is a tremendous amount of emotions when you have parents of a SEAL, their only son, and they're so proud that their son is a SEAL, and he gets killed."

*   *   *

Zinke was elected to the Montana State Senate in 2008 and now represents District 2, which includes the cities of Whitefish, Columbia Falls, and all of Glacier National Park.

He has been asked by many to run for the U.S. Congress in 2014. He may be on his way to joining another elite club, with its own traditions, rules, and initiation rites. If he does enter national politics, one of his goals will be to protect the SEALs from excessive bureaucracy. The United States, he said, still needs its pirates.

CHAPTER 4

Drago's War

We will call him "Drago," because that is how he is known in the teams and because he remains under threat from terrorists.

His tale has never been told before,[1] and it illustrates the openness of SEALs to new talents. He was one of the oldest men, and one of the few Polish immigrants, to join the SEALs. More tellingly, his story illuminates a key chapter in the development of the SEALs.

He was also the only SEAL to serve a prison sentence before joining the teams—but that was in another country, in a brutal time.

* * *

Drago came screaming into the world in 1962, in Lodz, Poland. A crowded industrial city beset by food and fuel shortages. Most of the damage of World War II, which had ended in 1945, remained unrepaired. Bomb craters in parks became muddy wading holes, and the rusting ruins of factories became playgrounds for poor kids like Drago.

As with most Poles, his family was divided between the pull of its centuries-old Roman Catholic traditions and the new totalitarian Soviet Communist ideology imposed by Poland's Russian masters.

The conflict simmered and flared not just in Drago's country but inside his family. His parents had met as teachers, but their lives veered in different directions. His father became a local leader of the Communist Party in Western Poland. He quit his job teaching art history to devote himself full-time to the Communist cause. In time, his father's faithfulness to the Communists would be rewarded when he was made department director for theaters and museums at the Polish Ministry of Art. His mother never stopped loving her life in the classroom, and she became an accomplished teacher. She received few raises or praises for her hard work, but she believed her reward was in the next life. She was a devout Catholic.

His parents' views of human nature and morality were antagonistic opposites. Drago's father, and the Communists generally, saw masses of men who were entitled by History to commit atrocities, because the ends justified the means. Drago's mother believed that each individual would be judged at the end of time by a fair but firm God, and that every needless misery inflicted on another would be punished. The love his parents shared could not bridge their dueling values.

His parents fought around the clock, most often on Sundays. Communists are required to be atheists; the Soviet leader would tolerate no other gods before him. Yet Drago's mother wanted to take her son to church.

By the time Drago was four years old, the cold peace between his mother and father became molten opposition. One Sunday morning, his father blocked the door as his wife and his young son were dressing for church. In those days, Poles proudly wore their finest clothes to Sunday Mass.

His father was adamant and would not move from the doorway. "You cannot go because I will lose my job," he pleaded. "They are going to fire me. You cannot go to church."

Drago's mother wouldn't listen to her husband. She was more worried about her son's soul than her mate's job.

As the couple argued, Drago watched as his mother calmly opened the window to the street. In the window frame, his grandmother appeared. As his father continued to bar the door, his mother passed the boy out of the window. His grandmother took Drago into her arms. She set the boy gently on the sidewalk and led him by the hand to church.

Her defiant plan had been worked out in advance. His father was furious.

Drago learned a life lesson that would later aid him in the SEALs: Every obstacle can be overcome with persistence and creativity.

* * *

Later, Drago's father took the young boy on a train trip to see his own mother. She was delighted to see her grandson, but the boy asked her a question that touched off a conversational firestorm. Since he often heard his parents arguing about Communism, he asked his grandmother: "What is a Communist?"

He still remembers her answer. "They are Satan's henchmen. They are evil people, they are Satans. They murder innocent people."

"You mean like the real Satan?" Drago asked. He was picturing a red-skinned monster with horns and fire.

"Yes," she said without hesitation. "They have a hose, they breathe fire, and they are nasty and dangerous, and you need to avoid them."

His father had defined his life by the long climb up

the Communist ladder. And he was sitting in his own mother's kitchen as she called Communists like him "Satans." He tried to talk as quietly as he could. "Ma, you cannot talk that way. I am not Satan."

His own mother looked at her only son. "If you sold your soul to them, you are Satan to me."

Drago never forgot that moment. Both of his grandmothers and his mother were uncompromising in their principles—even if their views offended family members. Drago learned to hold on to his beliefs no matter what the world thought. This lesson would serve him well in prison and in the SEALs.

*　*　*

Dictatorship is always a slow-moving civil war of the rulers against the ruled. And civil wars divide families, too.

By the 1970s, the struggle between Communism and freedom divided his parents. They were exhausted by arguments and beyond reconciliation. His father joined the government bureaucracy in Warsaw, then a two-hour train ride away, and his mother stayed in Lodz. Drago lived with her and his younger brother and sister.

As a schoolteacher, his mother began attending secret nighttime meetings and helped form an independent trade union. Later that union secretly merged into Solidarity, a national union of unions that represented millions of workers standing up to Communism. The irony of workers organizing into unions in order to fight the Soviet "worker's paradise" was lost on no one.

Drago, too, joined the anti-Communist underground. Lech Walesa had emerged as the national leader of the Solidarity union, battling police in the Gdansk shipyards. By age twenty, Drago and a friend were printing an underground newspaper—really, a double-sided, single-sheet leaflet. It was a dangerous thing to do. "At the time," Drago recalls, "you could go to jail just for having a typewriter. They [the Communists] controlled everything."

Distributing the paper was the riskiest part of the job. After printing a few hundred copies at a friend's house, Drago would walk the streets of Lodz and press them into people's hands. "It was kind of naïve, because you know what you're doing, that you're going to get caught. But we didn't care at the time," he told us.

Drago soon felt a policeman's grip on his shoulder. He was arrested for a crime to be named later. At first, he was held in Lodz City jail, alongside common criminals, while the police brutally tried to learn the names of his accomplices. He didn't give in. He had grown up hard and tough, and they couldn't make him feel afraid.

Fighting the guards became a full-time job. "When I was in jail, I didn't obey the rules. We had our own rules. We were political prisoners, but we never considered ourselves criminals."[2]

The fight began with chairs. The prison chairs had no backs, and guards would beat prisoners who leaned against walls or slouched in chairs. When he arrived at the city jail, he was told to sit bolt upright, like a department store mannequin. Drago decided to break the rules, and lean back on the wall. A guard saw him and roughly dragged him out of the cell. The guard yelled and threatened.

Once he was back in the cell, Drago vowed to escalate his disobedience. He laid on the bed. "They came in, they dragged me out, and they beat the hell out of me."

Back in his cell, he immediately climbed back into bed.

Drago refused to give up. It was a contest of wills. Eventually the guards gave up, but not before writing a complaint letter to his mother saying that Drago didn't follow prison rules and was disobedient.

* * *

After many months and time in two prisons, Drago was released. The Communist rulers bowed to pressure from the Solidarity union, Pope John Paul II, President Ronald Reagan, and most of the civilized world. A general amnesty was announced, and Drago was set free.

But he was still watched. Often a policeman would stop Drago on the sidewalk and drag him into a patrol car. He would sit in the cage in the back as the police drove around the city in circles. Then, hours later, one would say: "Okay, get out." He would walk home wondering how long he would be free.

Drago realized that one day the police could pick him up and he would disappear, as so many Poles had vanished before. He had heard about their unmarked graves in the Katyn Forest. So he went to the U.S. embassy.

An American diplomat asked him where in America he wanted to go.

He said, "I don't ever want to be cold again. The hotter the place, the better."

He was asked: "How about Memphis, Tennessee?"

"Memphis, Tennessee?" he wondered. "I know Elvis Presley is from Memphis, Tennessee, but that is all I know." The diplomat showed him a map. Then he said it was warm there.

Drago shouted with joy. "Yes!"

Three anxious months later, in March 1984, he had a visa and a plane ticket to the United States.

He was thrown into an alien world with technologies and people he could barely understand. "I didn't speak English. Now, I know we were poor. At that time I didn't know that we were poor. I just was living my life, but I remember my mom had to put newspaper sometimes into our jackets as insulation to shield us from freezing winds during harsh Polish winters. We didn't have the right clothes. We could not afford it." In Poland he was often hungry. "We had the coupons for each month and we were allowed to eat only so much meat, so much sugar. I don't remember what the portions were, but they were very small. Even with coupons, I remember my mom had to stand in lines at five a.m. to buy bread. Sometimes, by the time she made through the line, everything was sold... well, that meant we were going to school hungry. She was trying her best, and my siblings knew it."

* * *

He began his American dream by working as a part-time janitor, sweeping out schools. Then he found a job answering the phones at a car-parts shop. He didn't have to use much English, but it was good practice. By

81

1988, by being friendly and working hard, he won a job as shop technician in a Mercedes-Benz dealership. "I was making really good money and enjoying life."

The first Gulf War came in January 1991.

* * *

He had just become a U.S. citizen and wanted to serve his new land. "I announced to my friends, I say, 'I'm leaving. I'm going to fight in the war.'"

"And they told me I was crazy. 'What do you mean?'" Drago said. "This is my country and it's fighting the war, so I'm just going to go fight the war for my country." He'd made up his mind.

At first, he tried to join the U.S. Army. He didn't know the difference between the Army and the Navy. Then, by chance, he met some Navy SEALs at a sky-diving event. They told him that the Army was like the post office with guns. If he wanted action, he should join the SEALs.

He went to see the Navy recruiter the next day. Most of the process had been completed by Army recruiters, so once the screening was complete, he went back to the Navy office. On Thursday, he asked, "When will I ship out to boot camp?" The answer was "Monday."

He was sworn in on a Friday morning, married on

Friday afternoon, and shipped out to basic training on Monday. "It was all very quick."

Months later, he graduated at the top of his boot camp company and won the excellence award as the number one recruit that training session. He was thirty-one years old.

But Drago still had to get into the SEALs, and his medical file showed that he had a kidney stone.

In Millington, Tennessee, he went to see a Petty Officer, who was a Navy SEAL motivator there. Drago explained that the kidney stone in his file would keep him out of the SEALs.

"Yes, I want to see your medical record," the Petty Officer said.

Drago handed him the file. The Officer opened it up, looked at it and saw the offending page. "Oh, that's it."

He told him to leave the room and a second later called Drago back in. "What page are you talking about? Can you show it to me?"

There was no page about a kidney stone in the file. "Do you see any kidney stones anywhere?" he asked.

Drago said: "Nope, I don't. I don't even remember any such page!"

"Neither do I."

Drago passed the medical exam for the SEALs.

* * *

Three weeks into BUD/S, Drago's leg was so swollen by flesh-eating bacteria that he couldn't put his pants on. He was sent to the infirmary and put into the next BUD/S class, number 185. He would have to start all over again.

He was determined not to quit. Hell Week came. He started Hell Week with size ten shoes. Soon, the severe training rubbed the skin from his soles and his heels. His feet swelled to size thirteen and a half. "My feet looked like a pepperoni pizza."

Still, Drago refused to quit. "It was nothing compared to a Polish prison," he said.

One night during BUD/S, a friend asked him why he was so determined. Drago realized that he was tired of hearing men say that they were "*trying* to be a SEAL" or "giving it their best shot."

So when he was asked, he had a powerfully simple response: "I didn't come here to *try* to be a SEAL. I came here to become a SEAL. I didn't come here to try. I'm not trying it. I'm going to be a SEAL unless you just kick me out for something or I break myself. I will be a SEAL."

The room was quiet. His powerful determination stunned them.

* * *

He passed and, in March 1993, received orders to report to SEAL Team Two.

At the time, the "welcome to SEAL Teams" was old-school and brutal. Today they may call it hazing...back then "it was just a welcome FNG (Fucking New Guy) to the Teams," Drago said.

Every Friday night, the new guys were required to join the older guys to share a keg of beer in the high bay, a tall space in the team compound with cranes and chain lifts. "We FNGs weren't there to drink beer—we were basically amusement for the experienced guys," Drago said.

Drago and the new guys would be dangled upside down by their feet, taped with rigger's tape, from the rafters or from a crane. They dangled like bats. Sometimes, mercifully they were lowered down to have some beer poured onto them. Other times, they would get beaten up. "It wasn't called hazing. It was called 'welcome to the teams.'"

The brutality had a purpose, as it did with other fraternities. It bonded the men together and it built trust. Once everyone was assured that the new guys were tough enough to take it, they knew they could trust them in battle.

That trust would prove to be essential when Drago was part of the SEAL platoon ordered to hijack a Russian oil tanker.

* * *

In the Persian Gulf, in the year 2000, some Russian tankers were illegally moving large shipments for Iraqi dictator Saddam Hussein. Violating U.S. and United Nations sanctions gave Hussein a river of cash to feed his war machine and his Baath party cronies—while his people starved. If the United States failed to dam this illegal tide of money, Saddam Hussein would again threaten Israel and America's Arab allies as well as fund terrorist groups, as he had in the past.

Drago knew that his mission was important. He, with his platoon, was stationed on an aircraft carrier, the USS *John F. Kennedy*.

The target: a Russian oil tanker called the *Volgoneft*.

As SEAL snipers circled in helicopters above the contraband tanker, Drago and his teammates fast-roped to the deck of the tanker.

Drago knew that the team would have to seize the ship before it escaped into Iran's territorial waters. (Though Iran and Iraq were enemies, they often protected each other's shipping to vex their shared enemy— Uncle Sam.) Drago's team would have only minutes.

They landed on the steel deck and ran toward the bridge. Within three minutes, they had tied up the captain and the bridge crew. Belowdecks, another SEAL team was surprising the engine room crew.

But the Russian captain wasn't ready to give up. He kept barking in Russian, telling his crew not to cooperate. He was betting that the Americans would not understand. But Drago did. He had been forced to learn Russian in Polish schools. Drago grabbed him by his cap and led him to a small access door into the ship's main chimney. He said, in Russian: "If you don't shut up, I am going to shove you in and lock you in this chimney, and if you don't fit I will beat you in and you'll be sitting there quietly."

The Russian captain, shocked by Drago's command of his language and his commanding personality, bowed his head. He would cause no more trouble.

Drago enjoyed his moment with the Russian. After a childhood of pain, it was a little justice.

* * *

Life in the SEAL teams is dangerous, but it is always leavened with humor.

In planning a snatch-and-grab mission in Iraq, the intelligence briefer warned that there were two large dogs hidden behind twelve-foot-high concrete walls in the target's Baghdad compound. The target was a terrorist leader. If the dogs barked, any hope of surprising the insurgent leader would be lost. Still, Drago didn't like the idea of killing the dogs. "I like dogs. I like animals, so I didn't like that idea, but you have to do what you have to do."

It was a joint operation between the SEALs and the GROM, a Polish Special Forces unit. The briefer was a part of the Polish team.

Later that night, the SEAL team approached the concrete wall of the target's compound. A teammate silently scaled the ladder and poked his head over the top of the wall, then scanned the yard with his night-vision goggles. At another place, a GROM lookout climbed into place.

The radio crackled. Drago heard, in Polish, an urgent whisper: "I see two huge dogs. Damn! Fucking huge!"

Drago sighed. This was going to be tough.

Yet, he followed the plan, climbed the ladder, and dropped into the compound. His teammates dropped in behind him. As Drago ran toward the house, he saw the "dogs" that the Poles were talking about—two skinny cows. They were mindlessly chewing grass.

They quickly entered the house and captured the target without firing a shot. It was a "perfect op"—

what SEALs call an operation when no shots are fired. Except for the cow-dog confusion.

They returned to base to debrief.

After the mission, Drago looked in the conference room and saw the poor guy who made the call about the two big "dogs."

His other teammates had made up flash cards, similar to the ones used to train soldiers to recognize aircraft by their outlines. One of the teammates held up a card. "What's this?"

The lookout looked glum. "Dog."

Another card was held up. "What's this?"

"Cow."

"What's this?"

"Chicken."

Drago walked out because he was laughing so hard.

*   *   *

In Iraq, Drago was a liaison officer between the SEALs and the GROM. "So I was sort of double-dipping. I was going on missions with GROM and with our guys."

Drago and his team were hunting an insurgent leader, a former general in Saddam Hussein's army who was organizing armed attacks on Americans.

When they found him, he was hiding in a house

with blast-proof doors. "So we prepared an appropriate charge capable to blast through such doors. As we were coming to the doors (I was the lead breacher on this mission) I noticed that the intel was wrong—there was a solid door but not as strong as the intel indicated. I am breacher, and it is my expertise. I need to know such things. Powerful explosive charges placed on weak doors would destroy the whole room and might kill the occupant. I changed the charge to a smaller one, appropriate for the construction of the door (our entry point). It happened that [the target] was awakened, possibly by the barking dogs, and for some reason decided to walk to the door and put his ear to it while holding the doorknob, as I blasted through his door."

The explosion just threw the door away and left him standing in place. "It didn't even throw him on the ground—he was dazed, he didn't know what was going on."

The general was left holding only the doorknob, like a cartoon character.

Drago used a zip-tie handcuff as a tourniquet for the general's bleeding hand.

As he came around, the Iraqi general heard the operators from GROM talking, he spoke to them in

Polish. "Hey! Hey! Stop for a second! You are Polish guys? Hey, get me out of here. The Americans are after me. Get me out of here! I have money! I have whatever! Get me out of here."

The Poles asked him to verify his name. He said, "Yeah, yeah, that's me."

The Polish commander said to Drago: "Hey, we have the son of a bitch."

The general started crying. "You bastards, I'm going to catch you. How can you do this to me?"

The general had learned Polish while he attended flight training in Poland, when that country was a satellite of the Soviet Union. Iraq was also a Soviet ally in the 1980s.

For Drago, he found that his unique history was constantly an unexpected asset in the SEALs.

He remains grateful to America and to the SEALs for giving him a new life. "But you know what, only in America, the only country in the world that you can come with nothing and through hard work and determination you can succeed and become a valuable member of this great society. I came with the bag of clothes, not even speaking English, and now I am on the tip of the spear of the most elite force of our country. It is amazing. It can't happen any other place in the world but America. I love America. Everything I have I owe to America and its wonderful people. Often people ask me: 'You're Polish American?' and I always say, 'No, I don't believe in that. I don't believe in being Something-American. You're either American or not, and I am an American.'"

CHAPTER 5

Afghanistan: Operation Red Wings

Ringed by razor wire, Asadabad is a lonely U.S. out-post in Eastern Afghanistan's Kunar Valley. Its outer concrete walls are pockmarked with bullet holes and the brown-red burns of exploded grenades. At night, the wind is cold and constant, blowing around debris of past battles.

Asadabad was called a forward operating base, because nothing lies in front of it except the shad-owy enemy. The attackers are mostly Taliban and a pickup crew of militants, who would climb up the steep, snaking goat paths from Pakistan. The border is unmarked and unfenced—an invisible line that the Americans knew by GPS and the enemy by tradition. All other American or allied forces lay to Asadabad's rear, a hard day's drive or a long helicopter journey from the south or the west. Help was far away and the enemy was close.

In June 2005, Asadabad was home to the U.S. Marines of the Second Battalion, Third Regiment. The Taliban had welcomed them with a rain of rocket attacks. Day and night, the base was rocked by mortars and probed by sniper shots. No wonder the Marines called Asadabad "A-bad."

Every move against the enemy failed to stop the attackers. The Marines had sent foot patrols into the steep, dry hills, fired fusillades of mortars, and called in air strikes. The explosions echoed down the rocky valley walls. But, the next day, the attackers were back.

To rid themselves of the constant assaults by Taliban forces, which were led by a warlord named Ahmed Shah, the Marines called Special Operations Command (SOCOM) for help.

Operation Red Wings was born. Some accounts refer to it as "Operation Red Wing," but that is incorrect. It's named after an NHL franchise team (the Red Wings), as are all other operations in that operational series.

That fateful call set in motion the bloodiest battle in the forty-five-year history of the SEALs and the largest air search-and-rescue mission since the end of the Vietnam War, and it yielded the first Medal of Honor for a SEAL in the war on terror. It was a horror show that produced heroes and corpses.

* * *

Senior Crew Chief Dan Healy was in charge of planning the SEAL component of Operation Red Wings.

He had grown up near the New Hampshire coast and drifted into the Navy with a friend. Soon, he was determined to join the SEALs, and he made it through BUD/S on his first attempt. He spent the bulk of his SEAL career shuttling between Southern California and Hawaii, usually as an instructor. He won high marks from his SEAL students for his patience and his gung-ho attitude. And, they said, he was fun to party with.

Healy was determined to prove himself. Ever since the September 11 attacks, he was bucking to get in combat. Now in Afghanistan, in 2005, he finally got his chance. He was a few months into his first deployment in Afghanistan when his commander asked him to plan the SEAL component of Operation Red Wings. Working out of a cubicle choked with maps and intelligence reports, he became obsessed with finding the Taliban warlord killing the Marines in A-bad.

On the morning of June 27, 2005, Healy called together four members of SEAL Team Ten: communications officer Dan Dietz, sniper Matthew Axelson, medic Marcus Luttrell, and Lt. Michael Murphy, the unit's commanding officer.

Raised in Littleton, Colorado, Dietz as a youngster wanted to be a ninja until he found out it wasn't really a profession, his mother said. After becoming a SEAL, he slept through his alarm one morning. As Dietz rushed in late for duty, he impressed everyone with his abject apology and even volunteered his own punishment. A SEAL officer remembers that day well: "He gave himself a harsher punishment than I would have given him"—in this case, running in combat boots and cleaning out a storage locker. His willingness to hold himself accountable impressed everyone, the officer said. Dietz had recently married Maria. She went by the nickname "Patsy" and was madly in love with him. Their long overseas phone calls were legendary.

Matthew Axelson was a sniper. "Axe," as the team called him, was a high achiever whose family lived off a quiet cul-de-sac, a few miles from Apple Computer's headquarters in suburban Cupertino, California. His plan was to serve his country until he turned twenty-five and then become a schoolteacher in Chico. His wife, Cindy, was impressed by his humility. When people asked Axelson what he did, he would just say he was "in the Navy." Besides golf, good beer, and California, Axelson loved being a SEAL. Tall and good-natured, he was respected in the teams for his hard-core training regimen and his uncomplaining professionalism.

From the small ranch town of Willis, Texas, medic Marcus Luttrell had trained since he was 15 to join the SEALs. He and his twin brother, Morgan, both dreamed of becoming SEALs. The twins found a Texan who agreed to train them before they joined the Navy at eighteen. They ran for hours down dusty country roads with concrete blocks on both shoulders. They climbed ropes and spent hours in cold-water pools. After high school, they joined the Navy and were selected for SEAL training. They each made it through BUD/S on their first try. Later, the twins commissioned a special tattoo: each would have half of the SEAL trident tattooed on his back. When they stood together, the tattoos formed one large SEAL insignia. Tattoos are a common way to celebrate the successful completion of BUD/S, but the ambitious size and complexity of their back tattoos quickly became the talk of the teams.

Lt. Michael Murphy, the team's commander, hailed from Patchogue, New York. He stitched a patch from the New York City Fire Department inside his uniform. The September 11 attacks were "a major motivator" for him, one team member recalls. He proposed to his fiancée, Heather Duggan, under the Rockefeller Center Christmas tree in 2003. She immediately said yes, as the ice skaters circled on the rink below. The couple planned to marry as soon as he returned from Afghanistan, and he counted the days on his cell phone.

Healy didn't waste time with preliminaries. The team would be going deep into enemy territory.

The plan was simple. A helicopter would insert the SEAL team at night a few miles from a village where the warlord Ahmed Shah was supposedly holed up, if the intelligence reports were right. They would rope down and find a concealed position. If they spotted Shah, they would radio "eyes on target," and an eighty-man Quick Reaction Force would swoop in to capture or kill him. If Murphy's team succeeded, the attacks on the Marines at A-bad would cease.

On an impulse or a premonition, Axe decided to pack a few extra magazines of ammunition. Luttrell saw him, wondered about the extra weight, and then took a few extra magazines for himself. Resupply would be impossible in the field, and running out of ammo in a firefight is a death sentence that the lazy impose on themselves. As it turned out, they would need every round.

* * *

With their weapons and gear, the four SEALs boarded a U.S. Army 160th Special Aviation helicopter. It thundered off toward the drop zone: a field of waist-high grass and rotting stumps. Illegal loggers had long since cleared the trees, making it ideal for a Taliban ambush. It was still dark when they arrived. The men slid silently down ropes from the hovering chopper.

The helicopter sound faded away into the night sky and was gone. The four SEALs were on their own in what they called "Indian country." They waited in frozen silence for 15 long minutes, straining their ears for the noise of enemy movement. They heard only the wind and the rattle of bony branches of shrubs. They were alone, on a high plateau, in the Taliban's backyard. And, so far, no one had spotted them.

As a thunderstorm crashed overhead, the SEALs lined up and hiked into the horizon, a jagged tooth-like line lit only by the dim moon. Using a special GPS, they found their way to a rocky nook overlooking the sleeping village. Then, storm winds pushed in a thick, gravy-like fog that cut off the team's view of the village. They had to move close—a dangerous decision so near to a Taliban stronghold.

Murphy found a finger of rock that looked down on the target—a perfect observation post, but a risky one. If they were attacked from behind, they could be trapped. Still, they settled in, hiding under brush and fallen trees. When the sun rose, the village would come to life and, the SEALs hoped, their target would emerge to relieve himself.

Shortly after dawn, the SEALs heard an eerie noise, a sort of tinkling sound that grew louder and louder. At first, they couldn't explain it. Then, it became obvious. Goats. Hundreds of them, with bells around their necks, flooded down the slope. Then came the shepherds, two graybeards and a boy, driving the flock right into the SEALs' position.

In a flash, Murphy and his men captured them.

Now came a painful choice. Shepherds often spy for the Taliban. And boys often support their siblings and parents by sitting on a high mountain lookout with a small mirror. A tilt of the mirror in their hand would flash a signal to the village below if American or allied forces approached. For these patient hours in the wind and rain, visiting Arabs or Pakistanis would pay as much as a dollar per day—a good wage for a boy in the remote slopes of Eastern Afghanistan. So these seemingly simple shepherds were likely employees or associates of the Taliban.

The team briefly considered shooting them, but they quickly decided against it. Gunshots would reveal their position. Morality was also a factor. "We are not murderers," Murphy said, according to Luttrell. He ordered the prisoners to be released.

As soon as the shepherds were gone, the SEALs ran over rocks and stumps, surging up the slope to their old location. They had to find a defensive position before the enemy found them.

They were under no illusions. The information about their presence was too valuable not to be immediately passed along. It was only a matter of moments.

The Taliban were not long in coming. Initial intelligence reports put Shah's forces at eighty fighters, but some forty Taliban appeared on the ridges above them. The enemy held the high ground and started flanking the SEAL team on both sides; they were about to be surrounded.

Luttrell began firing, followed quickly by Axelson and Dietz. Excellent marksmen, the SEALs started dropping the turbaned fighters. Still, they were outnumbered forty to four. Wood splintered all around them as the Taliban sprayed AK-47 fire. The SEALs couldn't hold out for long.

The radio spoke only static. There would be no air support or rescue.

Murphy ordered them to retreat down the ravine, gaining distance and time. But the Taliban pursued their prey relentlessly.

In a singular act of bravery, Dietz volunteered to climb to a nearby peak to get a radio signal out of the narrow, sharp-sided valley. He ran up a steep slope as bullets made the dirt jump behind his steps. At the top, he frantically worked the radio. A stray shot took off his right thumb. More bullets pulverized the radio. It fell in pieces from his injured hands. He couldn't get through to the base now. The cavalry would not be coming.

Dietz abandoned the pieces of the radio and climbed back down to rejoin his teammates. No one said a word. Whatever they would do next, they would do it together.

Most likely, Dietz took at least two shots as he scrambled down the mountain to rejoin the team. Without medical treatment, he would die within an hour. Still, he kept firing at the closing enemy.

Without an air rescue, or close-air support from above, the SEAL team was doomed.

Geometry, geography, and numbers were against them. The enemy outnumbered them and was closing in on them like the claws of a giant crab. The militants held the high ground and were encircling them. It was time for a Hail Mary pass.

The radio was gone, but Murphy still had his satellite phone. Stepping out of cover, the lieutenant walked into the open for a clear signal. He knew the enemy only needed seconds to target him. Murphy punched in the number for the SEAL command post at Bagram Air Base.

The seconds needed to transfer him to a senior officer were an agonizing eternity. When connected, he managed to report their dire situation at the moment that bullets showered the dirt and rocks around him. The officer said that help was on the way. Somehow, Murphy summoned the strength to respond, "Roger that, sir. Thank you."

As Murphy staggered back to his men, bullets rained down on him. Bleeding and dying, he had given his men a chance.

No matter the pain, the SEALs had to keep moving and shooting. They scrambled and stumbled down the hills, stopping only to fire back at their pursuers. It would take almost an hour for help to arrive—an eon in battle. Would their ammunition and luck hold?

* * *

Back at Bagram, Lt. Cmdr. Michael McGreevy instantly approved a daylight rescue, though standard procedure was to fly helicopters only at night, when they were less vulnerable to ground fire. No one disagreed with his decision. They knew the stakes. He burst out of the SEAL command, almost bowling someone over. "They're in a TIC!" McGreevy yelled. He meant "troops in contact," or a battle to the death.

McGreevy ran into the barracks to round up any SEALs or Night Stalkers (elite Army units) he could find. The men sprang into action, grabbing gear and guns while running for the door. They knew the stakes and the score.

Onboard trucks racing for the airfield, sergeants divided men into "chalks," or assault units.

Healy counted heads.

The posse was coming.

Rotors already were turning on the lead helicopter as the men clambered onboard.

The pilots had thundered through their preflight checklists.

Healy said to a nearby enlisted SEAL: "Get off. I outrank you."

Friends say it was typical of Healy. He was taking charge, consumed with saving the lives of his men without any atom of concern about himself. It was a fateful decision.

* * *

Four helicopters beat into the sky, climbing at top speed. Less than twenty minutes later, the pilot had bad news. The two Black Hawks, including Healy's, were too heavy to vault over the sharp spikes of the mountains of Afghanistan's eastern Kunar province. As precious minutes ticked past, the choppers diverted to Jalalabad, where sixteen men were ordered off the Black Hawks. Healy stayed onboard.

The men who climbed off were silent but unhappy to be left out. "We wanted to get those guys," one told us.

With more than ten minutes lost, the two helicopters decided to outrun their slower, armored escorts. Contact with the trapped SEAL team had been lost. There was no time to spare.

Soon, Healy's helicopter neared the SEAL team's last known location. The lead chopper moved into position. The SEALs and Night Stalkers stood up to rope down from the helicopter.

The door opened and the wind roared in. No one saw the two-man Taliban crew, on the ground below, load a rocket-propelled grenade launcher. In less than a second, the grenade found its mark (the open door), and a fireball erupted inside the helicopter.

The SEALs onboard the second Black Hawk were horrified to see the lead chopper explode, tilt its nose upward and spill men to the ground. The remaining air crew, belted in, were trapped inside a flaming comet, plunging down into a boulder-choked ravine. Flames speared out of every opening and as the craft splintered in the rocks.

Healy, McGreevy, and a dozen others were gone. The sudden loss of fourteen special operators was the largest one-time loss of naval special warfare personnel since World War II.

Inside the second helicopter, the SEALs desperately wanted to land and make the enemy pay. But the radio gave different orders: Leave now. No one had to explain. They had lost one aircraft and fourteen men; no one wanted the losses to grow. Murphy's men were likely gone, too. Why risk lives to retrieve corpses? The decision was logical but emotionally unwelcome. Full of quiet, angry, and sad men, the second helicopter lumbered home.

As night fell, the SEALs planned another rescue mission for their comrades. Survivors (if any) would be saved, and the fallen would be taken home with honor. The agonizing mystery: No one knew the fate of Murphy's team. Could they still be alive?

* * *

Gloating, Ahmed Shah phoned the *News*, a daily in Islamabad, Pakistan. He said his men had killed five commandos and brought down a helicopter. He would release a video soon, he promised. Such a victory over the Americans had to be exploited so that Shah could rise in the Taliban's ranks.

The news reached the United States the morning of June 29. No names were released. As the rest of the country prepared for the July Fourth weekend, several frantic families scattered across America waited for news of their loved ones.

They phoned and e-mailed each other, desperate for news. In a New Hampshire trailer park, Dan Healy's mother, Natalie, awoke from a fearful dream. *Is Dan OK?* she wondered.

Back in the vicinity of Asadabad, rescue teams had landed and were moving toward the crash site and the ground team's last known position. Nearly every type of U.S. Special Forces—Rangers, Night Stalkers, SEALs—joined the mission. Afghan Special Forces provided translators and guides. Overhead, Navy and

Air Force planes filled the sky, searching for the missing Americans and pounding enemy positions. The cavalry had come.

* * *

On the ground, Luttrell climbed through the brush. Alone and burning with thirst, he had spent the night hiding in a shallow cave as Taliban footsteps crunched around him. He had no way to contact the Americans flying overhead. If he showed himself, the Taliban would shoot him before they could land.

Dizzy and blurry-eyed, Luttrell collapsed on a mountain trail. He stirred as a shadow covered him. He looked up at a bearded shepherd. The man gave him a thumbs-up sign. Should he trust him? Could he? Luttrell snatched a hand grenade off his vest and pulled the pin. Only the Texan's thumb prevented the explosion. Undaunted, the man helped Luttrell to his feet. Together, they lurched toward the village of Sabray, where Luttrell was deposited on a heap of cushions in a stone hut.

* * *

Under heavy fire, rescuers scoured the battlefield. Within two days, they found Dietz. His autopsy report later revealed he had sixteen mortal wounds and many other injuries. He had died fighting, killing at least a score of Taliban, whose bodies lay nearby.

Close by, they found Murphy. Riddled with bullets, he, too, had died a warrior.

As the search went on, the Taliban seemed to hide behind every tree, squeezing off a few shots and running. But they were being beaten back. The Americans had arrived in force.

All the men lost on the helicopter were recovered by July 3. Their bodies were respectfully prepared for transport to the United States, as the search continued for Axelson and Luttrell. Could they still be alive?

*   *   *

On July 4, in Willis, Texas, the phone rang. Holly Luttrell answered it, fearing the worst. She listened intently and then told her friends the good news: her son was alive. One of the SEALs at Luttrell's house was his swim buddy from BUD/S, J. J. Jones. A proud Texan, Jones was one of the few African-Americans in the SEALs. He and Marcus were close friends. Jones ran into the yard, asking the crowd of relatives, neighbors, and SEALs to be quiet. Then he shouted, "They got him, guys! Marcus has been rescued!"

As the crowd roared its approval, Jones gave the rest of the news:

Luttrell was taken to safety by helicopter and was already in the air to Landstuhl Regional Medical Center in Germany for emergency medical treatment.

* * *

Still, the SEALs kept searching for Axelson. They found him July 10, among fallen timber. His distance from the other SEALs indicated that he had kept fighting, alone, for perhaps an hour, maybe more. The Taliban found him incredibly hard to kill.

That day in 2005 proved to be the deadliest day in the history of naval special warfare since the June 6, 1944, Normandy landings.

But the operation was a success, though a costly one. Operation Red Wings and the rescue effort broke the back of the Taliban in Afghanistan's eastern Kunar province. The Taliban would not return in force to that region until 2010, when the Obama administration signaled that it would gradually withdraw from Afghanistan.

In August 2005, the Marines launched Operation Whalers (like Red Wings, also named after an NHL franchise) to destroy Taliban remnants. The eighteen-day campaign of mountain battles drove the last of Shah's men into Pakistan. As a result of the sacrifice made by the SEALs, Night Stalkers, Rangers, and Marines, the people of Kunar province were able to vote in that September's parliamentary elections, the first free elections in decades.

Shah reportedly died in Pakistan in 2006, in a shootout with a villager. The dispute that ended the warlord's life, according to a Pakistani press report, was over the custody of a chicken.

Luttrell, Dietz, and Axelson received the Navy Cross, the nation's second-highest decoration for valor.

A memorial service for Healy was held in Exeter, New Hampshire, on July 17, 2005—which would have been his thirtieth birthday. The funeral procession was a mile long and traveled not far from the stony Atlantic Beach where he had swum as a boy.

In a White House ceremony, President George W. Bush posthumously awarded Lt. Michael Murphy the Medal of Honor; his parents tearfully accepted it on his behalf. Murphy's grave at Calverton National Cemetery in New York later received a special Medal of Honor headstone.

Murphy was the fourth Navy SEAL to be awarded the Medal of Honor, the first since the Vietnam War, and the first U.S. service member in Afghanistan to receive the nation's highest award for heroism. In a private meeting before the ceremony, Dan and Maureen Murphy gave the president a gold dog tag as a tribute to their son.

The official commendation tells the tale:

"For conspicuous gallantry and intrepidity at the risk of his life above and beyond the call of duty as the leader of a special reconnaissance element with Naval Special Warfare Task Unit Afghanistan on 27 and 28 June 2005. While leading a mission to locate a high-level anti-coalition militia leader, Lieutenant Murphy demonstrated extraordinary heroism in the face of grave danger in the vicinity of Asadabad, Konar [*sic*] Province, Afghanistan. On 28 June 2005, operating in an extremely rugged enemy-controlled area, Lieutenant Murphy's team was discovered by anti-coalition militia sympathizers, who revealed their position to Taliban fighters. As a result, between 30 and 40 enemy fighters besieged his four-member team. Demonstrating exceptional resolve, Lieutenant Murphy valiantly led his men in engaging the large enemy force. The ensuing fierce firefight resulted in numerous enemy casualties, as well as the wounding of all four members of the team. Ignoring his own wounds and demonstrating exceptional composure, Lieutenant Murphy continued to lead and encourage his men. When the primary communicator fell mortally wounded, Lieutenant Murphy repeatedly attempted to call for assistance for his beleaguered teammates. Realizing the impossibility of communicating in the extreme terrain, and in the face of almost certain death, he fought his way into open terrain to gain a better position to transmit a call. This deliberate, heroic act deprived him of cover, exposing him to direct enemy fire. Finally achieving contact with his headquarters, Lieutenant Murphy maintained his exposed position while he provided his location and requested immediate support for his team. In his final act of bravery, he continued to engage the enemy until he was mortally wounded, gallantly giving his life for his country and for the cause of freedom. By his selfless leadership, courageous actions, and extraordinary devotion to duty, Lieutenant Murphy reflected great credit upon himself and upheld the highest traditions of the United States Naval Service."

When justice is done, Dietz, Axelson, and Healy will also receive the Medal of Honor. Their heroism continues to inspire the teams. Their willingness to sacrifice their lives for the teammates illustrates the core of the SEAL culture.

A narrow bar called Danny's, a few blocks from the SEAL base in Coronado, California, is a regular hangout for off-duty SEALs. Its ceiling is built like a boat bottom, and its high chairs and vinyl booths have seen better days. On the wall are pictures of Murphy, Axelson, and Dietz (along with eleven recently deceased SEALs). No names or ranks adorn the photos. But, if you're a SEAL, you know their faces and their legend. The only words written under the photos are "Long Live Brotherhood."

CHAPTER 6

Fallujah: The Perfect Op That Led to Prosecutions

Glowering over the Euphrates River, Fallujah is a dirty, crowded Iraqi city of some three hundred thousand people. In 2004, it was notorious for killing Americans for sport.

In Fallujah's basements, they mixed chemicals, in its kitchens they made bombs, in its open-air markets they sold machine guns, and in its mosques they justified it all. Boys were lookouts and couriers, girls snapped photos of American patrols, women assembled fuses, local men trained to fight, and bearded men from abroad, with sweaty wads of cash, paid for it all.

Forty-three miles west of Baghdad, Fallujah was the heart of the "Sunni triangle" and the center of

115

anti-American opposition. It was the headquarters for the insurgency, which used foreign fighters and foreign money (to pay out-of-work Iraqis as much as $600 per attack) to kill Americans and thousands of Iraqi civilians in the name of "Iraqi independence."

Like Belgium in World War I, Iraq was fast becoming a blood-stained land where distant foreign forces came to war and recruit natives for both sides. Iraq's neighbors—mainly Iran and its Arab ally, Syria—smuggled in and supplied bomb makers, sharpshooters, and money men. Al Qaeda, which American air power had smashed on the plains and treeless hills of Afghanistan, was eager to face and fight their nemesis in the urban canyons of Iraqi cities, where America's famed reluctance to kill civilians would diminish its artillery and air power advantages.

Fallujah had not been brutalized in the occupation. Indeed, it had not seen any air strikes during the March 2003 invasion of Iraq, but it got itself into the war by ambushing coalition forces in April 2003. That first battle raged for only a fraction of an hour, but it lingered in the minds of American military commanders. Any real battle for control of the city, they knew, would be a bloodbath. Locals were well stocked with belt-fed machine guns and rocket launchers. Meanwhile American commanders faced intense political pressure to keep American casualties to an absolute minimum. These two realities combined in the minds of U.S. military commanders, and patrols became shorter, quicker, and, soon enough, rarer.

Meanwhile, large numbers of foreign fighters, including al Qaeda elements, flooded into the city to become either murderers or martyrs, as Allah decided.

They were impatient to realize their destiny.

Everyone knew that a blood-drenched house-to-house Armageddon was coming. It was a grim task that few Americans looked forward to. They knew the body count on both sides would be high. The insurgents had months to dig in and booby-trap the city. Once they had fortified their positions in the city itself, they were able to export their activities throughout the area by setting IEDs and staging other attacks on the coalition forces. The coalition forces knew that the city would have to be taken and cleaned out in order to bring peace to Iraq.

As the city and the soldiers waited for the final showdown, four Blackwater employees, including a former SEAL named Scott Helvenston, were sent into Fallujah to retrieve some kitchen equipment left behind by another contractor on March 31, 2004. It was a routine mission that quickly became international news.

It sparked one of the bloodiest battles in a generation of American war fighting and, years later, inspired one of the strangest secret missions of the U.S. Navy SEALs.

* * *

Scott Helvenston, born on June 21, 1965, was the youngest U.S. Navy SEAL in history. After graduating from BUD/S at the age of seventeen, Helvenston deployed with SEAL Team Four and served for two years. Then he was transferred to Coronado, California, where he deployed with SEAL Team One. An outstanding athlete, even among SEALs, he became an instructor at BUD/S, leading physical training every day for four years.

During a routine parachute jump in 1994, his main chute failed and his backup chute only partially inflated. He landed hard. He injured his back, wrist, and ankles, and after months of treatment, he was discharged from the Navy for medical reasons. That hurt more than his injuries.

It was a turning point in his life. He was disappointed and disillusioned. He didn't know what to do with himself. He had never imagined a life outside of the active-duty SEALs. His SEAL buddies would still share a beer with him. But it wasn't the same.

Still, he couldn't allow himself to wallow in despair and regret. He bounced back in 1997 and formed a fitness company, Amphibian Athletics, with the goal of teaching civilians the outdoor fitness skills he once taught SEALs. He was climbing up a cliff of despair by renewing his SEAL-like focus with daily achievements and dogged determination. His SEAL training camps were successful, drawing people from across Southern California, eventually including Hollywood stars. Through his new friends, and an old SEAL buddy, he was hired to coach Demi Moore in the film *G.I. Jane*.

Then he reinvented himself again, becoming an actor in his own right, appearing in reality shows such as *Combat Missions* and *Man vs. Beast*. In *Man vs. Beast* he raced a chimpanzee on an obstacle course and is said to be the only human to have bested the animal.

Then the Hollywood work petered out and the call of war sounded. He reinvented himself again, as a military contractor. He joined Blackwater, an outfit formed by a former SEAL to train SWAT teams and military units in a special facility in the swamplands on the Virginia–North Carolina state line. The company was originally named Blackwater because of the dark mud in its remote training facility, where government teams could rehearse storming buildings in its fake, purpose-built town using live ammunition. As the company grew, it opened more training facilities and soon became one of the best and the largest private training operations in the world. When the September 11 attacks dragged America into war, Blackwater diversified into supplying guards and trainers to U.S. military operations overseas. Contractors were paid higher salaries than soldiers, but cost Uncle Sam less overall, due to lower training, housing, and supply costs. More important, Blackwater's network among SEALs and other former commandos brought in skilled personnel who didn't want to work for the government—but didn't mind going to war. It didn't take long for word to reach Helvenston that Blackwater was looking for former operators like him.

He signed up as a security specialist and shipped out to Iraq. He was sent to the hottest part of the "Red Zone," Fallujah. He was looking forward to it.

Helvenston met three other Blackwater contractors: Jerry "Jerko" Zovko, Wesley Batalona, and Michael Teague on March 31, 2004. It was their first day together and their last.

* * *

Helvenston and others left the staging area outside Fallujah at approximately 10:00 a.m.

The operation was flawed from the start. None of the members of the team had ever worked together before. The four men were driving in two nonarmored SUVs, with only two men per car: one driver and one navigator. The SUVs with foreign nationals stuck out; in fact, they were known as "bullet magnets" because they were easily identified as American. Iraqis rarely, if ever, drive American-made SUVs, preferring their Mercedes or Toyota equivalents.

Both the State Department and the CIA strongly recommended that teams going into Fallujah be no fewer than six men per unit. Because there were only four men and two SUVs, there was only one man to drive and another to navigate Fallujah's winding and unmarked streets. There was no one to ride shotgun and defend the vehicles if they were attacked. And if the navigator was forced to fight, it was easy to become lost and trapped in a maze of Fallujah's medieval streets. In a gunfight, shooting and map reading are tough to do simultaneously.

There were other operational shortcomings. Since the operation was apparently organized at the last minute, the routine preoperation intelligence assessment to review the threat level along the travel route was not made available to Helvenston or his ill-fated comrades.

Finally, and in an apparent direct violation of the terms of the Eurest Support Services contract signed by both Blackwater and its partner, Regency Hotel and Hospital, the contractors were supposed to operate only armored vehicles...and the men were not given any such vehicles. None of the vehicles they were riding in were even fitted with bulletproof glass, let alone armored with reinforced steel plates.

This was, apparently, a policy designed to save money. "The original contract between Blackwater/Regency and ESS [Eurest Support Services], signed March 8, 2004, recognized that 'the current threat in the Iraqi theater of operations' would remain 'consistent and dangerous,' and called for a minimum of three men in each vehicle on security missions 'with a minimum of two armored vehicles to support ESS movements.'...But on March 12, 2004, Blackwater and Regency signed a subcontract that specified security provisions identical to the original except for one word: 'armored.' It was deleted from the contract, allegedly saving Blackwater $1.5 million," according to a noted Blackwater critic, Jeremy Scahill in his book "Blackwater: the Rise of the World's Most Powerful Mercenary Army."[1] (Blackwater has disputed some of the claims in his work and with good reason.) In addition, the contract wasn't followed regarding the number of men per vehicle. Only two men per vehicle were available on the day Helvenston was sent into Fallujah.

Helvenston and his colleagues would have to take their chances.

* * *

About a half hour later, on a narrow street, masked gunmen jumped in front of the vehicles and sprayed them with automatic fire. All four men, including Helvenston, were killed almost instantly. They never had time to return fire.[2]

The windows of the unarmored vehicles were smashed and then doused with gasoline. Then, a burning rag set them ablaze while a group of men with scarves covering their faces, hurled bricks into the blazing vehicles. They danced and sang with joy as the column of black smoke climbed into the sky.

When the fire died, the jihadis ripped the burnt bodies from the vehicles, hooked them on chains, and dragged them through the streets of Fallujah. Ultimately hundreds, perhaps thousands, of Fallujah residents gathered, chanting, "Fallujah is the graveyard of Americans."

They hung some of the charred bodies from a city bridge over a dirty tributary to the Euphrates. Tipped off by the insurgents, news crews arrived to videotape the tragedy. Their lenses feasted on the atrocity.

American soldiers saw the smoke rising from the city and did not know what had taken place. Yet, like cavalry soldiers in the stockades of the Old West, they knew that a pillar of smoke on the horizon meant that something evil was heading their way.

* * *

As the images of the American bodies dangling from a Fallujah bridge made their way around the world, the coalition's top civilian leader, Paul "Jerry" Bremer, consulted with senior officials in the White House and military officers in Centcom over a secure video-conference link. The options were debated.

Four days later, a mixed ground-assault force of Army and Marines arrived. Supported by tanks and close air support, a house-to-house battle raged for days in Fallujah. It would prove to be one of the bloodiest battles of that war.

Fallujah was a magnet for jihadis, the place to make your mark as part of your generation. It was a gathering place that few wanted to miss. They came from every part of the Muslim world, from the mountains of Pakistan, the hills of Chechnya, and the villages of Bosnia to the dry reaches of Libya and the slums of Cairo. They came to kill Americans and to die as "martyrs."

Among them was Ahmed Hashim Abed, a top al Qaeda leader.

Numerous intelligence reports and interrogation memos pointed to Abed as the ringleader responsible for the massacre of the four Americans. He didn't come to die; he wanted his paradise on this Earth. He slipped away in the chaos of combat. He remained a ghost, a killer who couldn't be tracked.

Ahmed Hashim Abed was listed as an HVT (High Value Target), a top priority. The SEALs who had served with Helvenston vowed to capture or kill his murderer. They would hunt that deadly ghost for years.

Five years later, in 2009, they found their man.

* * *

Carl Higbie's platoon, part of SEAL Team Ten, made finding Abed their highest personal priority.

The SEALs had plenty of motivation. Abed was the leader of the group that they knew had killed, dragged, burned, and hanged the body of former Navy SEAL Scott Helvenston and three other Blackwater employees. None of Higbie's platoon had served with Helvenston. They had either joined after his departure or were

East Coast SEALs while Helvenston was on the West Coast, but the bonds of the brotherhood were strong. In addition, the SEALs knew that killers never struck once. They would kill until captured or killed themselves. Finding Abed was also a military necessity.

Higbie was team leader in charge of SEAL Team Ten. Higbie and his team spent months poring over reports and working with snitches. American intelligence databases are vast. It is easy to miss clues if they are scattered across dozens of reports among millions of files. It takes patience and focus to collect and collate information for a single individual. Painstakingly, the SEALs gathered the files and put together the mosaic. Finally, they found Abed—the killer of Helvenston. Now they wanted to swoop in and get him.

Their own chain of command proved to be the toughest obstacle.

*　*　*

The officer in charge of Higbie's platoon turned down the mission. Higbie thought he was a career officer serving a short hitch in the SEALs, who hoped to burnish his résumé and move up the ladder. While ambition makes some men bold, it makes more men cautious. The officer was more career cautious than Higbie thought necessary. But Higbie didn't argue. In the new, professional SEAL teams, enlisted men were not supposed to challenge officers.

Instead, Higbie made revisions.

He thought that a perfect plan would be impossible to turn down. The officer turned it down again. He denied the mission for various reasons real or contrived, in Higbie's opinion. Higbie wouldn't give up. He kept making revisions.

Higbie's officer preferred goodwill missions to ones in which lives were risked. He ordered SEALs to rebuild school walls in Iraqi cities and instituted a program, called "180 Lunches," in which each SEAL was supposed to have lunch with a different Iraqi civilian every weekday. The enlisted SEALs silently resented this. It wasn't what they trained for; it wasn't why they became SEALs. It was like using a Ferrari to deliver the mail. "They would make us go out during the day and make us engage local Iraqi people just to say 'Hi, how's it going? We're American.' We helped build a fence in downtown Fallujah during broad daylight in 130-degree heat, out in the street. That was the kind of stuff that they made us do."

Meanwhile, the officer kept denying his approval for an operation to seize a SEAL killer.

* * *

Then Higbie learned that it was not the faceless higher-ups who were turning down his mission plan, as he had been led to believe. He learned that the officer was not even passing his request to the officers above him. It was just dying on a junior officer's desk.

The Iraqi SEAL base was less than a quarter-mile long. There were few places to hold secret conversations. One night, Higbie and his teammates met in a dark corner to plot a countermove. One teammate had a high-ranking contact in Washington. They decided to take a chance.

"Finally, my buddy went around the chain of command and went way higher in order to get approval for it. Basically they put a lot of pressure on our direct command and they approved it," Higbie said. When the officer was asked about approving the mission, he "didn't mention that he had denied it like ten times."

While going over the cautious officer's head proved to be the right thing to do in getting the operation approved, it also enraged the officer. That officer would ultimately get his revenge.

These kinds of bureaucratic workarounds have become more common as the SEALs were "professionalized" under Admirals Olson and McRaven. Officers who had come up through the ranks ("mustangs") were seen by many enlisted SEALs as more likely to put missions ahead of their careers and were more comfortable communicating with enlisted men, who usually came from humbler backgrounds and lacked elite educations. The "college men" on career tracks were seen by Higbie and others as more careful and more schooled at bureaucratic infighting. Higbie was about to find this out the hard way.

* * *

Mission planning soon became a passive-aggressive battle of its own.

Since the operation was approved, the argument shifted to equipment, as the officer in charge withheld the helicopters needed for the mission.

As usual, the officer [whose name is withheld because he remains on active duty] did everything he could to deny Higbie's ability to get the job done: "He would find reasons why; he would say 'You don't have enough assets,' which is why we had three helos instead of two. Normally we have two helos for that body count [the team needed for the mission]. He said we needed two, so we got two, then they said we need three."

Securing the equipment for the mission was more difficult than Higbie had anticipated. "It was crazy how much of an ass pain it was to coordinate assets.

We ended up getting three helos, and it was like we were trying to get it, trying to get it, trying to get it, and they wouldn't give it to us. Finally, we had to call the Army, to get a Navy asset in the battle space area, because they [the Navy officer in charge] didn't want to give us assets for it. That was their little back-door thing to try to keep us from accessing assets and hitting the target."

Ultimately, the transport and the operation were ready. Higbie thought they were finally going to get the "go" order.

Then the officer threw him another curveball. They would have to dump one of the SEALs assigned and replace him with a combat camera operator, who was ordered to videotape all operations with the team. The combat camera operator was a middle-aged woman with little combat experience. As Higbie knew from previous missions, the camera operator was not physically fit enough to keep up with the SEALs. "We all liked her, but she smoked two packs a day and couldn't run and couldn't shoot." Her presence meant the loss of a gun, and also a loss in speed and agility on the entire team making the assault. She couldn't defend herself and, Higbie feared, would likely become a liability if things went badly. If she were wounded, someone would have to carry her. If she were taken hostage, she would be a propaganda prize for the enemy.

And, most worryingly, in a gunfight you want as many guns on your side as possible. She shot videos, not bullets. How could she defend herself in a firefight?

When Higbie was absorbing this blow, his superior landed another right cross. The officer told Higbie to cut other SEALs from the operation so that they could include a number of Iraqi police, the Iraqi SWAT. The SEALs were concerned about them, too: "In a gunfight, these guys will turn around and shoot you. It was so counterproductive to me. These guys were awful. I mean, they had been training with SEALs for five years and they still can't shoot a fucking paper [target] at ten yards."

The officer, Higbie said, seemed obsessed with the "right ratio" of Americans to Iraqis. "The whole deployment, you can't go on this op because you don't have the right ratio. What is the right ratio [between SEALs and Iraqis]? Well it's not this, just submit another one and we'll tell you if it's right." He would never give Higbie an exact number; they would have to keep guessing while the officer kept changing his mind. Sometimes it was two Iraqis per SEAL, sometimes it was three. On this mission, it was four.

While ratios may seem unimportant, the importance

becomes real very quickly in a gunfight. SEALs who train together can almost read each other's mind in battle. And they have excellent fire control—they can hit targets without killing friendlies. The Iraqis, by contrast, were notorious for shooting civilians and even coalition forces by accident or design. Many SEALs, including Higbie, were reluctant to take them on fire missions. It was too dangerous.

Finally, after a bureaucratic battle of epic proportions, every element of the mission was approved. Zero hour would come several hours after darkness fell.

* * *

In the hangar, the small number of SEALs assembled. Given the few Americans, everyone would have to do two jobs. Higbie was both a team leader and communications guy. "I was carrying three radios, I had four magazines, three on my body and one in the gun. I had two grenades, flashbang, and a shaped charge on my leg. I had a pistol, too. That's pretty standard. I had my M4 and then the pistol."

The SEALs, the camerawoman, and the Iraqis boarded three helicopters and roared out into the night. It was an unwieldy combination, but somehow it had to work.

*   *   *

Some eight miles south of the city of Fallujah, the village of Amiriyat Falujah was basically a walled, fortified complex set up to defend itself from potential invaders.

The aerial surveillance photos were intimidating. Ringed by dunes, the interior was an interlocking series of buildings that would provide ample opportunity for snipers to fire on the SEALs. "It was a fortress," Higbie said.

The group was dropped by the helicopters just over two miles from the target village. The night was dark, humid, and hot. The SEALs were sweating just standing still. The CH-60 helicopters lifted off in a spray of sand that the SEALs called "rotor wash." They knew to put their backs to the bird and not watch it dust off.

As the dust cloud cleared, the SEALs listened as the helicopter engines died away in the starry sky.

It was silent, save the wind ruffling their desert camo pants.

The team was shaped in a V pattern, a standard defensive move for a nighttime SEAL movement.

While the land was flat, it was treacherous—with soft, almost quicksand-like soil. Higbie called it "moon dust." SEALs, heavily laden with weapons and equipment, sank up to their knees. With every step, each SEAL had to pull his boot out of the sucking sand, shift his weight, and then pull the other boot out. During the 2.5-mile trek, each person had to pull his boots out some forty-five thousand times.

It was slow going. The camerawoman and the Iraqis demanded rest stops repeatedly. Higbie scanned the horizon nervously as the non-SEALs took frantic gasps of air. He knew that they were exposed and vulnerable in the badlands.

*   *   *

Higbie used a careful strategy in "stacking" his air assets. An AC-130 helicopter gunship was silently overhead, almost a mile above the struggling team. Its job was to keep eyes on the team and provide aerial gunfire if needed. Its electric-powered machine guns and cannons could put thousands of rounds downrange in minutes.

Above the AC-130 and five hundred yards ahead was a Predator drone plane.

"The sole reason we had that Predator was so that our commanding officer could see what we were doing. That's why I pushed it ahead of us instead of keeping it on us. He was like 'I want to see what you guys are doing right now.'" Instead, the Predator showed the terrain ahead, so that the officer who didn't support the mission was not able to micromanage it. (The officer couldn't see the video feed from the AC-130.)

This was a little passive-aggressive pushback from Higbie. He didn't want to give the officer video that could be used against his team later. It would turn out to be a wise strategy.

* * *

The high dune walls of Amiriyat Falujah loomed above the team, blocking out stars and the horizon. Slowly, they scanned for sentries. They heard only the wind and saw only empty sand slopes. They found a narrow gap in the walls and filed through it. Inside the dune walls was a sprawling concrete complex of ramshackle buildings and dusty cars. They heard the hum of the diesel generators. The village seemed asleep.

They approached cautiously and quietly. The target building had been marked by an informer, who used a sign that could be seen only through infrared goggles.

They moved silently along the concrete walls, looking for the infrared sign. When they found it, it was time for action.

The team stood at the front door, discussing the entry plan using only their hands and eyes. Higbie waited outside. "So my job was to deal with the AC-130 and the Predator, and to keep scanning the town to make sure that there was no movement at any time, and I was in charge of making sure no one entered the building without us knowing."

The Iraqi police were deployed as perimeter guards.

Then the village began to come to life. Doors and windows opened, voices in Arabic wanted to know what was going on. The villagers were armed, and tension was building in their voices. They knew something was up, but they just weren't sure what it was yet. The operation would have to be completed quickly and efficiently, or it could turn into a bloodbath in a heartbeat.

*   *   *

The SEALs burst through the door. A SEAL new to the Iraq war, Mathew McCabe, spotted Abed, the target, lunging for a gun. He tackled him.

"This happened for two reasons," Higbie said. One, inexperience, because he was a new guy and he wasn't allowed to get experience by our commanding officer. He was hesitant to shoot because, this is the second reason, because the commander told everybody that if they killed somebody, they'd better have a damn good reason."

The tackle was a risky move. If Abed had been a few seconds faster, the SEAL would be dead. In the normal course of "threat/no threat" analysis Abed would have been instantly shot. As it happened, shooting Abed would have been a better outcome for almost all concerned.

* * *

With Abed in white plastic zip ties behind his back, the team moved rapidly out of the village. They needed to go before the villagers had the chance to wipe the sleep from their eyes and open fire with their automatic weapons.

Higbie radioed the helicopters to land a few hundred yards from the village's high dune walls. (Retreating over the "moon dust" would have been a death sentence.)

The choppers landed, the team and prisoner were loaded, and helicopters dusted off into the night sky. It was a perfect op, Higbie said. Mission accomplished and no shots fired.

The detention center at Camp Baharia, a nearby SEAL base, was a twenty-foot-long conex box, a shipping container with doors and windows cut out with welding torches.

Higbie turned Abed over to the master-at-arms,

a young navy enlisted man on his first deployment overseas.

It was time to celebrate a little. "We debriefed with the helo pilots on site, we gave our high fives, and we say we got this motherfucker." No alcohol was served, but Higbie treated himself to a hot shower and went to bed.

In the predawn hours, fate soured for the SEALs.

* * *

Higbie was shaken awake and told to report to the officer who never liked the mission. When he arrived, his other teammates were there, ashen faced. The officer was apoplectically angry. He held up Abed's tunic. It was spotted with blood. "There is going to be an investigation," the officer said.

Someone had given the prisoner a bloody lip, and criminal charges would be brought.

NCIS arrived the next day.

It was possible, if not probable, that the prisoner gave himself the bloody lip. Al Qaeda operatives knew America's strict rules on treating prisoners—and they were known to use these rules against their captors. Al Qaeda handbooks, captured by U.S. forces in Afghanistan, teach them how to bring false charges while in American custody. It was another case of using America's assets against her. Just as al Qaeda used America's planes against her on September 11, 2001, it now used America's military legal system against her war fighters.

Another, perhaps more likely possibility, is that the young master-at-arms beat up Abed. He later made comments that Higbie took to be an admission of guilt.

NCIS investigated and determined that no SEALs were ever alone with the prisoner and that no evidence or testimony implicated them. Abed fingered the master-at-arms as the culprit. The investigation of the SEALs conduct continued anyway.

NCIS briefed the officer who never liked Higbie's mission, telling him there was no evidence of wrongdoing. The officer told the NCIS investigator: "I don't care, find something. I am not going to go down for this."

* * *

All eight of the accused SEALs quickly got lawyers. Four of them were eventually charged.

The officer insisted on a captain's mast, an informal disciplinary procedure that doesn't involve lawyers.

The SEALs, citing naval regulations, demanded a court-martial. Higbie said: "You're charging us with a serious offense here and we're not going to take captain's mast, we're going to take court-martial, because we know we didn't do anything wrong."

The SEALs were separated and sent home. It would take months before the trial began. After the U.S. Army's Abu Ghraib scandal, Navy commanders were taking no chances with the politicians or the press. They would go strictly by the book, no matter what they privately thought about the charges.

* * *

The trial ultimately took place in Baghdad. Higbie's testimony was mercifully short. The first thing the prosecutor asked was "Did you abuse this prisoner?"

Higbie was sitting upright, looking straight out, as he addressed the courtroom. "No, sir."

The prosecutor put his hand on his forehead, looked down, and shook his head. Higbie got the impression that the young prosecutor didn't like the case or even being made to ask these questions.

The military jury exonerated Higbie and, in a separate tribunal, the other SEALs.

A post on a Facebook page called "Support the Navy SEALs Who Captured Ahmed Hashim Abed" summed it up best: "SEALs 3—Terrorist 0."

Higbie and his team had captured a notorious

killer and defeated the charges brought by a politically correct commander. But the politics and bureaucracy made him lose trust in his leaders. He left the SEALs with sadness. While they were exonerated of all charges, the careers of the other SEALs were also damaged. The trial was a black mark on their records that they would have to explain for the rest of their careers. A Big Navy mentality—designed for regulating life among other American sailors aboard the closed world of ship at sea—treats accusations as evidence that a man can't get along with teammates. If the accused sailor were more diplomatic, the charge would not have occurred, or so goes the thinking. This attitude isn't well suited to SEALs who take prisoners on the battlefield. Accusations made by enemy prisoners are a natural product of war and should be treated differently as a result. But the Big Navy culture makes no such allowances for the SEALs when evaluating men for promotion.

In the end, the navy lawyers did what the terrorists could not—effectively end the careers of Higbie and other SEALs.

CHAPTER 7

Benghazi, Libya:
SEALs Alone

Benghazi is a city of high walls and narrow streets perched on Libya's Mediterranean coast.

Once the capital of Libya, where Arabs gathered to trade fish and gossip on its shores while sheikhs and captains plotted intrigue on its leafy terraces, whatever charm the city once had was stolen away by World War II, when the Allies and General Erwin Rommel's Afrika Korps fought over the coast roads that were the city's lifeline. After the war came waves of migrants from Libya's hot, poor interior. By the time Col. Moammar Gadhafi's bloody coup succeeded in 1969—driving out a pro-American king—the city was a crowded slum, and all economic and political power had shifted to its longtime rival city, Tripoli.

Benghazi briefly reverted to relevance when it became the center of the anti-Gadhafi rebellion in 2010. The tribes that called Benghazi home never liked Gadhafi. With the help of U.S. air power overhead and special forces on the ground, the Arab world's longest-serving dictator was driven from power and ultimately killed in October 2011.

The new Libyan government, the Transitional National Council, was temporarily based in Benghazi, but it had little control over the city or the country.[1] The police had shed their uniforms and were hiding in the homes, fearing retribution. A welter of competing militias had taken control of the streets, often setting up roadblocks to demand "taxes." Criminal mafias moved in, and radical Islamic militants soon followed. As night fell and the call to prayer drifted away, gunshots echoed.

This was the cauldron of chaos that the U.S. ambassador to Libya, Christopher Stevens, called home in April 2011. He helped coordinate with Libyan officials during their long fight with Gadhafi's forces in the spring and summer of 2011. While the security situation remorselessly worsened over the next twelve months, senior officials in the State Department's Washington headquarters kept reducing Stevens's security detail. They did this for budgetary reasons (the Benghazi station was temporary and therefore bureaucratically difficult to assign security personnel and equipment to) and for political reasons (the State Department wanted to present the Libyan war as "won" and downplay any risks that might smudge the banner of victory). This proved to be a miscalculation.

While the war against Gadhafi was over and Libyans overall remained very pro-American (in polls, Libyans had a higher opinion of Americans than citizens of any other Arab country), the war weakened the central government and invited opportunistic interlopers, including al Qaeda.

* * *

Stevens, a debonair Arabic-speaking career foreign-service officer, put up a brave front.[2] He kept extending his stay throughout 2011 and 2012, knowing that few would volunteer to take his place.[3]

He set up temporary headquarters in April 2011 at the Tibesti Hotel, which the German newsmagazine *Der Spiegel* describes as "a monstrous concrete tower on the shore road" that is home to representatives from nine European countries, with the European Union renting an entire wing.[4] The guest list made the hotel an obvious target for terrorists.

Stevens was still registered at the Tibesti Hotel on

June 1, 2011, when a car bomb exploded and rocked the hotel.[5] Stevens was unharmed. But the bombing vividly showed that even interlocking sets of security agents couldn't safeguard foreign diplomats in the rebel capital from terror attacks.

The attacks would continue to escalate over the next fourteen months, while Washington repeatedly reduced security forces in Benghazi because, officials told us, they "thought the war was over." In fact, a new war on America and her allies was just beginning.

* * *

Stevens tried appealing directly to Washington-based policy makers at his only in-person appearance at the State Department press briefing on August 3, 2011. He was emphatic about the rising dangers in Benghazi: "There was a security vacuum when the regime fell, and they [the rebels] had to stand up very quickly to this organization called the TNC [Transitional National Council]. The police, for the most part, just left their posts because they were afraid of popular reaction against them because they had committed abuses in the early days against the people. So there's hardly any police around, and because of that vacuum, militias started to form and step in. And so looking after the security of Benghazi and eastern Libya, you've got a lot of militias and a few police. And this had led to some security challenges that you've already read about and know about."[6]

Later that month, American diplomats moved into a walled compound. The compound was surrounded by concrete-block walls and set back almost three hundred yards from the main road. "We need that much room to provide the best possible setback against car bombs," Stevens said.

By December 2011, the perimeter wall was raised to nine feet and topped by three feet of concertina wire. Large lights were hung to flood the street with bright light. Jersey barriers, long concrete blocks reimbursed with rebar, were positioned outside and inside the main gate to slow vehicular traffic into the compound and deter car bombs.[7] Yet all of these security measures are backward looking—they are designed to stop the car bombs that bedeviled diplomats at the Tibesti Hotel. They weren't designed to defeat new types of attacks, such as an armed invasion.

No one, in Washington at least, worried about the growing threat of an armed assault on the tiny piece of American real estate in Benghazi. After all, the war was over.

* * *

In addition, throughout 2011, angry demonstrations become a daily occurrence. Fifteen commanders of the Protective Security Brigade protested in front of the Transitional National Council headquarters, saying they weren't getting proper gear, and the menace of the militias made their jobs impossible.[8] Several hundred other protesters demanded the removal of "climbers," survivors from the Gadhafi era who were still working for the Libyan government.[9]

Belatedly, the State Department hired Blue Mountain Libya, a British security outfit, to guard the American compound in Benghazi. The firm used its $783,284 contract to hire twenty Libyans to act as guards.

Embassy staff flagged problems with the Blue Mountain Libya guards almost immediately. Eric Nordstrom, former regional security officer for the U.S. Embassy in Tripoli, told congressional investigators: "It's my understanding that there was a very high turnover with those people." This is diplomatic understatement. Some guards lasted only a few weeks.

Two former Blue Mountain employees told Reuters they had "minimal training," and they described "being hired by Blue Mountain after a casual recruiting and screening process."[10]

Then the kidnappings began. An American running

a nonprofit humanitarian group in Libya was attending a friend's bachelor's party when armed men stormed into the room on December 1, 2011. They called themselves the Zintan Martyrs Brigade. They claimed the power to arrest the revelers and held everyone for thirty-six hours. Finally, after a botched attempt to secure ransoms from family members of the Libyans present, the police arrived. The Martyrs Brigade agreed to turn over their captives in exchange for the police investigating the "crimes" of those that they held. The police soon released everyone due to "lack of evidence."[11]

This may have been a test run for a larger attack. The Brigade was learning just how quickly authorities would respond and what arms they would bring to the fight. The seizure of the American embassy in Tehran in 1979 was preceded by months of minor attacks as a way to test America's resolve and to devise countermeasures to local police and American firepower.

In another parallel with Iran in 1979, demonstrations increased. Three thousand young people protested in Benghazi's Shajarah Square on December 12 and 13. The activists were angry that opening a business still required bribes and that large numbers of former Gadhafi-era officials were still on the government payroll. Members of the Committee of Wise

Men, a pro-TNC group, joined a second demonstration on the second night.[12] The demonstrators eventually went home. But it was clear that the public was splintering into factions, undermining the unity that would be needed to keep extremists at bay.

Behind the scenes, darker forces were relaxing for a fight.

In a surprise raid, Libyan police and military seized 150 rocket launchers and arrested scores of suspects in a warehouse hideout. A government spokesman said that the group claimed loyalty to the deposed Libyan dictator and were plotting to attack embassies and oil fields over the Christmas and New Year's holidays. The operation, according to the government, was code-named Papa Noel[13]—a reference to Santa Claus. They wanted to drive all Westerners from Libya and rule it as an Islamic dictatorship.

* * *

By January 2012, militant radicals were operating freely in the city. One extreme group invaded the Sufi cemetery of Sidi Ubaid in Benghazi. The group considers Sufi Muslims to be heretics. They dug up some thirty-one corpses and carried away the bodies.[14]

The new year, 2012, brought more brazen assaults. Azza Ali Orfi, a political activist, was attacked and beaten by two men in broad daylight as she left the Al-Fadhel Hotel in Benghazi on January 12, 2012.[15] The hotel was considered a safe place for Westerners to meet with Libyan activists. She was pro-democracy and pro-American, making her a double enemy to Islamic extremists.

The following week, protesters assaulted Transitional National Council vice chairman Abdul-Hafiz Ghoga after he attended a memorial service at Garyounis University for victims of the Libyan civil war. Ghoga subsequently resigned from the transitional government, saying he did not want to contribute to an "atmosphere of hatred" surrounding the government.[16] In reality, he feared for his life.

The Libyan government was coming dangerously close to losing Benghazi to the forces of anarchy.

* * *

Lt. Col. Andrew Wood arrived in Benghazi in February 2012. His account was sobering and clear-eyed. "Shooting instances occurred; [and] many instances involved the local security guard force we were training," he later told CBS News. "Constantly, there were battles going on between militias, criminal activity, and that became [an] increasing danger as time went on as well."

Wood said that Ambassador Stevens "was constantly concerned about the threats to not just himself but the entire staff there."[17]

No additional security measures were announced.

* * *

American diplomats were driving in marked vehicles from Benghazi's Benina Airport in April 2012, when a militia group blocked their way. As they pulled off the road, armed men surrounded the car. One asked for identification, but it seemed clear he wasn't part of the rebel police force. Perhaps he wanted a bribe or hostages. After a few tense minutes, the Americans were allowed to drive on.

Soon diplomats were running a dangerous gauntlet of militia checkpoints. One diplomat compared it to toll-booth stops on I-95, except, he said, people don't shoot you at toll booths in America. One diplomat later reported there were now twelve checkpoints between the airport and the embassy, with militia members aggressively trying to open doors and check contents of diplomatic vehicles.[18]

By appearance alone, there was no way to know if militias were friendly or hostile to Americans. Diplomats wondered: Who was running Benghazi anyway? The men moving paper in downtown offices or the armed ones commandeering the streets as private fiefdoms?

Despite this and other reports, the number of security personnel assigned to the diplomatic facility in Benghazi continued to plunge. By April 2012, the number of American diplomatic security agents in Benghazi fell to one person.

The State Department cited "visa problems" for security personnel but the Libyan government continued to insist that it would supply visas for any security personnel that the U.S. government required. Instead, it appears that the State Department simply did not forward the paperwork to their Libyan counterparts in time.

(Eventually, the "visa problems" were resolved. At the time of the attack on September 11, 2012, there were five diplomatic security officers—three at the compound and two accompanying Ambassador Stevens.)[19]

* * *

Explosions rocked the U.S. compound on March 8, 2012. The bombs detonated less than 400 meters (437 yards) from the diplomatic compound. There were no injuries or damage reported at the ambassador's complex.[20] But it was a warning sign.

Meanwhile, demonstrations and armed attacks continued to roil Benghazi.

Pro-federalism demonstrators marched in Benghazi on March 16, 2012, demanding that Benghazi and Tripoli be declared Libya's co-capitals and that seats in the Libyan parliament be evenly divided among all regions of the country.[21]

Two days later, six gun-wielding thugs wearing ski masks and military fatigues broke into the British School in Benghazi, terrifying teachers and stealing handbags, wallets, watches, and cars.[22]

On March 22, 2012 at 2:27 a.m., seven militia members arrived at the main gate of the U.S. diplomatic compound. They kicked the gate and demanded to be let inside. The local guard fled, but set off a silent internal security alarm that alerted security personnel and members of the 17 February Martyrs Brigade, a friendly, pro-democracy militia. They came quickly. The militia was part of the El Awfea Brigade of the Libyan Ministry of Defense; the militia members said they were investigating a fire. No one bought their story. The El Awfea Brigade left without incident.[23] It was another sign that local security guards could not protect the Americans inside their Benghazi outpost, and that the goodwill of friendly militias was vital.

Meanwhile, the number of new "police forces" continued to multiply.

Shortly thereafter, on March 28, 2012, Eric Nordstrom cabled the State Department in Washington to request five Diplomatic Security Service agents for Benghazi on forty-five- to sixty-day rotations, as well as four drivers. They would be slow in coming, and the original contingent would be gone before the attacks on September 11, 2012.

Nordstrom's cable said there was a problem with the Libyan government, which would issue gun permits only for periods no longer than seventy-two hours.[24] The Libyans deny that the regulation was applied to U.S. personnel. The CIA, and its contractors, certainly didn't have any trouble with Libyan gun permits, one Libyan official told us. Nor were most Libyans bothered by any kind of gun restrictions. More likely, said one American official familiar with embassy security in Libya, Nordstrom was complaining about the State Department's interpretation of an old, Gadhafi-era restriction on gun possession.

As if to underscore the need for additional security, a British diplomatic armored vehicle was attacked a few days later. Some 150 members of the Traffic Police Force, or Murur, opened fire on local militia members.

Caught in the crossfire, a British vehicle was shot up, as each side believed the vehicle belonged to the other side. A third security force called (variously) Al-Nayda or Al-Shorta swept in and broke up the fighting, allowing the diplomatic convoy to proceed.[25] If not for this timely rescue, the British diplomats would likely have been killed.

Next, the American diplomatic compound was bombed on April 6, 2012. A homemade bomb was launched over the concrete wall of the embassy compound. The bomb type, known to Libyan intelligence officials as a "fish bomb" or "gelateena," exploded in an empty parking area. No one was harmed. But the bombing showed that the American outpost could be attacked without any fear of consequences.

Libyan investigators traced the bomb to two men. Ominously, one was a current security guard at the U.S. complex and the other was a former security guard. Both were Blue Mountain Libya employees— the very firm hired to protect the American officials.

The former guard had been fired for "gross misconduct," including covering the inner walls of the compound with anti-American graffiti.[26] Could the other Blue Mountain Libya guards be trusted? As doubts deepened about the security firm, no one in Washington moved to replace the firm with American forces

or, even, another security firm. It was as if the State
Department was on autopilot.

* * *

Another "fish bomb" was thrown at a U.N. convoy
carrying the U.N. special envoy to Libya on April 10,
2012. The bomb exploded twelve feet from the convoy.[27] Again, no injuries. But the attackers were getting bolder.

The cemetery attackers moved to Western targets
later in April 2012. The Commonwealth Graves cemetery holds the bodies of British, South African, Austra-
lian, and other British Commonwealth soldiers killed
in Libya during World War II. They died to keep Libya
free from the Nazis. Over two hundred tombstones in
this cemetery were desecrated.[28] It was seen as another
message to the British delegation: leave Libya now.

* * *

Security guards at the International Medical University shoved and punched guards protecting a U.S.
trade delegation visiting Benghazi on April 26, 2012.
The fistfight lasted only a few minutes. A senior U.S.
diplomat, accompanying the trade delegation, realized that anti-American sentiment was worsening.

Terrorist attacks on the Libyan government were

increasing, too. Three bombs exploded at the main Benghazi courthouse on April 27.[29] If the new government couldn't protect itself, how could it safeguard American diplomats?

That same day, a militia kidnapped two white South Africans working for the United States in Benghazi as part of an American-funded effort to secure weapons and dismantle land mines. The hostages insisted for hours that they were not Americans. When they proved that they were South Africans, they were released.[30] It was yet another clue that anti-American forces operating freely in Benghazi were looking to kill or capture Americans.

Terror attacks continued against Libyan government officials in Benghazi. A hand grenade exploded in the Libyan Military Police headquarters in Benghazi on May 15, 2012.[31] That same day, the director of the Benghazi Medical Center, the city's most prestigious hospital, Dr. Fathi Al-Jhani was shot in the chest as he was leaving work. He survived, largely because he was attacked only steps from his own facility's emergency room.[32] He may have been targeted because he had met briefly with American officials in the hopes of getting new equipment for his hospital. Even casual encounters with Americans were enough for jihadis to target someone.

Other government officials were luckier. Two Benghazi-based members of the Transitional National Council, Khaled Saleh and Fathi Al Baaja, dodged bullets at Benghazi Airport on May 17. Neither man was hurt.[33]

But the pattern was clear: both the American officials and the Libyan government officials that they supported were now in the crosshairs of terrorists.

Terror strikes designed to drive Westerners out of Benghazi soon became even bolder. Two rocket-propelled grenades were fired at the headquarters of the International Committee for the Red Cross/Red Crescent on May 22, 2012. One hit a shipping container and the second missed entirely. The Sheikh Omar Abdul-Rahman Brigades claimed responsibility, saying the Red Cross/Red Crescent was allegedly converting Libyan ethnic minorities to Christianity.[34] The name of this heretofore-unknown group (the Sheikh Omar Abdul-Rahman Brigades) is telling. It is named after the blind Egyptian cleric, who is now held in a New York prison for plots to bomb in the Lincoln and Holland Tunnels leading in to Manhattan as well as plans to murder civilians at a number of New York landmarks. Freeing the blind cleric had been a goal of radical Islamists since the mid-1990s.

The Red Cross/Red Crescent, a humanitarian

group, was named as an official enemy of al Qaeda in Dr. Ayman al-Zawahiri's autobiography *Knights under the Prophet's Banner*. Zawahiri became al Qaeda's global leader immediately after the death of Osama bin Laden in 2011. The Red Cross responded by withdrawing all personnel from Libya. While the Red Cross attack may or may not have been the work of an al Qaeda cell, it was a complete victory for the terrorists.

*   *   *

The U.S. Mission in Benghazi was bombed a second time on June 6, 2012. Local guards said they saw a man wearing "Islamic" clothes place a suspicious package three feet from the mission's front entrance, then they saw him run away in a flurry of long robes. The package exploded six minutes later, blowing a large forty-foot hole in the mission's front wall. No one was injured.[35]

The Sheikh Omar Abdel-Rahman Brigades subsequently claimed responsibility, the same group that claimed responsibility for the Red Cross attack.[36] This group seemed to be testing the resolve of Western interests to respond and seemed emboldened when no armed response was forthcoming. Unfortunately, they were learning a lot about Ambassador Stevens's defenses.

* * *

Over the next two days, militants held an open-air conference at Liberation Square in Benghazi. Some fifteen militias, or "kalibas," attended the conference, which, according to a report from the U.S. Library of Congress's research branch, "probably make up the bulk of al-Qaeda's support in Libya." Al Qaeda held an open conference in Benghazi, and no one dared to stop them.

According to the Arabic-language newspaper *Libya al-Youm*, the conference was sponsored by the al Qaeda affiliate group Ansar al-Sharia and included the Free Libya Martyrs, the Abu Salim Martyrs, and the Revolutionaries of Sirt.[37] A report from another Arabic-language paper said its reporter on the scene "witnessed gunmen out riding scores of cars and military vehicles, demanding the implementation of the rules of Islamic Sharia and raising black and white flags with 'There is no deity but God and Muhammad is the messenger of God' on them." These are the flags of al Qaeda. The meeting "was a message to the many intelligence apparatuses which had entered into Libya, including Syrian, Iranian, and Israeli and American, were attempting to sabotage, peddle drugs, and spread false beliefs in the country."[38]

NPR reporter Steve Inskeep saw some of the demonstrators at this meeting, and one said his goal was "to kill the infidels," or *kofar*.[39]

Ansar al-Sharia commander Mohammed Ali el-Zahawi told the *Washington Post* that while his organization disapproved of attacking embassies, "if it had been our attack on the U.S. Consulate [*sic*], we would have flattened it."[40] He was talking about the May 2012 bombing of the U.S. diplomatic compound—not the massive attack that burned the U.S. facility on September 11, 2012. That larger attack had not yet occurred. Yet the State Department never mentioned this terrorist conference to the press or the public.

Given the wide variety of Arabic and American press reports, it is hard to believe that State Department senior officials were unaware that al Qaeda affiliates had just held a massive rally less than a ten-minute drive from the U.S. compound.

The day after the terrorist conference, Islamic militants fired a rocket-propelled grenade at an armed convoy carrying British Ambassador Sir Dominic Asquith. Two security officers were wounded, but the ambassador somehow survived. Reporters saw a white diplomatic car with its windshield destroyed and blood on the car's front seat.[41] The driver was gravely wounded.

The British retreated from Benghazi.[42] All employees of the British government were evacuated from Libya within days. A lifetime ago, the British ruled one-third of the globe. In 2012, a single rocket attack sent them home.

With the British diplomatic presence gone, the stars and stripes became the last Western flag to wave over Benghazi. Still, America announced no new security measures. America was alone and wasn't adding guards. In fact, the security had been reduced and was never replenished as repeatedly requested by Ambassador Stevens. The perfect storm was brewing, and no one was doing anything to prepare for it.

* * *

Violent attacks continued to plague Benghazi. The Tunisian consulate in Benghazi was stormed by twenty young men on June 17, 2012. The invaders burned the Tunisian flag inside the building. The men claimed that the consulate was displaying anti-Islamic art.[43] Islamic radicals, including those in al Qaeda, believe that any images of any living things defy the laws of Islam. Thus, even pious portraits of the prophet Mohammed are forbidden, as are television broadcasts and movie screenings. Of course, this doesn't stop al Qaeda from releasing videos on al Jazeera. To veteran State Department officials, the Tunisian consulate attack showed that the militants feared no one, that they could attack even Arab governments with impunity.

That same month, another Libyan government official was gunned down in Benghazi. Juma Obaidi al-Jazawi, a military prosecutor who ordered the arrest of former Libyan rebel commander Abdul Fatah Younes for human-rights abuses, was killed as he left his mosque.[44] Once again, the Libyan government couldn't protect their own officials.

Alarmed by the rising violence, even U.S. government contractors began warning their paymasters in Washington. Reports began to flood in about dangerous developments in Benghazi. The Navanti Group, a U.S. military contractor firm, concluded: "Benghazi has seen a notable increase in violence in recent months, particularly against international targets. These events point to strong anti-Western sentiments among certain segments of the population, the willingness of Salafi-jihadi groups in the city to openly engage in violence against foreign targets, and their capacity to carry out these attacks."[45]

None of these developments seemed to shift the State Department's view on increasing security in Benghazi. They didn't want to send more guards to a country that was supposed to be a diplomatic triumph of democracy and peace. The complicated reality— that the new democratic government was pro-American and committed to making Libya a "normal country" but that its new institutions were too weak to counter the waves of radical Islamists crossing the border from neighboring Egypt—was seen as too hard to sell in an election year.

*   *   *

Meanwhile, attacks on the Libyan government in Benghazi escalated in July. A mob of some two hundred people sacked the offices of the High National Electoral Commission, burning election records and demanding more local control.[46]

Even State Department officials were sounding the warning bell by July 2012. A July 9, 2012, cable written by Eric Nordstrom concluded: "Overall security conditions continue to be unpredictable, with large numbers of armed groups and individuals not under the control of the central government, and frequent clashes in Tripoli and other major population centers." The Government of Libya "remains extremely limited in its ability to sustain a security support presence at USG [U.S. government] compounds."[47] In short, any hope of the Libyan government protecting U.S. diplomats in Benghazi was unrealistic.

Secretary of State Hillary Clinton and others on the seventh floor of the State Department, where policy is set, failed to divert from their course. Their position was immovable. The war was won, and more security was an unneeded expense.

*   *   *

At the same time, the U.S. military was paying close attention to events unfolding in Benghazi.

Gen. Carter Ham, head of Africa Command or AFRICom, read cables from Nordstrom, Ambassador Stevens, and others, urgently begging for more security.

General Ham phoned Stevens on August 16, 2012, and asked if he needed any more security. Stevens said he did not. In a meeting sometime later, Stevens again said that he did not need additional security.

Why would Stevens refuse offers of more security when all of his cables and communications pleaded for more security? A McClatchy Newspapers reporter attempted to decode the bureaucratic struggle inside the State Department: "One person familiar with the events," wrote Nancy Youssef, said Stevens might have rejected the offers because there was an understanding within the State Department that officials in Libya ought not to request more security, in part because of concerns about the political fallout of seeking a larger military presence in a country that was still being touted as a foreign policy success."[48]

In short, Stevens did not want to swim "outside his lane" and alienate his superiors at the State Department, even to get the additional security he desperately needed. He was a career foreign service officer, and he knew how the game was played—even if he didn't like the rules.

Meanwhile, the little security that Stevens had was being taken away. The contract between the 17 February Brigade, a local militia that guarded the outside of the U.S. diplomatic outpost, expired on August 29, 2012.

The State Department did not renew it, citing budget concerns. A memo from "the principal U.S. diplomatic officer in Benghazi," whose name was redacted from congressional reports, said the contract had expired "several weeks ago" and that the brigade "has been implicated in several of the recent detentions. We also have the usual concerns re their ultimate loyalties. But they are competent, and give us an added measure of security."[49]

Since the contract had expired, the brigade said it would not provide security for U.S. personnel, including Ambassador Stevens.[50] The U.S. diplomats lost more security just days before the anniversary of the September 11 attacks.

The perfect storm was gathering on the horizon.

CHAPTER 8

Benghazi 911: When SEALs Answer the Call

On the last day of his life, Ambassador Stevens wrote in his diary: "It is so nice to be back in Benghazi."[1]

He meant it. It was September 11, 2012, and the morning dawned beautifully. The rosy skies revealed few clouds, and a breeze off the Mediterranean promised a gentle day—much like the beautiful weather that came before the deadly terror attacks on American soil on that same day eleven years earlier.

At first, the morning kept its peaceful promise. The morning call to prayer, which sounded from the minarets just before dawn, didn't produce any large crowds outside the diplomatic facility. Instead, Stevens heard birds chattering in the trees, the grumble of trucks and squeak of donkey cart wheels on their way to market.

The ambassador had arrived the day before with information management officer Sean Smith and two Diplomatic Security Service (DSS) agents. There were three other DSS agents already on site. The compound held eleven people that day: seven Americans and four local Blue Mountain Libya guards.

Then, as the morning sunlight was moving down the side of the buildings, a Blue Mountain Libya security guard spotted something suspicious. A wink of something metallic flashed in the sun from the scaffolding of a building directly across the street. It was 6:45 a.m. in Benghazi—a little too early for the construction crews to arrive.

The guard looked more closely. He saw a man, wearing a Libyan Supreme Security Council uniform, taking photos of the U.S. compound from the construction site. The second-story scaffolding gave the man a commanding view of the compound, and the photos would be useful in planning any assault. It was an ominous development.

The guard rounded up a colleague and walked across the street to confront the mysterious photographer.

The uniformed man angrily refused to talk to the Blue Mountain Libya guards and, instead, climbed into a parked police car and sped off.[2]

The incident was reported, but its true importance would not become obvious for hours. By then, it would be too late.

* * *

Meanwhile, the diplomatic staff went through their daily routines. A memorandum drafted by David C. McFarland, later sent by the U.S. embassy in Tripoli to the State Department in Washington, details the official responsibilities that day: Ambassador Stevens planned to open American Space Benghazi, a cultural organization, while staff met with a thicket of nonprofit groups, including the Libyan Society for Industrial Engineering, My Environment Society, and the cancer-fighting Cure Foundation.[3] All meetings occurred inside the compound to avoid alerting militias that their number one target had returned to Benghazi.

Somehow, the enemy knew anyway. Did they have a source on the inside?

Ambassador Stevens's last scheduled meeting ended at 7:20 p.m., as he walked Turkish Consul General Ali Kemal Akin to the main gate.[4] In his diary, Stevens noted that Akin "helped me land in Benghazi last year." The Turks had some one hundred thousand citizens working in Libya as oil engineers, electricians, and technicians. They often use these informal networks to alert Americans to developing threats. But the Turkish consul issued no warnings that day.

By 8:30 p.m., the last British security team drove its armored cars through the main (or C1, or "Charlie 1") gate.[5] They were returning borrowed equipment as previously arranged. The British quickly left the compound as night fell. The only guards left outside the gate were two local Benghazi police in a marked car. (Five other guards remained inside the compound, along with four local guards.)

Then the police mysteriously sped away at 9:42 p.m. Why? Did the police know that something was about to happen? A local Libyan newspaper quoted a Supreme Security Council official saying that the car was ordered to leave "to prevent civilian casualties." A guard interviewed by *Al-Sharq Al-Awsat*, a London-based Arabic newspaper with unusually good sources in the region, said that "my colleague guards and I were chatting and drinking tea. The situation was normal."[6] The disappearance of the local police was never fully explained.

Within a minute of the police car's departure,

masked men appeared at the main gate. They were members of Ansar al-Sharia and al Qaeda in the Islamic Maghreb, two known al Qaeda affiliates.

The masked men carried a rocket-propelled grenade launcher. They fired it at the main gate, shouting "God is great!" in Arabic. The RPG exploded in a thunderclap, blasting open the gate. More masked men emerged from the shadows and swarmed into the compound.[7]

The local guards, perhaps knowing what was coming, ran off into the night. They were armed only with clubs, not guns. They knew that they were no match for an army of armed men. Two guards were captured and beaten. After pleading for their lives and reassuring the invaders that they are observant Muslims, they are released.

Compound guards interviewed by *Al-Sharq Al-Awsat* estimate that some fifty attackers flooded into the compound in the first wave, led by four men who wore masks and "Pakistani clothes."[8] The turbans and long shirts worn by Pakistanis are markedly different from clothes usually worn by Libyans, especially to Arab eyes.

The invaders fired their AK-47s into the air—a rolling growl of automatic fire.

The Americans were now alone. State Department staff methodically locked doors and windows. The compound's Tactical Operations Center coolly notified the State Department in Washington, the embassy in Tripoli, and the Annex (a facility operated by the CIA, also called Villa A) within four minutes of the blast at the main gate.[9] The DSS officer in charge of the Tactical Operations Center radioes Scott Strickland, another DSS officer. Find the ambassador, Strickland was told, and bring him to safety.

Moments later, Strickland forcefully knocked on Ambassador Stevens's door. Stevens noticed that the man was carrying an M-4 automatic rifle and a 9 mm pistol. The ambassador's quarters were far enough from the main gate that he likely didn't hear the blast over his television set.

Strickland told Stevens and Sean Smith, who was nearby, to put on their body armor and to follow him. He led them to a safe room in a single-story concrete structure, in the rear of an office building. Strickland bolted the door.

Moments later, the jihadis broke down an exterior door and looted the office outside the safe room.

Inside the safe room, the Americans heard angry shouts in Arabic and the sounds of smashing furniture. How long would it take before this fury shattered the safe-room door?

* * *

In Tripoli, Libya's capital city across the Gulf of Sidra from Benghazi, Gregory Hicks was at home watching television. He was finally off duty after a long day. Hicks was second only to the ambassador in the Libya delegation and was the highest-ranking State Department officer in Tripoli that night. A foreign service officer knocked on his door and said, "Greg, Greg, the embassy's under attack."

He meant the facility in Benghazi.

Hicks saw that he had received a call from an unknown phone number on his cell phone and returned the call. It was Strickland's cell phone. Ambassador Stevens answered and said, "Greg, we're under attack," before the phone call is cut off.[10] These turned out to be the ambassador's last known words.

Hicks notified Washington.

The State Department requested that military assets be deployed to gather intelligence on the emerging emergency in Benghazi. A drone plane over Libya was retasked to fly over the U.S. compound in Benghazi.

The unarmed surveillance aircraft was directed to reposition over Benghazi and arrived on station by 9:59 p.m.—less than ten minutes after the ambassador's call.[11]

The images that the drone transmitted were frightening. Armed men were thronging the compound, and some vehicles were on fire.

* * *

Ambassador Stevens, information security officer Smith, and DSS officer Strickland were holed up in a safe room in Villa C, the diplomatic portion of the U.S. compound. This was where they were trained to run in the event of an attack. They had locked themselves in, behind steel-bar gates, in the inner room.

Inside the single-story concrete structure, on the other side of the safe-room door, the attackers set the office furniture on fire. The militants quickly located the diesel fuel drums, which were to be used to power new generators that hadn't been installed yet, and rolled the barrels toward the safe house. They beat them open with tools found in the equipment shed. They poured the fuel on the walls and doors of the ambassador's safe house. Then they set it ablaze. In seconds, the house was a howling inferno.

The building filled with noxious smoke. Strickland opened a window to draw in breathable air, but more smoke surged in. So the trio crawled to a bathroom in the rear of the safe room.

Now they had to make a life-or-death choice: stay

and die choking on the bathroom tile, or climb out the window and take their chances in the open compound. Strickland shouted for Stevens and Smith to follow him. He couldn't see them in the dense smoke.

Strickland leaped out a back window, but amid the acrid black smoke he lost contact with Stevens and Smith, both of whom seemed to have separated in the smoke. They were last seen by Strickland crawling on the floor, desperate for clean air to breathe.

Boldly, Strickland reentered the building several times, but he failed to find Stevens or Smith.[12] The smoke was too thick, and he knew the fire would be through the door in minutes. Coughing from the thick smoke, he plunged from the window and, dodging gunfire, made his way across the darkened compound.

* * *

Six minutes after the arrival of the surveillance drone, the State Department Operations Center transmitted an "Ops Alert," notifying the White House Situation Room, senior department officials, and others that Benghazi was under attack: "approximately 20 armed people fired shots; explosions have been heard as well."[13] (The actual number of attackers would prove to be far higher.)

The Tactical Operations Center on the Benghazi compound was a concrete structure with steel-barred windows and doors. Most of the DSS officers were using the makeshift fortress as their Masada, a place to make a last, desperate stand against enormous odds. Then, they heard knocking. The Americans exchanged surprised glances. After peeking out, one saw Strickland. Relieved, he opened the door to let Strickland inside.

Strickland reported that both Stevens and Smith were missing and that the terrorists had overrun their last known position. The two men were now either casualties or captives. They could do nothing to help either man now.

Everyone in the room knew one more thing: They would be next. And soon.

The DSS officer in charge placed an urgent call to the CIA Annex roughly five hundred yards away: "We're under attack, we need help, please send help now..." Then the line went dead.

* * *

At the CIA Annex, Tyrone Woods discussed the call with the Global Response team leader. Together, the two men walked over to see the CIA's chief of base, who was adamantly opposed to mounting a rescue. Woods persisted, saying, "If we don't act, people will die."

It was clear that Woods would go against orders if he was ordered to remain. He and the chief of base argued.

People who knew Woods knew how hardheaded he could be. He refused to back down when he believed he was right.

Tyrone Snowden Woods, known as "Ty" in the teams, was born in 1971 and served for twenty years in the U.S. Navy SEALs. He was awarded the Bronze Star, with combat "V" device, for leading a series of dangerous raids and reconnaissance missions that captured thirty-four enemy insurgents in the volatile Al Anbar province of Iraq. That province proved to be the turning point in the Iraq war. When tribal leaders switched their support from insurgents to Americans, the enemy was soon routed in that large, lawless province. The surge in 2007 built on the SEALs' success in Al Anbar. Woods served multiple tours in Iraq, Afghanistan, and other battlegrounds. He retired from the SEALs as a chief petty officer in 2007, but he didn't retire from dangerous assignments. He joined the State Department's Diplomatic Security Service and, ultimately, was sent to Libya.

* * *

Woods, who didn't like to take no for an answer, gathered six other heavily armed men. They climbed into two Toyota Land Cruisers and raced over to the embattled compound, arriving at 10:07 p.m.

Woods's plan was to avoid a suicidal frontal assault through the compound's main gate. Instead, he and his men parked their vehicles along the diplomatic facility's outer perimeter wall. They radioed the men trapped in the Tactical Operations Center (TOC) not to open fire on their position, a wise precaution. Using their own Land Cruisers as ladders, they scaled the wall.

The jihadis soon spotted them and opened fire. Woods and his team were running and gunning, shooting at attackers while moving toward the ambassador's last known location. The CIA team, composed largely of former special forces (including SEALs) were more accurate shots, and they drove back the attackers. They gained entrance to the burning building and dragged out Smith's body.[14]

Ambassador Stevens remained missing. Could he still be alive?

*   *   *

The U.S. National Military Command Center notified the Office of the Secretary of Defense and the Joint Chiefs of Staff of the situation at 10:32 p.m. Benghazi time.[15] At this stage, the attack had been underway for more than forty minutes.

Another half hour passed before Defense Secretary Leon Panetta and Joint Chiefs of Staff Chairman Gen. Martin Dempsey discussed the Benghazi situation with President Barack Obama during a regularly scheduled weekly meeting. That meeting started at 11:00 p.m. Benghazi time.[16]

It is unclear why the defense secretary was unable to see the president sooner. Yet, based on the timelines made public by the Obama administration, it seems likely that the president either denied the secretary's request for an earlier meeting or didn't acknowledge his request. It is mind-boggling that the president did not convene an immediate meeting, given the nature of a direct attack on an ambassador of the United States. By the time the defense secretary and chairman of the Joints Chiefs sat down with President Obama, the attack in Benghazi had been raging for more than one hour and fifteen minutes.

* * *

At the same time, Gregory Hicks asked the defense attaché at the Tripoli embassy if any military help was forthcoming. The attaché said that it would take two to three hours for the nearest fighters to get on-site from Italy—and that there would be no refueling aircraft available for the fighters to return to their base. Hicks said: "Thank you very much."[17]

He now knew that Washington had not authorized any military rescue and that the military wasn't going to offer false hope.

A second drone arrived over Benghazi at 11:10 p.m. and immediately began transmitting a live video feed back to Washington.[18] All of the president's men were watching the real-time images as the diplomatic villa burned and Americans struggled to save their own lives. In Washington, they watched and waited, as if it were just another television show. As if they were merely spectators, not decision makers with the power to send rescuers.

* * *

On the ground in Benghazi, Woods and the Global Response Staff (GRS) realized that they couldn't hold the diplomatic outpost. They had searched for the ambassador without success and grimly retrieved the body of Sean Smith.

Now they had to fight their way to the TOC, where all of the surviving diplomats were trapped. With their single MK-46 machine gun and Heckler and Koch rifles they were picking off attackers, but the enemy was relentlessly returning automatic fire. One GRS officer hurled grenades, pushing back the enemy. But it was like sweeping away water, which just runs back to fill the gap.

They cleared a path to the TOC, but the enemy quickly regrouped behind them. The attackers were becoming bolder and their numbers were growing. It was time to retreat.

Then the news got worse. The overhead drone aircraft revealed that more enemy reinforcements were arriving at a staging area less than three hundred yards from the trapped Americans. They would now either have to fight their way out or battle a much larger force in a matter of minutes.

Woods led the diplomats across the open compound. He helped the men vault over the nine-foot-high perimeter wall and into the Land Cruisers. Miraculously, despite the bullets bursting around them, none of the Americans were shot.

As they climbed into the SUVs, a jihadi lookout spotted them.

Bullets pockmarked the windows of their vehicles as they roared off to the CIA Annex. As they sped down the narrow, snaking streets, the drivers had to be careful not to flip the heavy armored vehicles. If the Land Cruisers overturned, they would be trapped and quickly surrounded by the pursuing attackers.

The lead driver radioed the guard at the CIA's main gate: "We're coming in hot."

By 11:15, both of the Toyota Land Cruisers arrive at the CIA Annex.[19] As the gate closed behind the last vehicle, bullets ricocheted nearby. They had been followed.

Woods and his men had saved them. But for how long?

* * *

Starting at midnight Benghazi time, Defense Secretary Leon Panetta held meetings with Gen. Martin Dempsey and Gen. Carter Ham. He was working to create rescue options for the president to approve. Panetta ordered a Marine Fleet Antiterrorism Security Team stationed in Rota, Spain, and a second Fleet Antiterrorist Security Team (FAST) platoon to deploy to Naval Air Station Sigonella. He ordered a special operations team based in northern Europe to deploy to Sigonella, an hour's flight away from Benghazi. A special operations team based in the U.S. was also ordered to deploy to Sigonella.[20] From this base in Sicily, forces could be ordered to Benghazi—if the president approved a "boots on the ground" operation.

However, a C-110 special operations team deployed to Croatia stayed in place. This team, known as EUCOM CIF (European Command's Commander's In Extremis Force), could have flown to Benghazi in three and a half hours. Of course, gathering men and materiel might have taken another hour or two.[21]

Yet no team was ordered to go directly to Benghazi.

Meanwhile, the enemy had pivoted to attack the CIA compound. As Panetta and the generals debated the options, mortar rounds exploded inside the CIA compound.

Woods climbed onto the roof of a building to direct fire at the attackers. The Americans' shots were accurate, dropping militants at one hundred yards. But the enemy force seemed to be growing larger.

Throughout the night, as Washington discussed and opined, Woods and the CIA team were fighting for their lives.

* * *

Meanwhile, Hicks and State Department officials were developing their own rescue option. The option amounted to one man: Glen Anthony Doherty.

The son of a former Massachusetts boxing commissioner, Doherty grew up as an all-around athlete in Winchester, Massachusetts. He surprised his family in 1995 by saying that he planned to join the Navy and become a SEAL. He was thirty years old. That made him a bit old to start a Navy career, but his family knew that nothing could stop him once he'd made his mind up.

Doherty got selected for BUD/S and made it through on his first attempt. He took additional schooling to be certified as a paramedic and a sniper. He was soon deployed all over the world. He was on the SEAL team that responded to the bombing of the USS *Cole*, the deadliest attack on a U.S. warship since World War II. Forty-four sailors were killed or wounded in that blast. (Bin Laden later released a poem celebrating the attack.)

In early 2001, Doherty was wondering about leaving the Navy. He was undergoing knee reconstruction surgery and weighing how much more punishment his body could take. The September 11 attacks on New York and Washington changed his mind. He went to serve in Afghanistan and Iraq.

Doherty and his team were assigned to secure oil fields prior to the invasion of Iraq in 2003. His mission was to prevent Saddam Hussein from setting the oil fields on fire, as he had during Desert Storm in 1991. Doherty then linked up with U.S. Marines fighting their way to Baghdad. As a sniper, he provided security for the advancing leathernecks in hellish fighting in Iraqi cities.

During his nine-year career as a SEAL, Glen served in both Iraq and Afghanistan.

Always on the lookout for an adventure, Doherty was a surfer, triathlete, white-water rafting guide, professional ski instructor, pilot, and self-professed adrenaline junkie. Other SEALs described him as "your quintessential SEAL."

Doherty was lifelong friends with some of his team members, including Brandon Webb, with whom he coauthored the 2010 book, *Navy SEAL Sniper: An Intimate Look at the Sniper of the 21st Century.*

After leaving the Navy, he worked for a private security outfit in Afghanistan, Iraq, Israel, Kenya, and Libya. In the month prior to the attack, Doherty gave an interview to ABC News. He surprised the reporter by saying that he was personally tracking down MANPADS, shoulder-fired surface-to-air missiles, in Libya and destroying them. He loved the job.[22]

* * *

After hearing from Hicks, Doherty quickly put together a ragtag team of government contractors and DSS agents. Finding no scheduled flights, he reportedly bribed the Libyan pilots of an aging Learjet with

$30,000 cash to fly his crew to Benghazi immediately.[23] The pilots agreed. The Learjet arrived in Benghazi at 1:15 a.m. local time.

They were unloading guns and equipment on the tarmac when they ran into trouble. In the midst of the attack, local police had not been alerted to their arrival and found the men to be suspicious. An argument erupted when Doherty could not tell the Libyans exactly where he was going with all of his firepower. (Doherty had only GPS coordinates, and the Libyans wanted an exact street address.) With his friend Ty Woods and other comrades under mortar and machine-gun fire, Doherty had no patience for the police runaround. More than an hour was lost trying to get his team out of the airport.

Meanwhile, Washington vetoed a request by Gregory Hicks to send a second team. Hicks has said he believed the veto came from the military. As the afternoon came to an end in Washington, D.C., the president went to dinner with his family in the upstairs residence of the White House. He did not appear to have been engaged at this stage.

* * *

Strangely, Ambassador Stevens seemingly arrived at Benghazi Medical Center, a local hospital, around

1:00 a.m. It is not clear who transported him to the hospital, or whether the ambassador was alive or dead when he arrived.

Hospital personnel picked up the cell phone that Strickland had loaned to the ambassador. They dialed the last number called by Stevens: Greg Hicks in Tripoli. "We know where the ambassador is. Please, you can come get him."

Hicks and other embassy officials feared the calls were a hoax, knowing Ansar al-Sharia militia had surrounded the hospital. The calls were likely a trap.[24]

A source the embassy trusted—known as Bakabar—went to the hospital to negotiate for Stevens or his body. By the time Bakabar arrived, the ambassador was a corpse. He might have arrived dead or dying. No one would tell Bakabar the story. He got custody of Stevens's body at around 5:15 a.m. The embassy instructed the hospital to place the name "John Doe" on the ambassador's death certificate. Bakabar and his associates transported Stevens's body to the Benghazi airport.

* * *

Overhead, one of the drone aircraft was running out of fuel. Another surveillance aircraft arrived over Benghazi at 5:00 a.m. to ensure a constant stream of video back to Washington.[25]

* * *

When Doherty finally arrived at the CIA Annex at approximately 5:00, he immediately asked for Ty Woods, his SEAL teammate.

Woods was on the roof, expertly using an MK-46 machine gun to thin the enemy's numbers. The rising sun had emboldened the attackers, who were surging for the wall.

Doherty climbed on the roof to join Woods. From this elevated position, they could pick off militants.

The two friends had less than a minute to discuss the situation. A French-made 81 mm mortar round exploded—killing Woods and putting the machine gun out of action. Another GRS agent was speared with shrapnel, and his blood coated the rooftop.

Doherty, by instinct and training, reached for the MK-46 and repositioned it. Before he could return fire, another 81 mm mortar round landed on him. He died instantly.

Cutting ropes from gym equipment, other GRS men climbed onto the blood-soaked roof and retrieved the wounded. As gunshots crackled around them, one wounded man was lowered by ropes into the building. Another was carried down by hand.

Mortar shells continued to explode throughout the CIA compound.

* * *

The drone overhead relayed frightening news. The enemy was gathering for a major assault. Their staging area was less than three hundred yards out—a single American aircraft missile could have dispatched them all. But no air support had been ordered. The CIA chief of base realized that they had to flee now or die in minutes when "the Indians" topped the wall of the stockade.

At 5:15 a.m., another mortar exploded inside the CIA compound. Others quickly followed. The assault lasted eleven minutes.[26]

* * *

The Americans raced by armed convoy to the Benghazi airport and departed on a 7:40 a.m. flight for Tripoli.[27] A second plane ferried the remaining Americans to Tripoli at 10:00 a.m. Later, on the night of September 12, the Americans departed for Germany. A C-17 aircraft left Tripoli for Ramstein Air Base in Germany with American personnel and the bodies of the four Americans killed in Benghazi. It arrived at Ramstein at 10:19 p.m.[28] The Americans had gotten out of harm's way as a result of the heroic acts of Glen Doherty and Ty Woods, and a handful of other GRS agents at the CIA compound. They had held the wall just long enough for a plan to be hatched to extract the remaining personnel from the compound to the airport.

* * *

Help arrived too late and remained too far away. The EUCOM special operations force arrives at Sigonella, Italy, at 7:57 p.m. A Marine FAST platoon arrived at Tripoli at 8:56 p.m.[29] The special operations force from America arrived in Italy at 9:28 p.m.[30]

Almost twenty-four hours after the attack began, American Special Forces remained hundreds of miles over the horizon from the smoking ruins of America's diplomatic facility in Benghazi. For the first time in a generation, a U.S. ambassador had been murdered. Three other Americans had been killed in an armed assault. And dozens more had been wounded, some so seriously as to require months of hospital care.

With a presidential election almost two months away, the search for answers began.

The big question—"Could they have been rescued in time?"—is addressed in the next chapter.

CHAPTER 9

The Rescue That Wasn't

The funeral of Ty Woods was silent, sobering, and sadly moving. At Fort Rosecrans National Cemetery, on a hill overlooking San Diego Bay and the Pacific Ocean, the afternoon sun falling on the bagpipers and Navy men in crisp white uniforms. Admirals stood side by side with enlisted SEALs, took their SEAL tridents off their chests, and pounded them in the top of the fallen SEAL's casket with their fists. A traditional SEAL farewell, sending another teammate, warrior, and friend to Valhalla. Glen Doherty was put to rest in a similar service in western Massachusetts.

There was no distinction, to the men in the teams, that Woods and Doherty were no longer active-duty SEALs when they had fallen. They were SEALs, and they died fighting to save American lives.

As the shock of the loss of two respected veteran SEALs reverberated across the secret brotherhood, a series of private calls, e-mails, and texts made it clear that many SEALs were angry with the president, the defense secretary, and the entire chain of command. Their rage was incandescent and inconsolable. Nothing had been done to try to save these two men after an eight-hour firefight?

Then the tone changed. The SEALs debated a series of options—steps that could have saved the lives of Woods and Doherty. We spoke with a number of SEALs as well as other fighter pilots and senior military officers to examine these options and to answer the two biggest unanswered questions: Could they have been saved? If so, how?

We combed publicly available records, congressional testimony, and State Department and Defense Department reports, and we reached out to Navy SEALs, mission planners, and veteran fighter pilots. We talked to witnesses and attorneys for witnesses who had been threatened to stay silent by their government supervisors. In the course of our investigation, we discovered five realistic scenarios—based on the presence of military assets, standard mission parameters, and capabilities— that reveal how the Americans encircled in Benghazi could have been saved.

* * *

The Obama administration offers two technical military defenses for its apparent inaction: There were no military assets that could be brought to bear in time to make a difference, and that there were no tankers available to support fighter aircraft if the fighters had been sent in to help. As we shall see, both statements are false and tactically irrelevant.

There were military assets available. There were options.

The following scenarios have been prepared based upon assets known to have been available to the United States at the time, as well as information provided to us by several career officers from different branches of the military. We provide realistic rescue scenarios to rebut the argument by President Obama and his senior officials: that there was nothing that could have been done to save American lives.[1]

The reason this story cuts so deep with Americans is because we, as a people, know that everything the government could have done was not done. A U.S. ambassador, a senior official, and two brave former Navy SEALs were killed as a result of the inability of those in power to protect our own. These rescue scenarios are consistent with the theme of this book—

that SEAL culture matters—and the creed of the SEAL teams:

We expect to lead and be led. In the absence of orders I will take charge, lead my teammates, and accomplish the mission. I lead by example in all situations.

I will never quit. I persevere and thrive on adversity. My Nation expects me to be physically harder and mentally stronger than my enemies. If knocked down, I will get back up, every time. I will draw on every remaining ounce of strength to protect my teammates and to accomplish our mission. I am never out of the fight.

We demand discipline. We expect innovation. The lives of my teammates and the success of our mission depend on me—my technical skill, tactical proficiency, and attention to detail. My training is never complete.

We train for war and fight to win. I stand ready to bring the full spectrum of combat power to bear in order to achieve my mission and the goals established by my country. The execution of my duties will be swift and violent when required yet guided by the very principles that I serve to defend.

Brave men have fought and died building the proud tradition and feared reputation that I am bound to uphold. In the worst of conditions, the legacy of my teammates steadies my resolve and silently guides my every deed. I will not fail.

* * *

These scenarios are dedicated to the memory of Tyrone Woods and Glen Doherty and to the Ty Woodses and Glen Dohertys of this nation's future. Without them, this great nation will not survive. Remember, they may have been ordered not to go and they went anyway. As a result of their unique and heroic efforts, dozens of American lives were saved. Woods and Doherty are already passing into legend. Doherty and Woods were not "bumps in the road." They were soldiers and heroes of this nation, and they should be honored as such.[2]

Rescue Scenario One
Date: September 11, 2012
Aviano Air Base
Mission Complete Time: 1:30 A.M.

Aviano Air Base is a NATO base located in northeastern Italy, in the Friuli-Venezia Giulia region. It lies at the foot of the Italian Alps, about ten miles from Pordenone, Italy.

Aviano is home to the United States Air Force's

Thirty-First Fighter Wing. The Thirty-First is the only U.S. fighter wing south of the Alps, and it is critical to operations in NATO's southern region. It maintains two fighter squadrons, the 555th Fighter Squadron (Triple Nickel), and the 510th Fighter Squadron (Buzzards).[3]

The Thirty-First Fighter Wing Operations Group ensures the combat readiness of two F-16CG squadrons, one air control squadron, and one operational support squadron conducting and supporting worldwide air operations. Each F-16 squadron maintains approximately twenty operational fighter jets.[4] The Thirty-First is the first permanently based fighter aircraft wing south of the Alps since World War II.

The Air Force defines the job of the Thirty-First as "expeditionary air combat in support of the Global War on Terrorism." Arguably, exactly the mission necessary for the job at hand: saving American lives under attack in Benghazi.

These fighter jets could easily have made it to Benghazi, with a single fuel stop at Naval Air Station Sigonella hours before the final battle that killed Glen Doherty and Ty Woods. The fighters would have arrived hours before Doherty and Woods died.

At a minimum, scrambling these jets toward Benghazi would have been consistent with the imperative expressed by SEAL Team Six assault leader Ryan Zinke: "immediately move assets forward to the theatre where needed."

In reality, assets were not ordered forward until six hours after the ambassador was killed. Secretary of Defense Panetta later testified before Congress that he did not have any direct conversations with President Obama after 6:00 p.m. (Washington time) on the night of the atrocities that killed the ambassador and three other Americans. This means that the president had either disconnected from the discussion or he had simply moved on after the news of the ambassador's death had reached him. Either way, Panetta was very clear on his timeline of discussions.

While these jets can be configured to hold a vast array of precision bombing ordnance—from Hellfire missiles to grenade bomblets—it is likely that flying them "naked" with only their 20 mm cannons loaded would have been more than sufficient to disperse or dispatch the mob outside the CIA compound being defended by Glen Doherty and Ty Woods and others in Benghazi.

The effective range of an F-16C, with external fuel tanks, is over 1,700 nautical miles. However, even assuming less range was possible here, due to the "need for speed" to the target (faster travel burns more fuel); the jets stationed at Aviano Air Base had plenty of range to get there, with a single hot refueling at any base en route, including Naval Air Station Sigonella, located on the island of Sicily 845 nautical miles south.

Dan Hampton is a recently retired Air Force pilot, a decorated veteran of both Gulf wars with over 4,500 hours of flight time in an F-16, and he is familiar with the flight wings based in Aviano. He has flown out of Aviano many times. He has more than seven hundred combat hours in the F-16 alone and author of the *New York Times* bestseller *Viper Pilot*. "The Air Force could have done the job from there, if they had been called upon," Hampton said. The problem is that the Air Force, and all other branches of the Department of Defense, were never called upon to mount a rescue. The president did not speak to the Secretary of Defense to order or allow military action.

The distance between Aviano Air Base and Benghazi is 1,050 nautical miles. F-16s have a range-fuel supply for approximately 1,700 nautical miles.

Based upon our discussions with current and former military officers, including Commander Zinke and Dan Hampton, the following basic plan could have and, more important, should have been put in place.

All times noted herein are local (Benghazi).

9:40 P.M.

Ambassador Stevens makes the initial call reporting the attack was taking place at 9:40 p.m. Stevens reports to Hicks in Tripoli: "Greg, we are under attack."

All other agencies, both local to Libya and worldwide, were then immediately informed that a U.S. ambassador was under attack in one of the most dangerous places on Earth. This call should have prompted the immediate initiation of an Emergency Response Plan.

9:40 P.M.–10:00 P.M.

General Ham (commander at Africa Command, or AFRICOM) is given notice that a U.S. diplomatic outpost facility in Benghazi is under attack and needs help. He is also informed that the U.S. ambassador to Libya and his related staff are at risk of capture or death, and that a U.S. facility is in danger of being overrun, or has already been overrun, by enemy militants. Instead of being told to "stand down,"[5] along with others in Tripoli, the order is given for him to immediately mount and execute a rescue operation.

General Ham and his commanders are aware that the closest permanently stationed air fighter assets in the theater are located at Aviano Air Base in Italy. It is very possible, if not likely, that other assets were also located in the Mediterranean (including the entire Sixth Fleet carrier group, a flotilla of more than a dozen ships and a nuclear-powered aircraft carrier with over seventy-five planes) that were even closer than the permanent assets at Aviano.

10:00 P.M., *Aviano Air Base*

The jets stationed in Italy should have immediately been called in to action no later than 10 p.m. Had the F-16s scrambled from Aviano, then hot-refueled at Naval Air Station Sigonella, they could have easily been on-site in time to save Woods and Doherty. While there may not have been fighter jets already at Sigonella, there were certainly fighters located at Aviano, which could have been at Sigonella in approximately one hour and fifteen minutes.

The distance between Aviano and Sigonella is 845 nautical miles. A commercial flight between Aviano and Sigonella can cover the distance in approximately two hours, including takeoff and approach time. Hence, to estimate that an advanced fighter jet travelling at just under Mach 1 can cover the same distance in 1.25 hours is conservative.

According to Dan Hampton, who has flown into both Aviano and Sigonella on multiple occasions, 1.5

hours from Aviano to Sigonella is imminently achievable, even with a wide array of ground attack ordnance hanging from the fighter. Different ordnance packages dictate different flight speeds and fuel consumptions. While the speed achievable by the fighter, and gas consumption used is a factor, it certainly would have been achievable here, he said.

The American jets could have arrived in time to save the encircled diplomats and contractors. In fact, given the undisputed fact that Glen and Ty were alive until at least 5:15 a.m., at least four hours after help could have and should have been there.

11 30 p.m., Arrive NAS Sigonella, Hot Refuel F-16
12:30 a.m., Wheels up en route to Benghazi

Allowing the F-16 pilots one hour at Sigonella to refuel and replenish is more than sufficient time, according to veteran pilots, including Dan Hampton. A hot refuel of an F-16 can be done in 30 minutes or less. Essentially, a hot refuel is similar to refueling a NASCAR car during a race. The aircraft's engine is not shut off, and the fuel pump is attached to the aircraft. This allows the refilling procedure to begin immediately after the aircraft is wheeled off the runway. Practiced refueling crews have been known to accomplish the procedure in ten minutes.[6]

Given that the Navy personnel on the ground at Sigonella would have nearly certainly known what was taking place in Benghazi, and that there were two former Navy SEALs in a firefight with more than one hundred terrorist attackers, you can bet your last United States dollar the refueling crew at Sigonella would have been working like a NASCAR team at Daytona getting those birds fueled and ready to bring the fight to the enemy. Allowing one hour to achieve this task is more than reasonable.

Sigonella to Benghazi
Distance: 468 miles
Time to Target: (Speed 0.9 Mach) 45 minutes
Arrival Time: 1:15–1:30 A.M.

With refueled jets and less than five hundred miles to the fight, the F-16s would have had a variety of options upon arrival in Benghazi. One thing is certain: while it is difficult, even by the U.S. State Department's timeline, Glen Doherty and Ty Woods were alive and fighting until at least 5:15 a.m.

Benghazi is located on the Mediterranean shore and would have been easily visible on the night of September 11, which was clear with no overcast conditions.

On their approach, the F-16 pilots would have had two distinct advantages in accessing and planning their attack. The first was that they would have been in constant contact with the Air Force personnel operating the drone over the battle since 11:10 p.m., according to the Department of Defense timeline. The cockpit of the F-16C has the capability to get real-time images from the drone shown on their equipment, not dissimilar to watching a live TV report on one's television in your living room.

From these images, the pilots would have had the capability to assess the number of attackers, potential antiaircraft capability, and the correct approach. The second advantage the pilots had was two battle-trained and hardened Navy SEALs on the ground who had experience with forward air controlling of aircraft, and also had working laser designators to highlight the targets at night.

According to Dan Hampton, he could have deposited ordnance on board the F-16s within feet of the target: "Especially with two ex-SEALs, because they're all qualified in forward controlling of aircraft. And they had laser pointers, which kind of takes all the error out of it. Normal weapons aside, we've always got the cannons, which I've used in a pinch myself, and in an absolute environment, the cannon might have been the best."

Even if the Rules of Engagement (ROE) allowed

by the Defense Department for the pilots did not include use of missiles or cannons, still the effect of a low-altitude afterburner "blast" of two F-16s would have bought the Americans valuable time.

When asked whether he had an opinion as to what effect a low-altitude pass over the scene with afterburners engaged might have had on the attackers in Benghazi, Dan Hampton responded: "Well, the same effect it has on most people. These weren't trained soldiers. These were just basically insurgents. I think it would definitely make them pause. I think they might rethink their attack if they thought there was heavy overhead support from the Air Force or Navy."

The roar of deep-diving American jets literally might have scattered the enemy permanently without firing a shot.

The former top diplomat in Libya, Greg Hicks, told congressional investigators that more could have been done by the military on the night of September 11 and morning of September 12 to spare the lives of those being attacked in Benghazi. He wondered why the military did not send a plane as a show of force into Libyan airspace: "The Libyans that I talked to, and the Libyans and other Americans who were involved in the war, have told me also that Libyan revolutionaries were very cognizant of the impact that American and NATO airpower had with respect to their victory," in the war against Libyan dictator Moammar Gadhafi.

Hicks, then the U.S. deputy chief of mission in Libya, told investigators on April 11, 2013: "They are under no illusions that American and NATO airpower won that war for them. And so, in my personal opinion, a fast mover flying over Benghazi at some point, you know, as soon as possible might very well have prevented some of the bad things that happened that night." Hicks went on to say he believed "if we had been able to scramble a fighter or aircraft or two over Benghazi as quickly as possible after the attack commenced"—after being reported around 9:40 p.m. that night—"I believe there would not have been a mortar attack on the Annex in the morning because I believe the Libyans would have split. They would have been scared to death that we would have gotten a laser on them and killed them."

Hicks also suggested that he believed the Libyan government would have granted the U.S. permission to fly the planes. "I believe that the Libyans were hoping that we were going to come bail them out of this mess," Hicks said. "And, you know, they were as surprised as we were that American—the military forces that did arrive only arrived on the evening of September 12."

Hicks said at approximately 10 p.m. in Tripoli on the night of the first attack, he was at the U.S. embassy in Tripoli talking to State Department officials in Washington, D.C., regional security officer John Martinec at the U.S. Embassy, defense attaché Lt. Col. Keith Phillips, and others. Phillips was reaching out to officials with the Libyan Ministry of Defense and to the chief of staff of the Libyan Armed Forces, as well as officials with the Joint Staff and the United States Africa Command.

Hicks recalled asking Phillips, "Is there anything coming?"

Phillips told Hicks that the nearest fighter planes were at Aviano Air Base, in Italy—"that he had been told that it would take two to three hours to get them airborne, but that there were no tanker assets near enough to support a flight from Aviano." The pre-flight checks can be time-consuming, but three hours is probably an exaggeration meant to let Hicks know that no one in Washington wanted to take the perceived political risk of mounting a rescue. The refueling issue is, likewise, a nonissue. If the jets didn't have enough fuel to return to Italy, they could land on a nearby carrier or at an allied landing strip in Libya itself.

In February 2013, Gen. Martin Dempsey, chairman

of the Joint Chiefs, was also asked why F-16s at Aviano Air Base in Italy were not deployed to Benghazi that night. "This is the middle of the night now, these are not aircraft on strip alert," Dempsey said. "They're there as part of our commitment to NATO and Europe. And so, as we looked at the timeline, it was pretty clear that it would take up to twenty hours or so to get them there." Again, it could take several hours to put jets in the air and several more to put them in the skies over Benghazi—but twenty hours is an outrageous political exaggeration. It is even more outrageous when coming from the chairman of the Joint Chiefs. A man who should know better and expect better from the men and women he commands.

"Twenty hours?" Why twenty hours? Possibly of greater importance, given the array of issues that had been going on in Benghazi for the last several weeks, why were the planes not on alert, as was suggested should have been the case by Dan Hampton and others? Officials from the Obama administration have testified that the military assets were not in place to conduct a rescue of the besieged U.S. officials in Benghazi.

"This is not 9/11," Panetta said in a February interview on CNN's *State of the Union*. "You cannot just simply call and expect within two minutes to have a team in place. It takes time. That's the nature of it. Our people are there, they're in position to move, but we've got to have good intelligence that gives us a heads-up that something's going to happen."[7]

Excuse us, Mr. Panetta—it *was* 9/11, just a different year and a different group of terrorists killing Americans. The United States spends more money on its military than the next ten largest militaries in the world. It is hard to believe that a fighter response couldn't be managed within six hours.

Rescue Scenario Two
Date: September 11, 2012
10:00 P.M.
Gaeta, Italy

As the call came in from the commander-in-chief of AFRICOM, the U.S. Navy pilots in Gaeta knew the situation was dire. They didn't wait for orders but were already getting ready as the orders came in. They immediately jumped into their G-suits and headed for the planes being readied for takeoff. America's diplomatic outpost in Benghazi was under attack.

Knowing the powder keg where the call was made from, it caught none of the pilots by surprise that a 911 call could be made from this part of Africa on 9/11.

The pilots knew that the closest facility that could

potentially have any firepower ready was Sigonella. Although Sigonella was a Naval Air Station, it had no permanently stationed attack aircraft based there. There might have been helicopters in Sigonella, but not the type needed for an armed assault. The wing commanders were already debating options for what might be needed in the newly formed Republic of Libya, when the flight crews were told to "light the fires" on the FA-18E Super Hornets. Takeoff was imminent.

As chance would have it, all but one of the four flight crews selected had already been involved in battles in the skies over Libya, during the overthrow of Col. Moammar Gadhafi in 2011. The U.S. Air Force and the U.S. Navy were instrumental in driving the Arab world's longest-serving dictator from power through strategic air strikes and close air support of the Libyan rebels, usually with the help of SEALs on the ground acting as forward air controllers.

The flight leaders knew what ordnance to load on the fighters. They chose the new stealth, air-to-ground missiles, primarily for their precision and ability to cause the least amount of collateral damage in the concrete-walled neighborhood where snipers hid and mortar crews worked. Collateral damage was clearly not in the "game plan" for the brass setting the mission parameters. No one wanted another Stalingrad or Dresden; they wanted a carefully calibrated attack that spared civilians.

As was generally the case, even in war zones, the Rules of Engagement (ROEs) could change on an hourly basis. Given the political sensitivity—the U.S. was less than eight weeks from a presidential election—the pilots knew that the ROEs might change several times while they were en route to the target. What they did know was that Americans were trapped, that some Americans were already dead, and that the survivors desperately needed close air support to save the diplomats, spies, and contractors caught on the ground. That was enough for them. After a very brief rundown of the limited information available, the orders were then given: "Go!"

Here was what they knew for sure: the U.S. ambassador's last words were: "Greg, we're under attack." They were also aware that as many as forty-two other American lives hung in the balance.

Of equal importance, there were an unknown number of attackers. Some estimates put the number of attackers in the hundreds. Further, the pilots had no idea of what type of antiaircraft capability the attackers may have. Enemy rockets that could threaten aircraft, such as the Soviet-made SA-7, were as common as camels in Libya. Did the attackers also have captured antiaircraft artillery from the Gadhafi days? It was unlikely, but the sobering possibility could not be ruled out.

Gaeta is a sprawling U.S. Navy base on Italy's west coast, south of Rome and north of Naples—near the ankle of Italy's boot. It is just under six hundred nautical miles from Gaeta to Benghazi. In fact, enforcement of the no-fly zone (Operation Odyssey Dawn) was routinely done from Gaeta during the overthrow of Gadhafi.[8]

Given their strategic location in Gaeta, the FA-18 jets on the deck of a carrier were launch ready. The amount of time to takeoff depended on command orders to light the fires and stretch the catapults. The twin General Electric F414 turbofan engines were "lit" and ready for takeoff on the deck of the nuclear-powered carrier.

There is good reason why a president's first question in a crisis is "Where are the carriers?" They are still the preeminent and undisputed master of force projection on the face of the planet. The United States maintains eleven carrier strike groups (CSGs): each consists of one aircraft carrier, two guided missile cruisers, two antiaircraft warships, and one to two antisubmarine destroyers or frigates. The United States Sixth Fleet is based in Gaeta, Italy. On September 11, 2012, the flagship for the Sixth Fleet, the USS *Mount Whitney* (LCC-20) had just finished commemoration services for the 9/11 victims.[9]

As the fighters were catapulted down the deck of the nuclear-powered carrier, the flight leader and his wingman would have already been running through the contingencies during the fifty-minute flight time to Libya.

Takeoff went down without a hitch, and the two planes leveled off at ten thousand feet. The night was calm with very little wind, and there was virtually no air traffic. The communications with the ground forces were now patched into the coms for the aircraft. The individuals on the ground were not identified by name or military branch, but they were clearly either current or former special forces personnel, responding coolly and professionally to the questions being posed to them by naval command. They were also clearly well versed in the terminology of forward aircraft control, and their need to direct fire "danger close" in the area in front of them. They were giving exact GPS coordinates of the attackers' positions and had indicated their ability to use their laser designators for guidance of precision ordinance onboard the approaching aircraft. They had clearly directed aircraft to targets while under fire before.

Approximately halfway into the flight, the pilots were told that the ground troops conducting the defense were former Navy SEALs and that the information given by them should be considered accurate and reliable in directing their fire. Neither of the pilots were surprised by this revelation. Both had had the honor of working with SEALs previously. Knowing they had naval brothers on the ground in need of help merely raised their resolve to get it done right.

The pilots were now also able to view the video being transmitted by the aerial drone circling over the scene of the attack in Benghazi. The images showed dozens of terrorists surrounding the position held by the SEALs and CIA officers.

The SEALs were now asking for immediate air support as soon as they could get it. They had their laser designators prepared to light up the targets as soon as the American aircraft arrived. The pilots directly radioed the SEALs on the ground. They said that they were "ten minutes out and hot."

The acknowledging voices of the SEALs on the ground seemed uplifted by this news, as the crackle of small arms fire erupted in the background.

The Heads Up Display (HUD) on the FA-18s illuminated the inside of the cockpit as the planes approached Libya's eastern coast. Clear, with very little cloud cover, the conditions presented no visibility issues from a pilot's perspective.

Now the ROE meant everything—their orders determined what the pilots had to do and not do. They had been given the green light to use precision-guided munitions as long as the offending individuals were clearly identified as "hostile" by the personnel on the ground. The approximate number of bad guys was one hundred, and they were concentrated fifty to one hundred yards from the compound where the Americans were sheltered. Dropping bombs with friendlies this close was difficult and required exact planning both in the approach and drop of the ordnance. While collateral damage was to be avoided if at all possible, dropping their bombs on the Americans that they were trying to save was their worst nightmare.

The two experienced naval aviators elected to do a single high-altitude pass before starting their bombing run. This approach had two advantages: It could provide a warning to those civilians who are not affiliated with the bad guys to flee immediately, as the roar of passing fighters was hard to mistake for anything else. It would also give the pilots a chance to do a final recon of the drop zone.

During the flyby, the pilots asked the Navy SEAL located on the roof of the CIA compound to activate the laser designator for identification and targeting. Ty Woods did so, just as he had many times in the past. The guidance systems immediately locked on the position "painted" by the laser.

Time to get final clearance to engage the enemy.

The lead pilot radioed the Tactical Air Command center and requested clearance to use Hellfire missiles to engage trucks and personnel that have been identified as firing mortars and rockets on the trapped Americans.

Clearance given, the pilots did a 180-degree, three-G turn, leveled off at approximately 3,000 feet, and requested that the position of the mortar crews again be painted by the SEAL on the ground through his laser designator. The SEAL lit up the bad guys for the final time, and he watched as the missiles left the FA-18s at almost identical times.

The missile blast was sudden and sun-hot. The blinding explosions were quickly followed by multiple secondary explosions, where the gas tanks of the trucks explode, as well as the mortars and other ammunition being carried in enemy vehicles.

The images from the overhead drones confirmed two direct hits on the vehicles and crews operating the mortars, with the immediate killing of over two dozen jihadis. Dozens more were injured, and they attempted to crawl away from the carnage.

Believing another bombing run imminent, the remainder of the attacking force dispersed. Some broke out in a wild run down Benghazi's serpentine streets. Others cowered in doorways or hid under burned trucks.

The pilots hit their afterburners as they turned in for another run, purposely identifying their intentions to hit the enemy again. Their ambassador had just been killed, and his body was still unrecovered and being dragged through the streets. They were far from exacting the payback this group of terrorists deserved.

There was no doubt left in the minds of the surviving attackers: the Americans intended on exacting some revenge, and the superpower's wrath was measured in precision-guided munitions. Forgetting the reasons they were there in the first place, several more attackers desperately tried to flee and were killed by the SEALs and other diplomatic security personnel sniping from the rooftops.

The overhead drone identified the area of escape of the greatest mass of the attackers. The fighter pilots requested permission to clean up the rest of the mob by using their 20 mm cannons.

They were asked if the attackers appeared to be dispersing or were still moving toward the compound.

The pilots and SEALs responded almost simultaneously that the attackers appeared to be melting away.

The order was then given for the FA-18s to return to base. There was no need to make the rubble bounce.

The next wave of FA-18s would remain at altitude to confirm there would be no more attacks on the American diplomatic personnel.

The SEALs responded to the planes with a heartfelt "Thank you, Bravo Zulu."

The leaders of the attacking party were identified through several of the people wounded on the night of the incident. Their camps east of Benghazi were also identified. The next day a single cruise missile was launched and detonated over the camps. The camps disappeared in a blinding blast.

The Libyan government in power was grateful for the extermination of the individuals who had attacked the American consular facility and killed the American ambassador, as these armed radicals were a threat to their government as well.

Since the fighter jets arrived within a few hours of the initial attacks, Woods and Doherty were not killed. (It cannot be forgotten that Woods and Doherty did not die until the mortar attack on the CIA facility at

5:15 on the morning of September 12. This was well over seven hours after the attack had begun the day before.)

Rescue Scenario Three
Drone Attack
10:00 P.M.

The original drone arrived over the Temporary Mission Facility (TMF) and started transmitting images at 9:59 p.m., barely seventeen minutes after from Ambassador Stevens's frantic call for help: "We are under attack." Even though dimly lit, the infrared cameras on the unmanned aerial vehicle (UAV) clearly showed the scene unfolding below it was one of complete pandemonium: Heat signatures from bodies laid out in the courtyard and areas surrounding the entrance to the TMF, not moving and clearly dead or dying, fire spraying from the barrels of the guns being carried by the attackers, and RPG blasts all over the area. The attackers numbered in dozens, perhaps over one hundred.

Eventually flames started shooting from various windows in the diplomatic outpost, showing that the attackers had set fire to the buildings in the compound. Desperate radio transmissions coming from the Diplomatic Security officers on site also made it clear that

219

some people there were still alive, and searching for the ambassador.

One thing was certain: amid the confusion, the Americans still alive on the ground were in need of help—now. Air Force personnel monitoring the images from the drone rang their superiors and put in the request for immediate help to be sent to Benghazi. They asked for clearance to send the only type of help they could personally supply, another armed version of the UAV: the MQ-9 Reaper. This drone could deliver thermal imaging showing militants cowering inside buildings.

(The original drone that arrived in Benghazi, minutes after Stevens's call, was unfortunately a Northrop Grumman RQ-4 Global Hawk. Unfortunate, because it was unarmed. Had it been armed, and if the controllers of an armed UAV had been authorized to use force to defend the lives of the American diplomats, there was a very real possibility, if not a probability, that the entire Benghazi debacle could have been nipped in the bud. Ambassador Stevens and Sean Smith very probably would also still be alive.)

Given its rapid response time, the Global Hawk was already in Libya observing other matters and was retasked immediately to Benghazi. The Global Hawk has a cruise speed of 404 miles per hour, and a range of more than 8,000 miles. However, this Hawk was based out of NAS Sigonella, only some 400 miles north of Benghazi.[10]

The Global Hawk's infrared camera systems easily identified dozens of heat signatures both in and surrounding the diplomatic post. Viewing these images dispelled any remaining doubt as to whether the ambassador and his staff were in grave danger. Clearly the situation had degraded to the point of complete chaos.

As senior officials viewed the images coming back from the Global Hawk, the decision was made to send another drone. This one would be armed: the fearsome MQ-9 Reaper. Given the widespread use of these drones over Pakistan and Afghanistan against the Taliban, our research and interviews made it clear that it could have been used effectively in this scenario. The armed version of the Reaper drone is a game changer.

The Reaper was aptly named.

Thirty-six feet long with a wingspan of 65 feet, the Reaper was first put into service in 2007. Built by General Atomics, the Reaper is powered by a 950-horsepower turboprop engine and is capable of speeds in excess of 300 miles per hour. Of greater importance to those under attack was the Reaper's payload. The Reaper sent to Benghazi was armed with four of the newest 14 AGM-114 Hellfire air-to-ground missiles. These missiles are capable of destroying tanks. Used extensively in Pakistan, Yemen, and Somalia, this drone has been responsible for total reported kills of over four thousand terrorists and others. Used against an armed mob as close air support for the trapped Americans, it would be a game changer.

Cruising at a speed of 250 miles per hour, the drone arrived in Benghazi at 1:30 a.m. The attack had now been going on for approximately 3.5 hours. Approaching at over five thousand feet, it could barely be heard over the gunfire and chaos going on below. However, the operators monitoring its video and missile guidance technologies immediately picked up the laser designator painting the mortar crew just two blocks from the CIA compound where the SEALs and other State Department personnel were holed up. The enemy could be hit without hurting the SEALs.

Even though the hostile forces were located two blocks from the compound, they were in a clear line of sight from the SEALs located on the roof of the CIA compound that the Americans had fled to. The laser was pointed directly at the side of one of the vehicles with the symbol for Ansar al-Sharia painted on it. A perfect and fitting place for the Hellfire to impact.

The guiding system for the Hellfire immediately

indicated that it had found and locked on the laser. Whatever was located at this point on Earth was about to experience the reason Hellfire got its name. The operators at the drone command confirmed, through their satellite patch, that the laser was in fact the target the SEALs had chosen for the strike. Even though distance was some two blocks from the SEALs' location, the operator gave the last warning: missile locked on and engaged, danger close.

The Air Force drone operators were given the green light by their superiors. They hit the Launch button on the computer joystick. The Reaper cameras recorded the flash as the missile left the wing of the UAV and reached supersonic speed almost instantly. The Reaper operator watched the red trail from the missile honing in on its target.

The leader of the mortar team only had an instant to realize that they were under air attack before the Hellfire hit them—within inches of where the laser had marked. The blast wave radiated outward like a fiery red circular saw, slicing apart all it touched. Twenty attackers vaporized into pink mist. The secondary explosions rattled off like an oil drum thrown down a flight of stairs.

Within seconds, two more trucks exploded in a shower of hot metal. The explosion showered engine parts into the mass of attackers, wounding them with their own war machines. The shattered chassis were licked by flames, sending plumes of oily black smoke into the night sky. Those not lucky enough to die in the first few seconds lay dismembered and dying.

The second Hellfire pulverized another clump of jihadis fifty yards closer to the safe house. Another fifteen terrorists died in the Hellfire's thunder. It also took out a militant leader, who had been barking out orders to his officers. The burning claws of the Hellfire explosion soon reached a cache of RPG rounds that the enemy had brought. The RPGs exploded immediately like a devilish series of fireworks.

The panicked remainder of the mob fled for their lives down the narrow streets. They couldn't see the circling drone overhead but felt its wrath. They abandoned their vehicles and started to run wildly away from the blast radius.

The battle for the CIA station was over within minutes of the first missile being fired. More than fifty attackers lay dead or dying. The broken remnants of the mob were running for their desert hideouts.

Both Ty Woods and Glen Doherty and almost forty other Americans were saved. The Americans were delighted by their sudden deliverance from evil.

Rescue Scenario Four
QRF (Quick Reaction Force)
10:00 P.M.

The Global Response Staff (GRS) is an elite group of fewer than 150 specialists worldwide. Hired by the CIA to work in the most despotic hellholes on the planet, they are modern-day gunslingers and quite possibly the most highly qualified set of warriors in the world. Their hiring qualifications are not put out in public government-bid documents. Instead, members are selected and quietly tapped to apply by those who are already part of the crew. More than 75 percent come from parts of three very elite groups: Navy SEALs, Delta Force, and Marine Special Operations Force.

The GRS's best are known as "scorpions" for good reason. Not only have they proven themselves in gunfights, but also their knowledge of traps, bombs, setups, ambushes, kill zones, and unconventional tactics separates them from an already bad-ass bunch.

True samurai that live solely by the warrior code, they know they could be betrayed by their masters at any time and would be left to fend for themselves in ungodly parts of the world. They are not asked to

225

learn foreign languages where stationed, and generally do not even interact with the local populace, unless it is to obtain a specific item they are sent to retrieve. Their job is relatively simple and dangerous: safe-guarding diplomats and spies in places where they are prized only as targets or captives.

The GRS use the full panoply of intelligence—human assets, signal intercepts, orbiting satellites—to identify and defeat threats. They protect diplomats and other government personnel in some of the most dangerous parts of the world. When left with no other options, they do what they arguably do best—they shoot their way out. This is probably one of the most dangerous paramilitary jobs in the world. Glen Doherty and Ty Woods were both highly respected members of this group.

The GRS agents in Tripoli received the word that an attack was underway almost immediately after Ambassador Stevens made his last fateful call for help at 9:40 p.m. The initial word was received from the State Department, as Greg Hicks was trying desperately to put together a force to help his friend Stevens in Benghazi. Not knowing the exact circumstances of the attack, it was enough for the GRS guys to know it was time to get ready to roll. This was what they trained for.

They were pumped and primed; other people's crises were their motivation. Soon thereafter they tapped into the communications networks in Benghazi and quickly realized Woods was on the scene and Doherty, his friend, was going in as well.

The agents in Tripoli were largely located in a CIA facility. Little more than a large compound that had been fortified with concrete block and concertina wire, it was a very permeable Fort Apache in Indian country, nothing more.

Those that were located in other parts of Tripoli began to appear at the safe house. They knew that the situation was dire. Thus, most of the men showed up with their usual load-out of weapons and were each also carrying an additional large military duffel bag filled with special weapons and ammo. They knew they were in for a fight and wanted to have enough ammo and gear to finish it.

The word was then put out through the secure CIA channels: the operators were to assemble at a designated hangar at the Tripoli airport for further instructions.

The group that showed up would have made Wyatt Earp happy. They were quiet, sober men who knew how to handle a gunfight. They were veterans, experienced at killing men within six feet of their gun barrels, with some having made sniper shots approaching a mile away. Among the fifteen men, there was nearly a century of experience in Bosnia, Afghanistan, Somalia, Iraq, and other war zones. Some had recently separated from the military. Others had been out for years and working for various security contractors from Blackwater to Triple Canopy. Each sidelong glance told the same story: *These are the brothers I go to war with, and some of us may not return.*

The gear on display looked like an arms deal gone bad on the streets of Mogadishu. M-4s were the common gun of choice, outfitted with multiple thirty-round magazines and ten-inch close-quarter combat barrels. All guns had some form of laser sighting. The next most popular weapon was the venerable AK-47 in various configurations. While cheap in this part of the world, it was still the most common assault weapon for very good reason. It was reliable, and very easy to get ammo for virtually anywhere in the world, even from the bodies of slain enemies. They also had an assortment of semiautomatic pistols (generally .45 caliber), and 40 mm (mic-mic) grenade launchers. Ammunition and other weapons were shared among the group, not so much because anyone was in need but more to assure them that they were in this to the last round that anyone was still able to fire.

The officer in command was on loan to the CIA from a special operations unit working elsewhere in the sands of North Africa. The distance between Benghazi and Tripoli is 406 miles. The cruising speed of a US C-130 is approximately 345 miles per hour. Therefore, the flight time between Tripoli and Benghazi was no greater than one hour fifteen minutes.

A C-130 airplane had been regularly scheduled for the Tripoli-to-Benghazi run, though usually it moved packets of interoffice memos and cases of bottled water. Even though it had been repurposed, there was no need to even log a new flight plan.[11] A total of two fire teams of eight men each were formed by the officer in charge. Each had a SAW (Squad Automatic Weapon) gunner, a radioman, and several others armed with various rifles and grenade launchers.

They had a clear set of objectives. First, get from the airport to the CIA station as soon as possible. Second, either engage those attacking the station from the perimeter and therefore flank the enemy, or clear a path to the station and assist those already in the battle.

They were the Quick Reaction Force (QRF), the posse riding in to the rescue. This was not the reason they were hired, but it became their mission when Americans were in jeopardy in a lonely and dangerous part of the world.

* * *

Reaching their objective would require that the group obtain vehicles for transport from the airport to the CIA station, which is approximately ten minutes away. The available intelligence, from radio traffic with the people at the CIA station, indicated that they were receiving some incoming sniper fire, and that the attacking force assembling at the CIA station seemed to be growing.

Upon arrival, the QRF was initially stopped at the airport. However, after making it clear that they were not going to take no for an answer, they quickly obtained six civilian vehicles—taxicabs that cost $500 a month to rent. A ten-minute ride, even into a shooting zone, for $500 was considered fair trade. If the taxi driver survived (and likely he would), he would make two months of wages in a few minutes.

The CIA kept reservoirs of cash for these kinds of contingencies. The men opened ziplock bags and fanned out the cash. As soon as the taxi drivers saw it, they reached for the money. "Not until we get there," a CIA man said.

They motioned to the old Mercedes taxis. Their attitude: *Let's get this done.*

A quick route was mapped out, and the two fire teams elected to break into two separate "trains" going into the compound area. This would allow each of them to act as backup in case the other was attacked along the way.

After confirming the precise location of the attackers from a review of overhead drone data, each fire team mapped a path on their handheld GPS units. The first unit left for the CIA compound. Given their rides in civilian vehicles, their infiltration into the CIA station went off without a shot.

The same was true when the second train of vehicles arrived at the location approximately ten minutes later, using a different route. The drivers took their cash and roared away in a cloud of diesel fumes.

After a few quick moments of updating with the GRS agents at the compound, the arriving GRS agents set up an immediate perimeter defense with sniper and machine-gun kill zones completely surrounding the area around the CIA compound. The overlapping machine gun kill zones would also allow the GRS agents to effectively repel the ability of the attackers trying to bracket the CIA compound with mortar fire.

By 4:30 a.m., the compound again began receiving probing fire from attackers; they were testing to see how close they were able to get to the perimeter. However, given the numbers and skill of the shooters on the roof of the CIA compound, the snipers were able to keep the attackers a few hundred yards away from the facility.

At approximately 5:00 a.m., the attacking groups had built up enough courage to attempt a frontal assault on the compound. The mob was met with a fusillade of fire from sixteen battle-hardened GRS agents. Within minutes, many of the attackers lay dead or dying in the streets surrounding the compound. Their banzai charge had failed. It did, however, produce martyrs. The losses were simply too great for them to sustain the attack.

The rising sun would make them even easier targets. Their will to fight was breaking down as they slunk away into the shrinking shadows. They were gone before the sun raised its disk over the eastern mountains.

The American diplomats looked at each other with relief and a certain measure of disbelief. As one made coffee for the group, another said what everyone was thinking: "You know, it could have been much worse—Ty Woods and Glen Doherty could have died defending us."

Rescue Scenario Five
Cruise Missile Launch
10:00 P.M.

Several of the ships stationed at the Gaeta naval base were equipped with Tomahawk cruise missiles mounted with conventional warheads. With a flight speed of just over five hundred miles per hour, the missiles could easily make it to Benghazi within 1.5 hours. Given the location of the attackers in one central area outside the CIA station, it was determined that the best missile to launch was that containing the softball-sized cluster bomblet warhead. The exact GPS coordinates of the attacking mob were provided to the missile's guidance control from the drone circling overhead.

The Tomahawk missile is guided by a combination of a precision GPS, a special terrain way-point radar map, and two types of terminal guidance systems to place a warhead with literal pinpoint accuracy. The missile is designed to fly through a one-meter-square window on Earth at an exact predesignated time, and it has proven its ability to do so on thousands of occasions.[12] The newest Tomahawks, called Block IVs or tactical Tomahawks, can be retargeted in flight.

Given the possibility that the attackers might break off the attack and/or change locations prior to the missile's arrival, it was determined that the BGM-109 Block IV would be used. Further, given the decisions to use the small bomblets, the amount of collateral damage to the surrounding structures and civilian populace would be minimized.

The missile was launched from the destroyer at Gaeta at 3:00 a.m., after it was determined by the Pentagon that no other human and/or drone assets were capable of being used. During the hour-long flight to target, the location of the mob changed by approximately half a block to a small open area two blocks from the CIA house. The drone provided the exact location to within inches, and the targeting system on the cruise missile was reset.

The missile hit the mob at 4:40 a.m., and essentially destroyed the entire area for an approximate 150-foot radius. All attackers within the radius were instantly killed.

What was remaining of the attacking force staggered from the area after witnessing the complete devastation an unknown device had wrought upon them.

*   *   *

Based on a careful scrutiny of the available facts and timeline and interviews with fighter pilots, SEAL assault element leaders, and others, there were five plausible rescue options available to President Obama. Fighters could have been scrambled, armed drones dispatched, a commando Quick Reaction Force deployed, or cruise missiles launched. Instead, the president had dinner and failed to press his staff for action.

As the experts that we interviewed made clear, none of these were exotic or Hollywood-only options. Each scenario was based on the men and equipment in the theater of operations at the time, and none required those forces to do anything beyond what they had trained relentlessly to do. They are realistic alternatives.

We may never know why the president didn't act. Was he concerned about the political ramifications of ordering air strikes or teams into harm's way some two months before a tough presidential election? Liberating Libya and killing bin Laden were the president's prime foreign policy achievements. Having to fight al Qaeda (or its affiliates) to save Americans in Libya would call each of those accomplishments into question. And if the rescue mission had failed, it could have been another Desert One, the Carter-era Iranian hostage-rescue effort that killed eight men and never came close to saving a single trapped diplomat (as we described in chapter 2). Surely, these were concerns that weighed on the president's mind.

Still, two important points remain: the tragedy reveals the extraordinary prowess of only two U.S. Navy SEALs (Doherty and Woods) against some one hundred attackers. These two men helped save the lives of more than forty Americans against overwhelming odds, and that speaks volumes about the training and caliber of these men as individuals and as part of the SEAL teams.

And the tragedy reveals why the SEALs are indispensible. If a team had been deployed in time, there is little doubt that Benghazi would be simply another story of these Navy commandos triumphing against seemingly impossible odds. If America is going to continue to hold the al Qaeda menace at bay, it will need men like Woods and Doherty; it will need the U.S. Navy SEALs.

Where do these heroes come from? They are sought out and selected, they are prepared using the most demanding methods possible, and they are trained continuously to maintain their extraordinary abilities. Beyond the physical strength, mental toughness, and incredible skills, these heroes are made by a unique culture that shapes and sharpens them.

Yet the subculture of the SEALs is dependent on a political class that understands their unique abilities and summons the courage to send them in. The SEALs cannot save anyone if the president does not send them in.

CHAPTER 10

Benghazi Timeline

The narrative of the Benghazi attacks, as presented in the American media, has been scattered and episodic at best. As a result, the public failed to grasp the full meaning of the terror attacks on September 11, 2012, and the vital role that SEAL culture played in both giving lives and saving them.

Drawing on official timelines released by the State Department, the Defense Department, and congressional reports, as well as major American news organizations and Arabic-language newspapers, we constructed what we believe is the most complete and authoritative timeline of the Benghazi tragedy.

APRIL 5, 2011: Chris Stevens arrives in Benghazi on a Greek cargo ship. State Department spokesman Mark Toner says Stevens is "meeting with members of the Transitional National Council."[1] The *Washington Post* reports that Stevens is expected to stay in Libya "for several days."[2]

APRIL 7, 2011: Mark Toner says that Stevens is going to remain in Benghazi "for several more days, at least."[3] Stevens stays for months, setting up a temporary headquarters in the Tibesti Hotel.

APRIL 26, 2011: State Department director of policy planning Jake Sullivan says that Stevens "is working on a daily basis to try to understand better who the opposition is, what they stand for, what their plans are, what their agenda is, and so forth."[4]

JUNE 1, 2011: A car bomb explodes outside the Tibesti Hotel.[5] Stevens is unharmed.

AUGUST 3, 2011: Stevens gives his only State Department press briefing. He states "there was a security vacuum when the regime fell, and they [the rebels) had to stand up very quickly to this organization called the TNC. The police, for the most part, just left their posts because they were afraid of popular reaction against them because they had committed abuses in the early days against the people. So there's hardly any police around, and because of that vacuum, militias started to form and step in. And so looking after the security of Benghazi and eastern Libya, you've got a lot of militias and a few police. And this had led to some security challenges."[6]

AUGUST–DECEMBER 2011: In August 2011, American diplomats move into the compound (known as Villa C) where the September 11, 2012, attack would take place. A senior State Department official describes it in October 2011: "The compound is roughly three hundred yards long—that's three football fields long—and a hundred yards wide. We need that much room to provide the best possible setback against car bombs. Over the next few months, physical security at the compound is strengthened. The outer wall is upgraded; its height is increased to nine feet. It is topped by three feet of barbed wire and concertina wire all around the huge property. External lighting is increased. Jersey barriers, which are big concrete blocks, are installed outside and inside the gate. Steel drop bars are added at the gates to control vehicle access and to provide some anti-ram protection. The buildings outside were strengthened."[7]

SEPTEMBER 27, 2011: Fifteen commanders of the Protective Security Brigade protest in front of Transitional National Council headquarters, saying they aren't being provided enough equipment and the government is trying to dissolve their militia.[8]

SEPTEMBER 27, 2011: In a separate protest, hundreds of people gathered in Benghazi to demand the removal of "climbers," holdovers from the Gadhafi era who were still working for the state.[9]

OCTOBER 2011: The State Department hires Blue Mountain Libya to be the primary security force protecting the American compound (Villa C) in Benghazi. The British company is little known at the time, but its $783,284 contract enables it to hire twenty Libyans to guard the compound. Eric Nordstrom, former regional security officer for the U.S. embassy in Tripoli, told congressional investigators: "It's my understanding that there was a very high turnover with those people." Some former Blue Mountain employees told Reuters they had "minimal training" and that they described "being hired by Blue Mountain after a casual recruiting and screening process."[10]

NOVEMBER 24–27, 2011: Students at the state-run Benghazi University hold three days of protests, claiming that they are being flunked and expelled from classes without due process.[11] They portray the new transitional government as linked to the old regime in a seamless garment of corruption.

DECEMBER 1–2, 2011: The "U.S. citizen chief of party of a U.S. based NGO" [nongovernmental organization] is held captive for thirty-six hours by the Zintan Martyrs Brigade, which raided a Libyan bachelor party attended by him to look for alcohol. The brigade detained everyone for thirty-six hours and transferred control of the men to the police, which let them go because of a lack of evidence."[12]

DECEMBER 12–13, 2011: Three thousand young people protest in Benghazi's Shajarah Square against corruption and the allegedly large number of former Gadhafi-era figures still working for the government. Members of the Committee of Wise Men, a pro-TNC group, join a second demonstration on the second night.[13]

DECEMBER 20, 2011: The Libyan government seizes 150 rocket launchers and makes scores of arrests as it claims pro-Gadhafi forces were planning to attack embassies and oil fields over Christmas and New Year's. The operation, according to the government, was code-named Papa Noel.[14]

JANUARY 2012: Salafists [Muslim radicals] destroy the Sufi cemetery of Sidi Ubaid in Benghazi and remove thirty-one corpses.[15]

JANUARY 12, 2012: Azza Ali Orfi, a political activist, is beaten by two men after she left the Al-Fadhel Hotel in Benghazi.[16] She is a pro-democracy, pro-American activist. Both the Libyan government and the State Department see the attack as a warning shot.

JANUARY 19, 2012: Transitional National Council vice chairman Abdul-Hafiz Ghoga is assaulted by protesters after he attends a memorial service at Garyounis University for victims of the Libyan revolution. Ghoga subsequently resigns, saying he does not want to contribute to an "atmosphere of hatred" surrounding the government.[17] His departure reveals that the new government cannot protect its senior officials.

FEBRUARY 2012: Lt. Col. Andrew Wood arrives in Benghazi and notes the security situation is disintegrating. "Shooting instances occurred,

[and] many instances involved the local security guard force that we were training," he tells CBS News in October 2012. "Constantly, there were battles going on between militias, criminal activity, and that became [an] increasing danger as time went on as well." Wood said that Ambassador Stevens "was constantly concerned about the threats to not just himself but the entire staff there."[18]

FEBRUARY 19, 2012: A militia detains U.S. Mission personnel in Benghazi after they drive through a previously unknown checkpoint. They were subsequently freed, but the diplomats report there are now twelve checkpoints between the airport and the embassy, with militia members aggressively trying to open doors and check contents of diplomatic vehicles.[19]

MARCH–APRIL 2012: The number of American Diplomatic Security Service agents in Benghazi falls to one because of visa problems. (At the time of the attack on September 11, 2012 there are five—three at the consulate and two accompanying Ambassador Stevens.) [20]

MARCH 8, 2012: Several explosions take place about four hundred meters from the embassy compound. No injuries or damage are reported.[21]

MARCH 16, 2012: Pro-federalism demonstrators march in Benghazi, demanding that Benghazi and Tripoli both be declared Libya's capital and that seats in the Libyan parliament be evenly divided among all regions of the country.[22]

MARCH 18, 2012: Six armed robbers wearing ski masks and army fatigues break into the British School in Benghazi, menacing staff and stealing handbags, wallets, watches, and cars.[23]

MARCH 22, 2012: At 2:27 a.m., seven armed militia members show up at the mission (Villa A), demanding to enter. The local guard flees, but trips an internal security alarm that cause security personnel and 17 February Martyrs Brigade members to respond. The militia was part of the El Awfea Brigade of the Libyan Ministry of Defense. The El Awfea Brigade leaves without incident.[24]

MARCH 28, 2012: A cable sent by Eric Nordstrom to the State Department in Washington requests five Diplomatic Security agents in Benghazi on forty-five- to sixty-day rotations as well as four drivers and another regional security officer. The cable says there is a problem with the Libyan government, who will issue gun permits only for a period not to exceed seventy-two hours.[25]

APRIL 2, 2012: At 6:15 p.m., a British diplomatic mission armored vehicle is shot at by some two hundred members of the Traffic Police Force, or "Murur," who were fighting with local militia members. A third security force called Al-Nayda (or Al-Shorta) breaks up the fighting and allows the diplomatic convoy to proceed. British security officials believe the traffic police thought the British vehicle was part of a local militia.[26]

APRIL 6, 2012: A homemade bomb is thrown over the wall of the embassy compound. The improvised explosive device, known as a "fish bomb" or "gelateena," causes limited damage. One current and one former security guard, both Blue Mountain Libya employees, are arrested. The former guard had been fired for "gross misconduct," including covering the inner walls of the compound with graffiti.[27]

APRIL 10, 2012: A similar "fish bomb" was thrown at a U.N. convoy carrying the U.N. Special Envoy to Libya. The bomb explodes twelve feet from the convoy.[28]

APRIL 11–12, 2012: Some gunmen try to steal new vehicles from the headquarters of Libya's Ministry of the Interior, some two miles from downtown Benghazi. The Interior Ministry controls intelligence and police forces in Libya. The gunmen were thwarted after a thirteen-hour firefight.[29]

APRIL 2012: Vandals break into the Commonwealth Graves cemetery, where many British and Commonwealth soldiers killed in Libya during World War II are buried. Over two hundred tombstones are desecrated.[30]

APRIL 23–MAY 9, 2012: Fifty protesters block the entrances to Libya's largest oil producer, Arabian Gulf Oil Company (AGOCO), and demand more transparency in the government, more jobs for young people, and the ouster of Gadhafi-era officials from the government. The protesters block all entrances to the plant. The standoff lasts for weeks. The company said it had cut production by thirty thousand barrels a day.[31]

APRIL 26, 2012: Guards protecting a trade delegation visiting Benghazi get into a fistfight with security guards at the International Medical University. The principal officer of the U.S. Mission was accompanying the trade delegation but is escorted away unharmed.[32]

APRIL 27, 2012: Three prisoners and three guards are killed in a failed prison break at Benghazi's main prison.[33]

APRIL 27, 2012: Three homemade bombs explode at the main Benghazi courthouse. It is unclear whether the bombs were thrown at the building or exploded inside, or how many people were hurt.[34]

APRIL 27, 2012: Two South Africans, working in Benghazi as part of an American-funded effort to capture weapons and dismantle mines, are taken hostage and then released "for their own safety." The entire incident lasts for about two hours.[35] Their captors initially think that they are Americans.

APRIL 28, 2012: Benina Airport is temporarily closed after members of the Qatar Battalion of the Barqa Militia protest because they have not been paid for some time.[36]

MAY 15, 2012: A hand grenade explodes inside Military Police Headquarters in Benghazi.[37]

MAY 15, 2012: Benghazi Medical Center director Dr. Fathi Al-Jhani is shot in the chest and wounded as he is leaving the center.[38]

MAY 17, 2012: Two Libyan government senior officials, Khaled Saleh and Fathi Al Baaja, are shot at while at Benghazi Airport, but neither man is hurt.[39]

MAY 22, 2012: Two rocket-propelled grenades are launched at the headquarters of the International Committee for the Red Cross/Red Crescent. One damages a shipping container and the second misses. The Sheikh Omar Abdul-Rahman Brigades claimed responsibility, claiming the Red Cross/Red Crescent is converting Libyan ethnic minorities to Christianity.[40] The terror group is named after the blind Egyptian cleric who is currently imprisoned in New York for plotting to bomb the Lincoln and Holland Tunnels leading into Manhattan. The group is believed to be an al Qaeda affiliate.

JUNE 6, 2012: The U.S. Mission in Benghazi (Villa A) is bombed a second time. Local guards said they saw a man wearing "Islamic" clothes place a suspicious package three feet from the mission's front entrance. The package exploded six minutes later, blowing a large hole in the mission's front wall. No one is injured.[41] The Sheikh Omar Abdel-Rahman Brigades subsequently claim responsibility.[42]

JUNE 7–8, 2012: A conference held at Liberation Square in Benghazi attracts fifteen militias that, a report from the Library of Congress concludes, "probably make up the bulk of al-Qaeda's support in Libya." According to the newspaper *Libya al-Youm*, the conference is sponsored by the militia Ansar al-Sharia and includes the Free Libya Martyrs, the Abu Salim Martyrs, and the Revolutionaries of Sirt.[43] A report from Misbah al-Awani of New Quryna, another Arabic news source, says on June 14 the conference "was a message to the many intelligence apparatuses which had entered into Libya including Syrian, Iranian, and Israeli and were attempting to sabotage, peddle drugs and spread false beliefs in the country."[44] NPR reporter Steve Inskeep sees some of the demonstrators at this meeting, and one says his goal is "to kill the infidels."[45] Ansar al-Sharia commander Mohammed Ali el-Zahawi tells the *Washington Post* that while his organization disapproves of attacking embassies, "if it had been our attack on the U.S. Consulate [sic], we would have flattened it."[46]

JUNE 11, 2012: A rocket-propelled grenade is fired at a British diplomatic convoy carrying British ambassador Sir Dominic Asquith. Reporters saw a white diplomatic car with its windshield destroyed and blood on the car's front seat. The ambassador was not hurt.[47] The event will ultimately cause the British to withdraw from

Benghazi, but they leave their weapons in the American compound, which will be subsequently stolen in the September 11, 2012 attack.[48]

JUNE 17, 2012: The Tunisian consulate in Benghazi is stormed by twenty young men who torched the Tunisian flag inside the building. The men claimed the consulate was showing anti-Islamist art.[49]

JUNE 22, 2012: Juma Obaidi al-Jazawi, a military prosecutor who ordered the arrest of former Libyan rebel commander Abdul Fatah Younes last year, was killed as he left his mosque.[50]

JULY 2012: A contractor for the U.S. Africa Command, the Navanti Group, reports in a memo that "Benghazi has seen a notable increase in violence in recent months, particularly against international targets. These events point to strong anti-Western sentiments among certain segments of the population, the willingness of Salafi-jihadi groups in the city to openly engage in violence against foreign targets, and their capacity to carry out these attacks."[51]

JULY 1, 2012: Some two hundred demonstrators sack the offices of the High National Electoral Commission, burning election materials and chanting pro-federalist slogans.[52]

JULY 9, 2012: A cable drafted by Eric Nordstrom to Washington reports: "Overall security conditions continue to be unpredictable, with large numbers of armed groups and individuals not under the control of the central government, and frequent clashes in Tripoli and other major population centers." The Government of Libya "remains extremely limited in its ability to sustain a security support presence at USG compounds."[53]

AUGUST 2, 2012: A cable drafted by Jairo Saravia of the U.S. embassy in Tripoli says that the situation in Libya remains "unpredictable, volatile, and violent."[54]

AUGUST 16, 2012: Gen. Carter Ham, head of Africa Command, reads a State Department cable from Ambassador Stevens, which asks for more security. Gen. Ham phones Stevens and asks if he needed any more security. Stevens says he did not. In a meeting sometime between this date and September 11, Stevens says for a second time that he did not need additional security. "One person familiar with the events said Stevens might have rejected the offers because there was an understanding within the State Department that officials in Libya ought not to request more security, in part because of concerns about the political fallout of seeking a larger military presence in a country that was still being touted as a foreign policy success."[55]

AUGUST 29, 2012: The contract between the 17 February Brigade and the U.S. Consulate expires and is not renewed. A memo from "the principal U.S. diplomatic officer in Benghazi" whose name was redacted said the contract had expired "several weeks ago" and that the brigade "has been implicated in several of the recent detentions. We also have the usual concerns re their ultimate loyalties. But they are competent, and give us an added measure of security."[56] Because the contract had expired, the brigade said it would not provide security for U.S. personnel, including Ambassador Stevens.[57]

September 11, 2012
Note: All times are Benghazi time.

SEPTEMBER 11, 6:45 A.M.: A Blue Mountain Libya guard spots someone wearing a Libyan Supreme Security Council uniform taking photos of the U.S. compound from a building under construction across the street. Guards confront the mysterious man, who steps in a police car and speeds off.[58] Those photographs would be essential in planning an attack.

DURING THE DAY: Everything seems normal. A memorandum sent by the embassy in Tripoli to Washington and drafted by David C. McFarland says that Ambassador Stevens plans to open American Space Benghazi, a cultural organization. The report also notes that the consulate staff has met with such nonprofits as the Libyan Society for Industrial Engineering, My Environment Society, and the cancer-fighting Cure Foundation.[59]

7:20 P.M.: Ambassador Stevens escorts the Turkish general consul, his last appointment, to the main gate.[60]

8:10–8:30 P.M.: A British security team returns armored cars that it has borrowed from the Americans.[61]

9:42 P.M.: A police car guarding the U.S. compound drives off. A press report in a local newspaper quotes a Supreme Security Council official saying that the car was ordered to leave "to prevent civilian casualties." A guard interviewed by *Al-Sharq Al-Awsat* said that "my colleague guards and I were chatting and drinking tea. The situation was normal."[62] The sudden departure of the Libyan police is never fully explained.

9:42 P.M.: Members of Ansar al-Sharia and Al Qaeda in the Islamic Maghreb (AQIM) storm the main gate. Shouting "God is great!" they surge into the compound.[63] About fifty attackers enter the compound, led by four men who wear masks and "Pakistani clothes."[64] The compound's Tactical Operations Center notifies the State Department in Washington, the Embassy in Tripoli, and the Annex operated by the CIA.[65]

9:45 P.M.: Gregory Hicks, second-in-command at the Tripoli Embassy, is at home watching television when a foreign service officer knocks on his door saying, "Greg, Greg, the embassy's under attack." Hicks sees an unknown phone number on his cell phone and dials it. Ambassador Stevens answers and says "Greg, we're under attack" before the phone call is cut off.[66]

9:59 P.M.: An unarmed surveillance aircraft is tasked to reposition over Benghazi.[67]

10:02 P.M.: Ambassador Stevens, information security officer Sean Smith, and Diplomatic Security Service officer Scott Strickland struggle to get to a safe room in Villa C. Attackers set furniture on fire. The building fills with smoke. Officer Strickland leaps out of a window, but contact is lost with Ambassador Stevens and Officer Smith, both of whom have left the safe room because the building was filled with smoke. Strickland enters the building several times but fails to find Stevens or Smith.[68]

10:05 P.M.: An "Ops Alert" is issued by the State Department Operations Center notifying the White House Situation Room, senior department officials, and others that Benghazi was under attack and "approximately 20 armed people fired shots; explosions have been heard as well."[69]

10:07 P.M.: The CIA Global Response Staff security team from the Annex arrives at the compound and engages in a firefight with the attackers. Officer Smith's body is found but not that of Ambassador Stevens.[70]

10:32 P.M.: The National Military Command Center notifies the Office of the Secretary of Defense and the Joint Chiefs of Staff.[71]

11:00 P.M.: Defense Secretary Leon Panetta and Joint Chiefs of Staff Chairman Gen. Martin Dempsey discuss the Benghazi situation with

President Obama during a regularly scheduled weekly meeting.[72]

11:00 P.M.: Gregory Hicks asks the defense attaché at the Tripoli Embassy if any military help is forthcoming. The attaché says that it will take two to three hours for the nearest fighters to "get on-site" from Italy—and that there will be no refueling aircraft available for the fighters to return to their base. "I said, 'Thank you very much,' And we went on with our work."[73]

11:10 P.M.: The surveillance aircraft arrives over Benghazi.[74]

11:15 P.M.: The security team from the Annex decides the compound cannot be held and decides to retreat to the CIA Annex.[75]

September 12, 2012

12:00 A.M.–2:00 A.M.: Secretary Panetta holds meetings with Gen. Dempsey and Gen. Carter Ham. He orders a Marine Fleet Antiterrorism Security Team (FAST) stationed in Rota, Spain, to deploy to Naval Air Station Sigonella (an hour away from Benghazi) and a second FAST platoon to deploy to Sigonella. He orders a special operations team based in northern Europe to deploy to Sigonella. A special operations team based in the U.S. is also ordered to deploy to Sigonella.[76] However, a C-110 special operations team deployed to Croatia stays in place. This team, known as EUCOM CIF ("Commander's In Extremis Force"), could have arrived in Benghazi in three and a half hours.[77]

12:30 A.M.: A special operations team leaves Tripoli for Benghazi in a Learjet, arriving at 1:15 a.m. However, a request by Gregory Hicks for a second team is vetoed. Hicks believes the veto came from the military.[78]

DURING THE NIGHT: Ambassador Stevens is transported to Benghazi Medical Center around 11:00 p.m. It is not clear who transported him to the hospital or whether the ambassador is alive or dead when he entered the hospital. Hospital personnel call embassy personnel, saying: "We know where the ambassador is. Please, you can come get him." According to Gregory Hicks, embassy officials fear the calls are a trap, knowing Ansar al-Sharia militia surrounds the hospital.[79]

A source the embassy trusts known as Bakabar retrieves Stevens's body around 5:15 a.m. Bakabar and his associates transport Stevens's body to the Benghazi airport.

5:00 A.M.: A second surveillance aircraft arrives over Benghazi.[80]

5:15 A.M.: A mortar attack takes place in the CIA Annex that lasts eleven minutes. Former Navy SEALs Tyrone Woods and Glen Doherty are killed, and two other security officers are wounded.[81]

7:40 A.M.: The first airplane carrying Americans leaves Benghazi for Tripoli.[82]

10:00 A.M.: The second airplane carrying Americans leaves Benghazi for Tripoli.[83]

7:17 P.M.: A C-17 aircraft leaves Tripoli for Ramstein Air Force Base in Germany with American personnel and the bodies of the four Americans killed in Benghazi. It arrives in Ramstein AFB at 10:19 p.m.[84]

7:57 P.M.: The EUCOM special operations force arrives at Sigonella. The special operations force from America arrives at 9:28 p.m.[85]

8:56 P.M.: The Marine FAST platoon arrives at Tripoli.[86] They arrive twenty-four hours after the attack began, in a city several hundred miles from Benghazi.

CHAPTER 11

The Teams: Why the Unique Culture of the SEALs Matters

For the SEALs, triumph's locomotive often drags tragedy's caboose. The teams know that in a crackle of radio static or a flash of text, teammates they have known for years—sweated with, bled with, partied with—could suddenly be gone. It is an essential reality that defines their unique culture; they know that death stalks them just as they bring it to our nation's enemies.

Nothing underlines that reality than the events of the spring and summer of 2011. Perhaps the best known of the SEALs' triumphs (the bin Laden raid) occurred within weeks of their greatest loss of their brothers in their history ("Extortion 17").

Their triumph immediately became world famous—the president saw to that. Shortly before midnight, President Obama appeared on television screens to announce Operation Neptune Spear and the death of archterrorist Osama bin Laden.

After weeks of rehearsals in secret locations in the Virginia wilderness and the Nevada desert, waiting days and nights in an Afghan staging area, SEAL Team Six was ordered to load out and stand by for the helicopters. After ten long years of waiting, and so many sure things that never materialized from the head shed [headquarters], they were chosen to go after not just a High Value Target...but HVT number one: bin Laden himself.

The day of reckoning had come for both Osama bin Laden and the U.S. Navy SEAL teams. The story of the raid has been endlessly told, and yet, as sources in the teams tell us, the real story has never been told. No one who knows the reality is yet in a position to give a full account of what actually happened on the ground at bin Laden's concrete castle in Abottabad, Pakistan.

Certainly the public record is full of official contradictions and corrections. The White House, in a series of confusing press conferences, changed the official timeline a number of times. The changes are too numerous to list here. But one example will serve to illustrate how the Obama administration dramatically altered its story. First, senior officials told reporters in the White House briefing room that there was a "forty-five-minute firefight" involving "hundreds of shots." Days later, other officials admitted that only six or seven shots were fired, and all of those occurred in a two-minute period. (The latter sounds more like a well-executed SEAL mission, while the former sounds like a Hollywood finale.) In the months that followed, two different SEALs claimed to have fired the fatal shot into bin Laden. Later a third name surfaced. It may be years before any of these details can be sorted out.

For our purposes, the most important part of the mission was that the SEALs were sent in to bin Laden's lair at all—instead of the U.S. Army's elite "Delta Force" (now known as "CAGG") or the Marine Special Operations force, or another "black" elite unit whose name is unknown outside of Special Operations Command. Why were the SEALs selected? That question has been endlessly debated among special operators. Yet one thing is certain: if confidence in the SEALs had been an issue, as it had been in the 1980s, then it had been restored to the point where they were handpicked to visit America's number one enemy. The days of question marks and competition to get missions were largely over.

Nor did anyone object that the SEALs would be operating hundreds of miles from any shoreline controlled by the U.S. Navy. The frogmen would be going far from the sea…and no one thought that strange. This emphasizes how much the SEALs have evolved from pirates to professionals in eyes of top military commanders. The cultural changes made in the 1980s and 1990s (as we saw in chapters 2 and 3) transformed the SEALs. Also, their decade of fighting in Afghanistan, Iraq, East Africa, and elsewhere made them the go-to force for this most important of missions.

Adm. Eric Olson, now in charge of Special Operations Command, chose the SEALs, a force that he remade through vision and will. Olson had personally commanded, trained, refined, redirected, and wrenched this group kicking and screaming from their days as pirates to become the professional force they were that day. Olson did not choose them because he was a SEAL, but because they enjoyed his confidence and the confidence of the White House. That signals a profound cultural change.

* * *

The SEAL credo provided a constant reminder to those in command of Special Operations Command:

> *Brave men have fought and died building the proud tradition and feared reputation that I am bound to uphold. In the worst of conditions, the legacy of my teammates steadies my resolve and silently guides my every deed. I will not fail.*

* * *

Every man in the Red Squad of Seal Team Six had been tested by years of combat. They had all worked together through hundreds of missions, thousands of hours of training, and dozens of firefights. There were no rejects or "turds" among the group. No second-tier operators who could compromise this mission. They had been weeded out by the selection process, by the years, the deaths, and the training. This was the culmination of fifty years of history of the SEAL teams, which had begun with their formation by President John F. Kennedy. While they would not be forced to use every skill they each possessed (Sea, Air, and Land), they would need those skills that had been honed in the thousands of direct-action missions that had preceded this one. They were building on their history.

* * *

My Trident is a symbol of honor and heritage. Bestowed upon me by the heroes that have gone before, it embodies the trust of those I have sworn to protect. By wearing the Trident I accept the responsibility of my chosen profession and way of life. It is a privilege that I must earn every day.

The officers were calling the shots, but the chiefs still controlled the battlefield as they always had. It is the SEAL way. The thinking and plan, taught by their former teammates, was now to be executed by those on the ground.

The most highly skilled and underpaid professional athletes on Earth were about to show what they were made of, in a real-time satellite feed in the White House's Situation Room and in the secure rooms of the Pentagon. Their immediate viewing audience ranged from their officers in charge to the commander in chief himself.

It was life or death, and every SEAL knew it. Their wills had been written years before, or not, depending on whether they had someone to leave "it" to. Every

SEAL had long accepted the fact that he could die on this day, or on any day, with the teams. Years ago they all had written and signed the ultimate blank check to the United States, for any amount up to and including their lives. Most of this group had already cashed the check several times, only to have some twist of fate pull them back from the abyss.

Their ranks had been thinned by deaths and injuries on many occasions. Each man on this mission had fought with, trained with, drank with, or knew of dozens of teammates who had died over the last ten years of war. Funerals had become so frequent that they had replaced reunions.

* * *

I will never quit. I persevere and thrive on adversity. My Nation expects me to be physically harder and mentally stronger than my enemies. If knocked down, I will get back up, every time. I will draw on every remaining ounce of strength to protect my teammates and to accomplish our mission. I am never out of the fight.

* * *

Many different versions of the bin Laden raid have been written. What remains undisputed is that almost immediately upon arrival over the target, one of the SEALs' helicopters crash-landed over the compound in Abottabad, Pakistan. Unforeseen mechanical failure. For any other group of commandos, this malfunction would have been mission ending.

The SEALs were determined that this operation was not going to be Operation Eagle Claw, the failed mission to rescue the hostages in Iran (described in chapter 2). The crews of the 160th Special Operations Aviation Regiment, a special U.S. Army unit that transports the SEALs, knew well the risks of crash or capture. They, too, had lost many in their battles, arm in arm with the SEALs. They, too, had been infected by the SEAL mantra and unwillingness to accept defeat.

Backup plans for loss of a chopper were put in place immediately. There would be no scrapping of the mission, as the world saw in the sands of Iran. They would fight on, somehow.

*　*　*

We demand discipline. We expect innovation. The lives of my teammates and the success of our mission depend on me—my technical skill, tactical proficiency, and attention to detail. My training is never complete.

* * *

The helicopter crash into the dung heap used by bin Laden's farm animals eliminated the element of surprise. The compound came to life, and men with AK-47s emerged from the compound's darkened buildings.

As the team piled out of the downed helicopter, they knew they had to move quickly and efficiently to clear the compound and find their target.

Speech was unnecessary; it was likely lethal. A kind of SEAL telepathy took over. This group had long abandoned the need to speak to one another while in the midst of battle. Eye movements and hand gestures took the place of words. The pirates-turned-professionals were on the hunt, and they knew the prey was at hand.

They cleared the outlying buildings in the compound surrounding the main house, and killed the sole male occupant of the smaller structure, who had opened fire on them with an AK-47. His wife, standing behind her gun-wielding husband, died from the same bullet that felled her mate. She was the only civilian casualty. The SEALs had secured the women and children safely.

The SEALs were searching for a man whom intelligence reports called "the pacer," a man the CIA believed was bin Laden himself.

Entering the residence, they expected fire at every corner, door, and hiding place—a 360-degree shooting game that the SEALs had become adept at playing through constant practice.

Their laser sights swept the area constantly, with their trigger fingers resting lightly on the trigger guards. SEAL fingers are trained not to move onto the trigger until a target is clearly in view and clearly hostile. Every SEAL weapon covered a different direction, as the counterattack could come from anywhere and everywhere at the same time.

Their minds struggled to process the thousands of stimuli invading their senses through sight, sound, smell, and intuition. But there was only a single thought in each of their minds, a thought beaten into their conscious and unconscious minds over the thousands of hours of training.

So simple, yet so vital it had been programmed into their muscle memory.

Threat/no threat. Identify and classify every human and do it instantly.

After thousands of hours of training, it all came down to such a simple analysis: does the human in front of my weapon represent an immediate threat to me or my teammates?

* * *

Accounts differ about bin Laden's final movements. Moving through the concrete structure, the SEALs instantly identified and killed threats as they emerged. "Threat/no threat" ran through their heads.

Eliminate the threat, and move on to the next threat until the objective is achieved. Speed and precision. The people shooting at them were killed, almost as if they had not been there. The SEALs' minds were on automatic, according to one of the SEALs who trained them.

Finally, a bearded face appeared from behind a door to a dark room above them. All they can see is that he is a tall male. They cannot see his hands or body, but they assume he is armed and very dangerous.

Threat.

Two controlled shots are taken by the lead man in the train within milliseconds of recognition.

Both bullets hit the target within inches of one another.

Bin Laden is gone.

* * *

We train for war and fight to win. I stand ready to bring the full spectrum of combat power to bear

*in order to achieve my mission and the goals estab-
lished by my country. The execution of my duties
will be swift and violent when required yet guided
by the very principles that I serve to defend.*

*   *   *

With bin Laden vanquished, the deeds of SEAL Team
Six are trumpeted in the headlines of every major
news organization on earth. They instantly became
heroes, legends, and targets at the same time. Credit
for their accomplishments were instantly taken by an
administration desperately seeking some victory for
its reelection.

Books are printed, movies are screened. Beyond the
triumph, the SEALs knew, sneered the waiting face of
tragedy.

*   *   *

The aftermath of the bin Laden raid was written in
the blood of the SEALs and still raises their blood in
anger.

The mission was the biggest single loss of life dur-
ing a SEAL operation since World War II. It was
August 6, 2011, less than three months after the bin
Laden raid.

A Chinook CH-47 (code-named "Extortion 17")

was shot down by a rocket-propelled grenade in Afghanistan. Thirty-eight men vanished in the fiery blast, including 15 members of SEAL Team Six, Gold Squad.

Many of the victims' families told us that they fault the Obama administration for "outing" SEAL Team Six some three months prior as the team responsible for bin Laden's death. The families, parents, and widows simply could not imagine that the attack was anything other than enemy retaliation for bin Laden's death. And al Qaeda had said as much in its propaganda videos.

This catastrophic loss by SEAL Team Six happened some ninety days after SEAL Team Six gunned down bin Laden as he reached for a Soviet-made firearm. Only two days after Bin Laden was killed, Vice President Joe Biden appeared at a Ritz-Carlton podium in Washington, D.C., and recklessly told the world press: "Let me briefly acknowledge tonight's distinguished honorees. Adm. Jim Stavridis is a—is the real deal; he can tell you more about and understands the incredible, the phenomenal, the just almost unbelievable capacity of his Navy SEALs and what they did last Sunday."

Through these comments, and others that would follow, the Obama administration had violated the

Essentially, the families want to know why their sons were flown into a combat zone in a helicopter that was older than they were. Why was such a large group of SEALs put on a single aircraft? Why wasn't additional air support available, which is standard military procedure when special forces are involved?

Karen Vaughn still suffers from a searing and searching kind of grief. Her pain led her to ask some powerful questions that deserve answers: "Why was there no pre-assault fire? We were told as families that pre-assault fire damages our effort to win the hearts and minds of our enemy," she told reporters. "So in other words, the hearts and minds of our enemy are more valuable to this government than my son's blood."

Usually, air assaults open with artillery or missile strikes to disperse and confuse enemy fighters. This "pre-assault fire" often saves American lives, but it can produce civilian deaths and be used in al Qaeda propaganda videos. In the Obama years, commanders have been told to be more careful of providing fodder for enemy videos. That decision may turn out to be war-winning (or not), but the new Rules of Engagement put Americans at risk.

Karen Vaughn was simply asking if the trade-off was worth it.

No one had an answer for her.

operational security needed for covert missions by pointing the finger at SEAL Team Six as the team that had accomplished the bin Laden mission. Even then Secretary Robert Gates was critical. Many special operations personnel, including former SEAL Team Six Commander Ryan Zinke, were publicly unhappy with the politicians' casual use of the SEAL teams.

Karen and Billy Vaughn, whose SEAL son, Aaron, was killed in the chopper crash, were interviewed by television reporters. Karen Vaughn was direct: "As soon as Joe Biden announced that it was a SEAL Team who took out bin Laden, within twenty-four hours, my son called me and I rarely ever heard him sound afraid in his adult life.... He said, 'Mom, you need to wipe your social media clean...your life is in danger, our lives are in danger, so clean it up right now,'" she said.

Her husband, Billy Vaughn, had no tolerance for the media's tolerance of the vice president's inexcusable breach of national security: "The media has let this man get away with saying 'Uncle Joe's gaffes,'" he fumed. "This is not Uncle Joe and he's not some senile old grandfather. He is the second in command of the most powerful country in the world, and he needs to take responsibility for the comments he makes and quit being given a pass."[1]

* * *

It is impossible to say with certainty that naming SEAL Team Six as bin Laden's executioners led to the loss of a SEAL team six helicopter a few months later. We may never know, and the enemy has more-than-sufficient reasons to fire on any American aircraft in a war zone. But it is a dark suspicion that we have heard from a number of SEALs and their widows. The Obama administration's actions certainly broke the bond of trust between the SEALs and the president.

Other political changes are also making the SEALs question the administration—and these changes are seen as threatening to the culture of the teams. Pressure is building to graduate more recruits from BUD/S. Yes, training costs are high, and increasing graduation rates will make BUD/S more efficient from a bean-counter perspective. But it will change the SEALs. It would require formally lower standards for those who are admitted and, even worse, be seen to lower those standards.

Battle-tested SEALs are already telling us that they will not be comfortable going to war alongside the seemingly second-rate SEALs. This could mean a wave of retirements and a lack of trust among those who remain.

Outsiders forget that a vital part of SEAL culture is the right to refuse a mission. At any time, for any reason. Why would lower BUD/S standards mean more refused missions? This is closely held information, and the public will never know. But presidents and policy makers will be told. What happens when Americans are in trouble and SEALs who could save them refuse to go—because they do not want to risk their lives alongside weaker men?

The SEALs survive because they train like they fight: to win. They surround themselves with others who they know have met the same standards. It is a brutally objective set of standards. It qualifies men to stand among the select few. Reduce those standards, and the Navy will do a disservice to all of those who have come before and all of those who will have to rely on their fellow teammates in the future.

*   *   *

We have attempted to provide the reader with a glimpse in the world of some of the operators, with both active-duty missions and missions that took place after they had left the ranks. While each of these missions may have required different tactics to get the job done, the actions of the SEALs who accomplished these missions were guided by the same principles hammered into them through fifty years of discipline and thousands of man-hours of training. Their overriding principle remains: SEALs do not quit until their mission is accomplished or they are dead.

In describing the tragic events leading to the deaths of Glen Doherty and Ty Woods in Benghazi, we attempted to give you an idea of what we felt was an outrageous and unacceptable injustice visited upon two heroic former Navy SEALs. In the finest tradition of the teams, they bravely battled an overwhelming number of enemies and saved American lives. They were not given the help they should have been given. The complete story, and the motivations behind the players involved, may not be known for years. Once again, though, the actions of the warriors involved were consistent with the finest traditions of the Navy SEALs.

We have also attempted to describe that the actions of the teams have not been without critics and courts-martial, as was the case with those charged with allegedly beating a known terrorist prisoner.

Here we have tried to explain some of the trials and tribulations in the storied history of the SEAL teams to give the reader an idea of how they got to where they are today. They may have matured from pirates to professionals, but they have not lost the will to fight that made them pirates in the first place.

Big Navy has had its issues with the teams, and it has severely thinned their ranks at times during their existence. The "great bloodletting" described in chapter 3 remains a hotly debated point in the history of the SEALs, but it made them who they are today.

While the growth of any person or team is never complete, the SEALs as a small but highly specialized group of warriors have suffered more than their share. Their losses have been great and the funerals too frequent.

*   *   *

The war on terror cannot be ended unilaterally. Since before the Benghazi attacks, the Obama administration has been claiming that the war on terror is "over." This is a cruel fantasy. If America tires of the fight, it cannot simply call back its drones and its SEALs. The terrorists will keep coming. Surrender only increases their thirst for victory.

The war can end only with the enemy's utter defeat. As long as al Qaeda and its affiliates retain the will to fight, their bombings and shootings will continue. The only way to keep those attacks from America's shores is to send the SEALs and other commandos far from home to hunt and kill them.

The SEALs must be a constant threat to those that would do harm to this nation and to civilization itself.

If not, the razor edge of the threat will point the other way—at the hearts of civilians going about their daily lives. A mother pushing a stroller in a crowded mall. A secretary sitting in an office cubicle. A passenger on a plane, thinking only of a Thanksgiving dinner. A commuter lost in his iPad or a teen lost in her iPhone. The music of these innocents' lives would suddenly stop if the SEALs stayed home.

*   *   *

We must, as a society, keep a group of warriors free of politics and bureaucracy, free of the distractions that keep them from doing their vital work.

That means that we have to protect the teams from political prosecutions for operations that are perfectly run but ruined in the custody phase, as we detailed in the chapter about Carl Higbie's sad saga. In the abstract, it may seem to make sense to show the world that we punish wrongdoers even when they wear our uniform. In the real world, the enemy has learned to use our legal procedures against us. They know that even false charges can effectively take SEALs out of combat, sometimes permanently. What the enemy cannot accomplish on the battlefield, it should not be able to do in the courtroom.

Politics must be banished from special operations. Vice President Joseph Biden's careless remarks that named SEAL Team Six have caused real and lasting harm to the teams. The warriors of the teams cannot do their lifesaving work if they are nagged by the worry that their families may be vulnerable to enemy retaliation. Special operations require special security, and that includes elected officials, who will always be tempted to advance themselves at the expense of the SEAL teams.

Politics is vital to democratic deliberation and deadly to the elite culture of the SEALs. Our elected leaders should give them targets but not make them targets. Politicians need to know that they are not a wayward fraternity that needs to be corralled or cowed, but a delicate instrument to be unsheathed carefully and used surgically.

Without these heroes, the Navy SEALs, horror and terror will come to our shores. With them comes honor and security. We forget this at our peril.

Interim Progress Report

INTERIM PROGRESS REPORT *for the*
Members of the House Republican Conference
on the Events Surrounding the September 11, 2012
Terrorist Attacks in Benghazi, Libya

Chairman Howard P. "Buck" McKeon, Committee on Armed Services
Chairman Ed Royce, Committee on Foreign Affairs
Chairman Bob Goodlatte, Committee on the Judiciary
Chairman Darrell Issa, Committee on Oversight & Government Reform
Chairman Mike Rogers, Permanent Select Committee on Intelligence

April 23, 2013

EXECUTIVE SUMMARY

An ongoing Congressional investigation across five House Committees concerning the events surrounding the September 11, 2012, terrorist attacks on U.S. facilities in Benghazi, Libya has made several determinations to date, including:

- Reductions of security levels prior to the attacks in Benghazi were approved at the highest levels of the State Department, up to and including Secretary Clinton. This fact contradicts her testimony before the House Foreign Affairs Committee on January 23, 2013.

- In the days following the attacks, White House and senior State Department officials altered accurate talking points drafted by the Intelligence Community in order to protect the State Department.

- Contrary to Administration rhetoric, the talking points were not edited to protect classified information. Concern for classified information is never mentioned in email traffic among senior Administration officials.

These preliminary findings illustrate the need for continued examination and oversight by the five House Committees. The Committees will continue to review who exactly was responsible for the failure to respond to the repeated requests for more security and for the effort to cover up the nature of the attacks, so that appropriate officials will be held accountable.

Appendix

TABLE OF CONTENTS

Introduction _____ **1**

Findings _____ **2**

Policy Considerations _____ **4**

I.   Prior to the Benghazi attacks, State Department officials in Libya made repeated requests for additional security that were denied in Washington despite ample documentation of the threat posed by violent extremist militias. _____ 5

II.   The volatile security environment erupted on September 11, 2012, when militias composed of al-Qa'ida-affiliated extremists attacked U.S. interests in Benghazi. _____ 11

III.   After the attacks, the Administration perpetuated a deliberately misleading and incomplete narrative that the violence grew out of a demonstration caused by a YouTube video. The Administration consciously decided not to discuss extremist involvement or previous attacks against Western interests in Benghazi. _____ 18

IV.   The Administration's investigations and reviews of the Benghazi attacks highlight its failed security policies leading to the attacks while undermining the ability of the United States government to bring the perpetrators to justice. _____ 23

V.   The Benghazi attacks revealed fundamental flaws in the Administration's approach to securing U.S. interests and personnel around the world. _____ 27

Appendix I: Oversight Activities by Committee _____ **31**

Appendix II: Consolidated Timeline of Events _____ **36**

Appendix

Introduction

On September 11, 2012, armed militias with ties to terrorist organizations attacked U.S. facilities in Benghazi, Libya, killing four U.S. personnel: Ambassador Christopher Stevens; State Department Information Officer Sean Smith; and two American security officers – and former U.S. Navy SEALs – Tyrone Woods and Glen Doherty. Given the gravity of these attacks and the loss of American life, the House Committees on Armed Services, Foreign Affairs, Intelligence, Judiciary, and Oversight and Government Reform initiated immediate inquiries into issues within each Committee's jurisdiction concerning the events surrounding the attacks.

In the course of their investigations, the Committees have interviewed dozens of officials and individuals with first-hand knowledge of the events, met with members of the military and diplomatic corps overseas, and reviewed tens of thousands of classified and unclassified documents, cables, emails, and reports. Members of Congress traveled on fact-finding missions to foreign countries, including Libya. The Committees paid particular attention to investigating allegations receiving public attention after the attacks and the associated findings are included in this report.

At the direction of the Speaker of the House of Representatives and the Majority Leader, the coordinated oversight work and assessments made to date are being presented to the Members of the House Republican Conference in this interim progress report. The Committees will continue to review available information, and to interview sources as they come forward. This progress report will be updated as warranted.

Appendix

Findings

This progress report reveals a fundamental lack of understanding at the highest levels of the State Department as to the dangers presented in Benghazi, Libya, as well as a concerted attempt to insulate the Department of State from blame following the terrorist attacks. The Committees' majority staff summarizes findings to date as follows:

Before the Attacks:

• After the U.S.-backed Libyan revolution ended the Gadhafi regime, **the U.S. government did not deploy sufficient U.S. security elements to protect U.S. interests and personnel that remained on the ground**.

• **Senior State Department officials knew that the threat environment in Benghazi was high and that the Benghazi compound was vulnerable and unable to withstand an attack, yet the Department continued to systematically withdraw security personnel.**

• **Repeated requests for additional security were denied at the highest levels of the State Department.** For example, an April 2012 State Department cable bearing Secretary Hillary Clinton's signature acknowledged then-Ambassador Cretz's formal request for additional security assets but ordered the withdrawal of security elements to proceed as planned.

• **The attacks were not the result of a failure by the Intelligence Community (IC) to recognize or communicate the threat.** The IC collected considerable information about the threats in the region, and disseminated regular assessments to senior U.S. officials warning of the deteriorating security environment in Benghazi, which included threats to American interests, facilities, and personnel.

• **The President, as Commander-in-Chief, failed to proactively anticipate the significance of September 11 and provide the Department of Defense with the authority to launch offensive operations beyond self-defense.** Defense Department assets were correctly positioned for the general threat across the region, but the assets were not authorized at an alert posture to launch offensive operations beyond self-defense, and were provided no notice to defend diplomatic facilities.

During the Attacks:

• On the evening of September 11, 2012, **U.S. security teams on the ground in Benghazi exhibited extreme bravery** responding to the attacks by al-Qa'ida-affiliated groups against the U.S. mission.

• **Department of Defense officials and military personnel reacted quickly to the attacks in Benghazi.** The effectiveness of their response was hindered on account of U.S. military forces not being properly postured to address the growing threats in northern Africa or to respond to a brief, high-intensity attack on U.S. personnel or interests across much of Africa.

286

APPENDIX

After the Attacks:

- **The Administration willfully perpetuated a deliberately misleading and incomplete narrative that the attacks evolved from a political demonstration caused by a YouTube video.** U.S. officials on the ground reported – and video evidence confirms – that demonstrations outside the Benghazi Mission did not occur and that the incident began with an armed attack on the facility. Senior Administration officials knowingly minimized the role played by al-Qa'ida-affiliated entities and other associated groups in the attacks, and decided to exclude from the discussion the previous attempts by extremists to attack U.S. persons or facilities in Libya.

- **Administration officials crafted and continued to rely on incomplete and misleading talking points.** Specifically, after a White House Deputies Meeting on Saturday, September 15, 2012, the Administration altered the talking points to remove references to the likely participation of Islamic extremists in the attacks. The Administration also removed references to the threat of extremists linked to al-Qa'ida in Benghazi and eastern Libya, including information about at least five other attacks against foreign interests in Benghazi. Senior State Department officials requested – and the White House approved – that the details of the threats, specifics of the previous attacks, and previous warnings be removed to insulate the Department from criticism that it ignored the threat environment in Benghazi.

- **Evidence rebuts Administration claims that the talking points were modified to protect classified information or to protect an investigation by the Federal Bureau of Investigation (FBI).** Email exchanges during the interagency process do not reveal any concern with protecting classified information. Additionally, the Bureau itself approved a version of the talking points with significantly more information about the attacks and previous threats than the version that the State Department requested. Thus, the claim that the State Department's edits were made solely to protect that investigation is not credible.

- **The Administration deflected responsibility by blaming the IC for the information it communicated to the public in both the talking points and the subsequent narrative it perpetuated.** Had Administration spokesmen performed even limited due diligence inquiries into the intelligence behind the talking points or requested reports from personnel on the ground, they would have quickly understood that the situation was more complex than the narrative provided by Ambassador Susan Rice and others in the Administration.

- **The Administration's decision to respond to the Benghazi attacks with an FBI investigation, rather than military or other intelligence resources, contributed to the government's lack of candor about the nature of the attack.**

- **Responding to the attacks with an FBI investigation significantly delayed U.S. access to key witnesses and evidence and undermined the government's ability to bring those responsible for the attacks to justice in a timely manner.**

287

Appendix

Policy Considerations

- **The events in Benghazi reflect the Administration's lack of a comprehensive national security strategy or a credible national security posture in the region.** The United States continues to maintain an inadequate defensive posture in North Africa and the Middle East as a result of the Administration's under-appreciation of the threat that al-Qa'ida and related terrorist groups pose in the region.

- **This singular event will be repeated unless the United States recognizes and responds to the threats we face around the world, and properly postures resources and security assets to counter and respond to those threats.** Until that time, the United States will remain in a reactionary mode and should expect more catastrophes like Benghazi, in which U.S. personnel on the ground perform bravely, but are not provided with the resources for an effective response. As those opposed to U.S. interests will continue to take advantage of perceived U.S. weaknesses, the United States will continue to lose credibility with its allies and face the worst of all possible outcomes in strategically important locations around the world.

- **Congress must maintain pressure on the Administration to ensure the United States takes all necessary steps to find the Benghazi attackers.** It has been more than seven months since the FBI investigation began, and there is very little progress. The risks of treating the Benghazi terrorist attacks as a law enforcement matter rather than a military matter are becoming increasingly clear. The failure to respond more assertively to the attacks and to impose meaningful consequences on those who planned and perpetrated them has contributed to a perception of U.S. weakness and retreat. Al-Qa'ida grew emboldened when the U.S. failed to respond forcibly and effectively to the terrorist attacks on the World Trade Center (1993), U.S. Embassies in East Africa (1998), and the U.S.S. *Cole* (2000). Active terrorist organizations and potential recruits will also be emboldened to attack U.S. interests if the U.S. fails to hold those responsible for this attack accountable.

- **Congress must also provide an effective counterweight to the Administration's failure to adequately communicate the nature and the extent of the threats our country faces today.** The Administration must do more to develop a coherent and robust national security strategy, and Congress must hold it accountable to do so.

APPENDIX

I. **Prior to the Benghazi attacks, State Department officials in Libya made repeated requests for additional security that were denied in Washington despite ample documentation of the threat posed by violent extremist militias.**

I said, "Jim, you know what [is] most frustrating about this assignment? It's not the hardship, it's not the gunfire, it's not the threats. It's dealing and fighting against the people, programs, and personnel who are supposed to be supporting me ... For me, the Taliban is on the inside of the building."

Testimony of Regional Security Office for the U.S. Mission to Libya Eric Nordstrom before the House Oversight & Government Reform Committee, October 12, 2012

Setting Up the Benghazi Mission

The Libyan revolution, which led to the overthrow of brutal dictator Muammar Gadhafi, was supported by the United States, most directly in the form of NATO air operations which lasted from March through October of 2011. After Gadhafi was killed in October of that year, the revolution's interim Transitional National Council (TNC) declared the country liberated, and began attempting to establish a democratically-elected government. Around this time, the TNC relocated its center of operations from Benghazi to Tripoli.

A State Department memorandum circulated at the end of 2011 recommended U.S. personnel remain in Benghazi.[1] It explained many Libyans were "strongly" in favor of a U.S. outpost in Benghazi, in part because they believed a U.S. presence in eastern Libya would ensure that the new Tripoli-based government fairly considered eastern Libyan interests.

The memorandum also outlined conditions for a U.S. mission in Benghazi (the "Benghazi Mission"), which were approved by Under Secretary for Management Patrick F. Kennedy.[2] These **conditions included the staffing of five Diplomatic Security (DS) agents**. Diplomatic Security agents manage embassy security programs for the State Department and generally serve as the first line of defense for diplomatic personnel when stationed abroad.[3] They include the Regional Security Officers (RSOs) who serve as each U.S. embassy's principal security advisor.

The Deteriorating Security Environment in Benghazi

In spite of the TNC's efforts after the revolution, U.S. officials were aware that Libya remained volatile. U.S. officials were particularly concerned with the numerous armed militias that operated freely throughout the country, including those in Benghazi with ties to al-Qa'ida

---

[1] (SBU) Action Memorandum for Under Secretary for Management Patrick F. Kennedy, "Future Operations in Benghazi, Libya." December 27, 2011.
[2] *Id.*
[3] "Securing Our Embassies Overseas." U.S. Department of State. Retrieved at: http://www.state.gov/m/ds/about/overview/c9004.htm.

and Ansar Al Sharia.[4] In August 2012, the State Department warned U.S. citizens against traveling to Libya, explaining that "inter-militia conflict can erupt at any time or any place."[5]

The deteriorating security environment in Benghazi throughout 2012 mirrored the declining situation in the rest of Libya. From June 2011 to July 2012, then-Regional Security Officer (RSO) for Libya Eric Nordstrom compiled a **list of more than 200 security incidents in Libya, 50 of which took place in Benghazi**.[6] These incidents included violent acts directed against diplomats and diplomatic facilities, international organizations, and third-country nationals, as well as large-scale militia clashes.[7] U.S. diplomatic facilities in Benghazi came under direct fire twice in the months leading up to September 11, 2012: first in April 2012, when disgruntled Libyan contract guards allegedly threw a small improvised explosive device (IED) over the perimeter wall; and in June 2012, when unknown assailants used an IED to blow a hole in the perimeter wall.

The decisions by the British Embassy, United Nations, and the International Committee of the Red Cross to withdraw their personnel from Benghazi after armed assailants launched directed attacks against each organization were additional major indicators of the increasingly threatening environment. These developments caused Lieutenant Colonel Andrew Wood, who led the U.S. military's efforts to supplement diplomatic security in Libya, to recommend that the State Department consider pulling out of Benghazi altogether. Lieutenant Colonel Wood explained that after the withdrawal of these other organizations, "it was apparent to me that we were the last [Western] flag flying in Benghazi. We were the last thing on their target list to remove from Benghazi."[8]

---

[4] Transcribed interview of Benghazi Assistant Regional Security Officer David Oliveira, October 9, 2012. *See also* "Al-Qaeda in Libya: A Profile," A Report Prepared By The Federal Research Division, Library Of Congress, Under An Interagency Agreement With The Combating Terrorism Technical Support Office's Irregular Warfare Support Program, August 2012, at p. 4.

[5] Travel Warning, U.S. Department of State, Bureau of Consular Affairs. Libya. August 27, 2012. Retrieved at: http://travel.state.gov/travel/cis_pa_tw/tw/tw_5762.html.

[6] U.S. Embassy Tripoli, Libya, Regional Security Office, "Security Incidents since June 2011."

[7] *Id.* See also, the State Department's Accountability Review Board Report for a list of security incidents in Benghazi, Libya, during 2012 that were directed at western interests. These include: a March 2012 event in which members of a militia searching for a suspect fire weapons near the U.S. diplomatic compound and attempt to enter; an April 2012 incident in which a U.K. armored diplomatic vehicle is attacked after driving into a local protest; an April 2012 event in which a homemade explosive device is thrown over the U.S. diplomatic compound's north wall; an April 2012 event in which an IED was thrown at the motorcade of the U.N. Special Envoy to Libya in Benghazi; an April 2012 event in which a Special Mission Benghazi principal officer is evacuated from International Medical University (IMU) after a fistfight escalated to gunfire between Tripoli-based trade delegation security personnel and IMU security; a May 2012, event in which the Benghazi International Committee of the Red Cross (ICRC) building was struck by rocket propelled grenades; a June 2012 IED attack on the U.S. diplomatic compound; a June 2012, event in Benghazi where the British Ambassador's convoy was attacked with a rocket propelled grenade and possible AK-47s; a June 2012, event in which a rocket propelled grenade attack is made on the ICRC compound in Misrata (400 km west of Benghazi); a June 2012, attack in which protestors storm the Tunisian consulate in Benghazi; an August 2012 event in which a small bomb is thrown at an Egyptian diplomat's vehicle parked outside of the Egyptian consulate in Benghazi.

[8] Testimony of Lieutenant Colonel Andrew Wood before the House Committee on Oversight and Government Reform, October 10, 2012.

Appendix

Security Arrangements for the Benghazi Mission

Despite mounting security concerns, for most of 2012 the Benghazi Mission was forced to rely on fewer than the approved number of DS agents. Specifically, while the State Department memorandum signed by Under Secretary Kennedy stated that five agents would be provided, this was the case for only 23 days in 2012.[9] Reports indicate the Benghazi Mission was typically staffed with only three DS agents, and sometimes as few as one DS agent.[10]

For its security, the Benghazi Mission used a combination of these few DS agents, as well as a U.S. Military Security Support Team (SST), and two Mobile Security Detachment (MSD) teams provided by the State Department. The SST consisted of 16 Defense Department special operations personnel. As commander of the SST, Lieutenant Colonel Wood reported to the U.S. Chief of Mission in Libya.[11] The MSD teams each consisted of six DS agents, all of whom underwent advanced training to augment security at high-threat posts.[12]

In addition to the security provided by U.S. agencies, the Benghazi Mission used local, unarmed guards, who were responsible for activating the alarm in the event of an attack, as well as four armed members of the February 17 Martyrs Brigade, who were to serve as a quick reaction force. The February 17 Martyrs Brigade was one of the militias that fought for Gadhafi's overthrow. Numerous reports have indicated that the Brigade had extremist connections, and it had been implicated in the kidnapping of American citizens as well as in the threats against U.S. military assets. In addition, on September 8, 2012, just days before Ambassador Stevens arrived in Benghazi, the February 17 Martyrs Brigade told State Department officials that the group would no longer support U.S. movements in the city, including the Ambassador's visit.[13]

Internal State Department Communications on Security

State Department officials in Washington acknowledged that the Benghazi Mission lacked sufficient resources to protect its personnel in a deteriorating security environment. However, in a cable signed by Secretary Clinton in April 2012, the State Department settled on a plan to scale back security assets for the U.S. Mission in Libya, including Benghazi. Specifically, despite acknowledging Ambassador Cretz's March 2012 cable requesting additional security assets, the April plan called for the removal of the two remaining MSD teams, the third initially deployed MSD team having been previously removed. This

---

[9] Department of State, Accountability Review Board for Benghazi Attack of September 2012, December 19, 2012, at p. 31; Interview of Regional Security Officer Eric Nordstrom, October 1, 2012.

[10] Interview of Regional Security Officer Eric Nordstrom, October 1, 2012. See also, email from James Bacigalupo to Brian Papanu and David Sparrowgrove, May 7, 2012, 1:01 p.m., Subject: FW: Special Agent Tony Zamudio's TDY Performance in Benghazi.

[11] Testimony of Lieutenant Colonel Andrew Wood before the House Committee on Oversight and Government Reform, October 10, 2012.

[12] "Securing Our Embassies Overseas." U.S. Department of State. Retrieved at: http://www.state.gov/m/ds/about/overview/c9004.htm.

[13] Email from Alec Henderson to John B. Martinec, "RE: Benghazi QRF agreement," (Sep. 9, 2012 11:31 PM).

reduced security footprint was of significant concern to U.S. Ambassador to Libya Gene Cretz, who had requested the continued deployment of both MSD teams, or at least additional DS agents to replace them, and the full five DS agents for the Benghazi Mission that the December 2011 Kennedy memorandum documented would be stationed in Benghazi. His successor, Ambassador Christopher Stevens – who replaced him in May 2012 – shared Ambassador Cretz's concerns.

Critical Cables

During 2012, in numerous communications with the State Department, officials from the U.S. Mission in Libya stress both the inadequacy of security as well as the need for additional personnel. Two critical cables warrant specific mention:

• On **March 28, 2012**, Ambassador Cretz sends a cable to Secretary Clinton requesting additional security assets.

• On **April 19, 2012**, the response cable from the Department of State to Embassy Tripoli, bearing Secretary Clinton's signature, acknowledges Ambassador Cretz's request for additional security but instead articulates a plan to scale back security assets for the U.S. Mission in Libya, including the Benghazi Mission.

In addition, the April 2012 cable from Secretary Clinton recommended that the State Department's Bureau of Diplomatic Security and the U.S. Mission in Libya conduct a "joint re-assessment of the number of DS agents requested for Benghazi."[14] This prompted one frustrated Embassy Tripoli employee to remark to her colleagues that it "looks like no movement on the full complement of [five DS] personnel for Benghazi, but rather a reassessment to bring the numbers lower."[15]

In May 2012, Ambassador Stevens replaced Ambassador Cretz and continued to make requests for additional security. In an email in early June, he told a State Department official that with national elections occurring in Libya in July and August, the U.S. Mission in Libya **"would feel much safer if we could keep two MSD teams with us through this period [to support] our staff and [personal detail] for me and the [Deputy Chief of Mission] and any VIP visitors."**[16] The State Department official replied that due to other commitments and limited resources, "unfortunately, MSD cannot support the request."[17]

---

[14] 12 STATE 38939, April 19, 2012, Signature: CLINTON.
[15] Email from Jennifer A. Larson to Eric Nordstrom, Ambassador Gene Cretz, et al., April 21, 2012, 1:57 p.m., Subject: Re: Tripoli – Request for DS DTY and FTE Support.
[16] Email chain between Ambassador Chris Stevens and John Moretti, June 7, 2012, 3:34 a.m., Subject: MSD/Tripoli.
[17] *Id.*

APPENDIX

Despite the denial of Ambassador Stevens' request, Embassy Tripoli officials persisted in their requests for additional security. In July 2012, for example, RSO Eric Nordstrom alerted DS officials in Washington that he intended to submit a formal cable request for an extension of the SST and MSD teams. DS personnel in Washington alerted Mr. Nordstrom that Ms. Charlene Lamb, the Deputy Assistant Secretary for Diplomatic Security, was "reluctant to ask for an SST extension, apparently out of concern that it would be embarrassing to the [State Department] to continue to have to rely on [Defense Department] assets to protect our Mission."[18] Moreover, in response to Mr. Nordstrom's intent to request an MSD extension, Ms. Lamb responded, "NO, I do not [I repeat] not want them to ask for the MSD team to stay!"[19]

Critical Emails

June 7, 2012: Ambassador Stevens asks the State Department to keep the two MSD teams the Clinton April cable ordered removed from Libya. This request is denied.

July 6, 2012: Deputy Assistant Secretary for Diplomatic Security Lamb strongly asserts that Embassy Tripoli should not make a formal request for an extension of the SST and MSD teams.

On July 9, 2012, Ambassador Stevens responded with a cable that stressed that the security conditions in Libya had not met the requisite benchmarks established by the State Department and the U.S. Mission in Libya to warrant initiating a security drawdown.[20] He requested that a sufficient number of security personnel, whether DS agents, or SST or MSD team members, be permitted to stay.[21] Under Secretary Kennedy rejected the request for the SST extension, and both the SST and MSD teams were subsequently withdrawn.[22] Although the State Department made some modest physical security upgrades to the Benghazi Mission, the systematic withdrawal of existing security personnel resulted in a security posture for the Benghazi Mission that the State Department's Accountability Review Board later determined was "inadequate for Benghazi."[23]

Multiple Committees have reviewed the State Department documents cited in the previous sections and remain concerned that the documents do not reconcile with public comments Secretary Clinton made regarding how high in the State Department the security

---

[18] Email from David C. McFarland to Ambassador Chris Stevens, et al., July 9, 2012, 12:24 p.m., Subject: (SBU) Tripoli O-I July 9.

[19] (SBU) Email from Charlene Lamb to State Department personnel. July 6, 2012, 2:59 p.m. Subject: Re: Tripoli – Request for extension of TDY Security Personnel.

[20] 12 TRIPOLI 690, July 9, 2012. Signature: STEVENS.

[21] Id.

[22] Briefing by Under Secretary for Management Patrick F. Kennedy to Congressional staff, January 2013.

[23] Department of State, Accountability Review Board for Benghazi Attack of September 2012, December 19, 2012, at p. 4.

situation and requests were discussed. Despite acknowledging a security request made on April 19, 2012, Secretary Clinton made the following statements before the House Foreign Affairs Committee on January 23, 2013:

- "I have made it very clear that the security cables did not come to my attention or above the assistant secretary level where the ARB [Accountability Review Board] placed responsibility. Where, as I think Ambassador Pickering said, 'the rubber hit the road.'"[24]

- "You know, Congressman, it was very disappointing to me that the [Accountability Review Board] concluded there were inadequacies and problems in the responsiveness of our team here in Washington to the security requests that were made by our team in Libya. And I was not aware of that going on, it was not brought to my attention, but obviously it's something we're fixing and intend to put into place protocols and systems to make sure it doesn't happen again. ... Well if I could – 1.43 million cables a year come to the State Department. They are all addressed to me. They do not all come to me. They are reported through the bureaucracy."[25]

In addition, it remains unclear why the State Department chose to reduce security in the face of such a challenging security environment and chose to deny multiple requests from Embassy Tripoli for more assistance. It is clear that funding – or a lack thereof – is not the reason for the reductions in security, as Deputy Assistant Secretary for Diplomatic Security Lamb testified and as emails reviewed by the Committees attest.[26]

Moreover, a lack of funding would not have been at issue with respect to the rejection of the request to extend the deployment of the SST, as that team was provided via the Defense Department at no expense to the State Department. The Administration owes the American people an explanation regarding these unanswered questions, which must be explored in greater depth in the weeks and months ahead.

---

[24] Testimony of Secretary Hillary Clinton before the House Foreign Affairs Committee on January 23, 2013.
[25] *Id.*
[26] Testimony of Deputy Assistant Secretary of State for Diplomatic Security Charlene Lamb before the House Committee on Oversight and Government Reform, October 10, 2012; email exchange between Assistant Secretary Eric Boswell and Diplomatic Security Chief Financial Officer Robert Baldre, September 28, 2012 ("I do not feel that we have ever been at a point where we sacrificed security due to a lack of funding...Typically Congress has provided sufficient funding.")

APPENDIX

II. **The volatile security environment erupted on September 11, 2012, when militias composed of al-Qa'ida-affiliated extremists attacked U.S. interests in Benghazi.**

The Committees have concluded that U.S. security personnel on the ground exhibited extreme bravery in conducting defensive actions and rescue operations in the face of coordinated and sophisticated attacks on the U.S. presence in Benghazi.

Ambassador Stevens' Visit to Benghazi

Ambassador Stevens previously served in Libya as Deputy Chief of Mission (2007 – 2009) and as Special Representative to the Transitional National Council (March 2011 – November 2011). He became U.S. Ambassador to Libya in May 2012. Ambassador Stevens traveled to Benghazi on September 10, 2012, to fill staffing gaps between principal officers in Benghazi and to allow him to reconnect with local contacts. He also planned to attend the establishment of a new American Corner at a local Benghazi school.[27] It has been reported to multiple Committee staff - but not confirmed - that an additional purpose of his visit was to personally assess the security situation in Benghazi in order to lend more urgency to his planned request for additional security resources from Washington.

The Attack on the Benghazi Mission Begins

On September 11, 2012, there were a total of 28 U.S. personnel on the ground at the Benghazi Mission and at the Annex in Benghazi, including Ambassador Stevens.[28]

At appropriately 9:40 PM,[29] dozens of armed men approached the Benghazi Mission and quickly breached the front gate, setting fire to the guard house and main diplomatic building. The attackers were members of extremist groups, including the Libya-based Ansar al-Sharia (AAS) and al-Qa'ida in the Lands of the Islamic Maghreb (AQIM). A State Department officer in the Benghazi Mission's Tactical Operations Center (TOC) immediately notified the Annex, Embassy Tripoli, and State Department Headquarters that the Benghazi Mission was under attack and requested assistance. At no point did U.S. officials on the ground report a protest.[30]

At the time of the attack, Ambassador Stevens, Information Officer Sean Smith, and a DS agent were located in Villa C, the main building of the Benghazi Mission. At approximately 10:00 PM, within 20 minutes of the attack, Ambassador Stevens, Mr. Smith, and the DS agent suffered debilitating effects from smoke inhalation due to the heavy smoke as the main diplomatic building burned. All three tried to escape by crawling along the floor towards a window. Due to the thick smoke, the DS agent unknowingly lost contact with Ambassador

---

[27] American Corners are partnerships between the Public Affairs sections of United States Embassies and host institutions. They provide access to current and reliable information from and about the United States via book collections, the Internet, and through local programming to the general public overseas or abroad.
[28] As described in this timeline, as the attacks were ongoing, seven additional personnel arrived from Tripoli to assist, **bringing the total to 35 U.S. personnel on the ground that night**.
[29] All times local.
[30] Emails from State Department Operations Center to various recipients, September 11, 2012, at 4:05 p.m. Eastern and 6:08 p.m. Eastern.

Stevens and Mr. Smith at some point along the smoke-filled escape route. After crawling out of a window and realizing the Ambassador and Mr. Smith were not with him, the DS agent, under gunfire, repeatedly re-entered the burning building to search for them. As he was doing so, the DS agent also used his radio to call for help. Security officers from other parts of the Benghazi Mission responded and joined the DS agent's search for the missing individuals.

Within 25 minutes of the initial assault, a security team at the Annex was notified and departed for the Benghazi Mission. The security team tried unsuccessfully to secure heavy weapons from militia members encountered along the way, and the team faced some resistance, including gunfire, in getting to the Benghazi Mission. Over the course of the next hour, the Annex security team joined the Benghazi Mission team in searching for Ambassador Stevens and Mr. Smith. Together, the teams repelled sporadic gunfire and RPG fire while assembling all the remaining U.S. personnel at the facility.

While the security officers were able to retrieve the body of Mr. Smith, they were unable to locate Ambassador Stevens. After 90 minutes of repeated attempts to enter the burning main diplomatic building to search for the Ambassador, the teams assessed the security situation had deteriorated to the point that they were forced to abandon their search. The Annex security team loaded all U.S. personnel into vehicles and started the process of departing for the Annex, with the first vehicle departing at 11:15 PM and the second vehicle departing at 11:30 PM. Meanwhile, at approximately 11:10 PM, Defense Department unarmed surveillance aircraft arrived overhead. As the vehicles exited the Benghazi Mission, they encountered heavy gunfire and at least one roadblock in their route to the Annex.

Escalation at the Annex

At approximately 12:30 AM, a team of seven U.S. personnel departed Tripoli. This team arrived in Benghazi at 1:30 AM. At around 5:15 AM, within 15 minutes of the Tripoli team's arrival at the Annex, a short but deadly and coordinated terrorist attack began on the annex.[31] The attack, which included small arms, RPG, and well-aimed mortar fire, mortally wounded two American security officers, Mr. Tyrone Woods and Mr. Doherty, and severely wounded two other U.S. personnel. At 6:05 AM, the 31 survivors from the initial attack on the Benghazi Mission departed the Annex for the Benghazi airport. The surviving Americans departed Benghazi along with three of the four fallen Americans at 7:40 AM on September 12, 2012. The C-17 deployed from Germany departed Tripoli at 7:17 PM, carrying the American survivors and the remains of Mr. Smith, Mr. Woods, and Mr. Doherty. The plane arrived in Ramstein, Germany at 10:19 PM on September 12, 2012.

---

[31] The Tripoli team spent the hours between the arrival at the airport and the arrival at the Annex focused on gaining situational awareness about its main mission, which at the time was locating Ambassador Stevens, who they thought might have been kidnapped.

Appendix

Timeline for Ambassador Stevens

Due to the deteriorating security situation and exhaustive, but unsuccessful search for Ambassador Stevens, the security teams made the decision to evacuate the survivors of the attack on the Benghazi Mission and the remains of Mr. Smith about 90 minutes after the attack began. The evacuation began at approximately 11:30 PM.

At approximately 1:00 AM on September 12, 2012, local Libyans found the remains of Ambassador Stevens in the main diplomatic building at the Benghazi Mission and transported him to the hospital. The Libyans apparently did not realize who the Ambassador was, but they alerted the State Department of his location by using the cell phone that was in the Ambassador's pocket. Libyan doctors tried unsuccessfully to resuscitate Ambassador Stevens upon his arrival at the hospital. At 8:15 PM that evening, his remains were transported from the hospital to the Benghazi airport to begin the journey to Tripoli, to Germany, and then finally home.

The Defense Department's Timeline

At 9:59 PM,[32] within twenty minutes of the initial attack, Defense Department officials directed an unarmed, unmanned surveillance aircraft to reposition overhead of the Benghazi Mission. The aircraft arrived at 11:10 PM, approximately 20 minutes before the evacuation of the Benghazi Mission began.

In Washington, at 10:32 PM, an officer in the National Military Command Center at the Pentagon,[33] after receiving initial reports of the incident from the State Department, notified the Office of the Secretary of Defense and the Joint Staff. The information was quickly passed to Secretary of Defense, Mr. Leon E. Panetta, and the Chairman of the Joint Chiefs of Staff, General Martin E. Dempsey. Secretary Panetta and General Dempsey attended a previously scheduled meeting with the President at the White House at 11:00 PM, approximately 80 minutes after the attack began. The Defense Department reported that principals discussed potential responses to the ongoing situation.[34]

Following the White House meeting, Secretary Panetta returned to the Pentagon and convened a series of meetings from 12:00 AM to 2:00 AM with senior officials, including General Dempsey and General Carter F. Ham, the Commander of U.S. Africa Command (AFRICOM), which is the Geographic Combatant Command responsible for U.S. military activities in Libya. They discussed additional response options for Benghazi and the potential outbreak of further violence throughout the region, particularly in Tunis, Tunisia; Cairo, Egypt; and Sana'a, Yemen.

---

[32] Again all times local.

[33] The purpose of the National Military Command Center (NMCC) is to support military command and control for the Commander in Chief and the Secretary of Defense (often referred to as the National Command Authority). It is operated by the Joint Staff, to coordinate joint actions and coordinate with the supported Combatant Command. Principally located at the Pentagon, the NMCC broadly consists of multiple people, organizations, command and control systems, procedures, and facilities.

[34] Unclassified timeline, Department of Defense.

Appendix

To help expedite the movement of forces after the receipt of formal authorization, Pentagon officials verbally conveyed orders to other Combatant Commands.

Specifically, Secretary Panetta verbally directed the deployment of:

1. two Marine Fleet Antiterrorism Security Team (FAST) platoons from Rota, Spain to the Benghazi Mission and Embassy Tripoli;
2. a U.S. European Command (EUCOM) Commander's in-Extremis Force (CIF) to an intermediate staging base in southern Europe; and
3. a special operations force based in the United States to an intermediate staging base in southern Europe.

Concurrently, at 12:30 AM, a six-man security team and one linguist stationed at Embassy Tripoli departed for Benghazi; the team landed in Benghazi at 1:30 AM. At 2:39 AM, officers in the National Military Command Center transmitted the formal authorizations for the deployments of the two Marine FAST platoons and the EUCOM special operations force. At 2:53 AM, the U.S-based special operations force received formal authorization to deploy.

Analysis of the Defense Department's Response

Despite the brave and honorable efforts of the individuals on the ground in Benghazi – reinforced by the team from Tripoli – serious concerns regarding the Defense Department's systemic response required extensive review. **Combined with the failure of the President to anticipate the significance of the day and to proactively authorize the Defense Department with an alert posture to launch offensive operations beyond self-defense, forces were provided no notice to defend diplomatic facilities.** Fundamentally, the progress report finds that the Benghazi Mission did not have a sufficient, layered defense designed to fend off an attack until a military response could be deployed to provide a decisive conclusion to an assault. The oversight review of the Defense Department's response, however, has highlighted serious deficiencies in the military's strategic posture in Africa – and the region – which require corrective action and necessitate further examination by congressional committees of jurisdiction.

The military command responsible for this region is U.S. Africa Command (AFRICOM), which officially became one of the Defense Department's six geographic commands in 2008. The Command is responsible for all Department of Defense operations, exercises, and security cooperation efforts on the Continent of Africa, its island nations, and surrounding waters. AFRICOM faces serious resource deficiencies: it does not have any Army or Marine Corps units formally assigned to the command; it shares Air Force and Navy components with U.S. European Command (EUCOM); and it did not have a Commander's in-Extremis Force (CIF) assigned to the command at the time of the attack on September 11, 2012. Moreover,

APPENDIX

AFRICOM still lacks a fully constituted CIF with vital and unique enabling capabilities.[35] As a result, when the U.S. needed to respond swiftly to the attacks in Benghazi, the Defense Department did not task AFRICOM. Instead, it was forced to task EUCOM's CIF to respond, which was engaged in a training mission in Croatia.

In addition, because AFRICOM does not have assigned Marine FAST platoons – which are limited-duration, expeditionary security forces capable of responding to emergencies – it had to rely on elements of a FAST unit assigned to EUCOM for response in Benghazi. The Marine FAST platoon in Rota, Spain was hindered in its response because it lacked dedicated airlift at its location; the airlift was in Germany. Even if the airlift had been co-located with the platoon, the platoon would not have been able to arrive in time to save the lives of the four Americans killed in the attack.

The House Armed Services Committee also examined the deployment of stateside-based response forces. The special operations force deployed from the continental United States (CONUS) reached the staging based in southern Europe approximately 24 hours after the initial attack, even though the force was forward-leaning in its preparations as it awaited formal authorization to deploy. The Benghazi attack highlights significant drawbacks of policy options that solely rely on a CONUS-based response force, and the Committee will continue its vigorous oversight of the global disposition of military forces to determine whether the Department of Defense is appropriately postured to more rapidly respond to similar incidents in the future.

In addition, the House Armed Services Committee conducted a review of air assets available to respond to Benghazi. No U.S. government element refused or denied requests for emergency assistance during the crisis. The evidence also does not show there were armed air assets above Benghazi at any time or that any such assets were called off from assisting U.S. personnel on the ground. According to witness testimony, the security officials on the ground did use laser sights, but they did so as an escalatory demonstration of force in an effort to deter some attackers. They were not lasing targets for air assets.[36]

The House Armed Services Committee also examined the question of whether the Defense Department failed to deploy assets to Benghazi because it believed the attack was over after the first phase. The progress report finds that officials at the Defense Department were monitoring the situation throughout and kept the forces that were initially deployed flowing into the region. No evidence has been provided to suggest these officials refused to deploy resources because they thought the situation had been sufficiently resolved.

Similarly, the evidence does not show that military commanders involved in the U.S. military's response to the terrorist attacks in Benghazi were relieved of command, transferred, or encouraged to seek early retirement as a result of their actions in response to the attacks. In the

---

[35] U.S. Africa Command Posture Hearing testimony at the House Armed Services Committee. March 15, 2013.
[36] House Intelligence Community staff briefing with key surviving personnel and U.S. security officials. December 14, 2012.

APPENDIX

case of General Carter Ham, Commander of U.S. Africa Command (AFRICOM), House Armed Services Committee staff were aware of General Ham's plans to retire well in advance of September 11, 2012.

The disposition of military forces is a reflection of policy, strategy, and resources. Because of a number of factors – including the lack of a coherent Administration policy toward North Africa; an ad hoc and reactive Administration strategy for addressing threats to U.S. interests in the region; a lack of resources for AFRICOM; and the short duration of the attack – the Department of Defense was unable to provide an effective military response to the Benghazi attacks. Although responsible military officers and civilian officials within the Department of Defense reacted quickly to the attacks in Benghazi, **the effectiveness of their response was hindered because U.S. military forces were not properly postured** to address the growing threats in northern Africa or to respond to a brief, high-intensity attack on U.S. personnel or interests across much of Africa.

Analysis of the Intelligence Community's Role

The Benghazi terrorist attacks did not constitute an intelligence failure. The Intelligence Community collected considerable information about the threat and disseminated regular assessments warning of the deteriorating security environment in Benghazi and risks to American interests, facilities, and personnel.

The House Intelligence Committee examined the question of why the U.S. Intelligence Community (IC) did not provide an immediate and specific tactical warning of the attack in Benghazi. **A review of relevant documents confirmed that the intelligence community did not possess intelligence indicating planning or intentions for an attack on the Benghazi facility on or about September 11, 2012.** The review, however, also demonstrated that any official responsible for security at a U.S. facility or for personnel in Benghazi or the region would have had **sufficient warning of the deteriorating security situation, the corresponding increasing threat, and the expressed intent of anti-U.S. extremists in the region to attack Western and specifically U.S. targets.**

Throughout 2012, there were more than 20 attacks against Western and international interests in Benghazi. The IC monitored these and other extremist activities in North Africa and published hundreds of reports and assessments related to threats to these interests in the region before the September 11 attacks.[37] These reports and assessments, which were available to senior policymakers in the government, including those at the State Department and the White House, made clear that there were serious and credible threats to American interests and facilities in the region and in Benghazi specifically.[38] In addition, these reports and assessments made

---

[37] HPSCI review of intelligence assessments, cables, and reports.
[38] *Id.*

clear that the Benghazi Mission was the subject of credible threats, although no reporting warned of the attack on September 11, 2012.[39]

Other U.S. facilities were raided in September 2012, and known al-Qa'ida-affiliated terrorists were involved in each of the incidents. Also on September 11, Egyptian protesters scaled the walls of the U.S. Embassy in Cairo, Egypt, which at least four senior jihadists with well-documented ties to al-Qa'ida helped instigate.[40] On September 13th, hundreds of Yemenis – including some al-Qa'ida-linked individuals – stormed the U.S. Embassy in Sana'a, Yemen, but were repelled by local security forces. On September 14th, Ansar-al-Sharia-Tunisia (an al-Qa'ida-affiliated group) participated in an attack on the U.S. Embassy in Tunis, Tunisia, and set fire to the nearby American school.

---

[39] *Id.*
[40] *Id.*

APPENDIX

III. **After the attacks, the Administration perpetuated a deliberately misleading and incomplete narrative that the violence grew out of a demonstration caused by a YouTube video. The Administration consciously decided not to discuss extremist involvement or previous attacks against Western interests in Benghazi.**

The U.S. government immediately had information that the attacks were conducted by al-Qa'ida-affiliated terrorists, yet Administration officials downplayed those connections, and focused on the idea that provocation for violence resulted from a YouTube video.

Analysis At the Time of the Attack

The U.S. government knew immediately that the attacks constituted an act of terror. In an "Ops Alert" issued shortly after the attack began, the State Department Operations Center notified senior Department officials, the White House Situation Room, and others, that the Benghazi compound was under attack and that "approximately 20 armed people fired shots; explosions have been heard as well."[41] Two hours later, the Operations Center issued an alert that al-Qa'ida linked Ansar al-Sharia (AAS) claimed responsibility for the attack and had called for an attack on Embassy Tripoli.[42] **Neither alert mentioned that there had been a protest at the location of the attacks.**[43] Further, Administration documents provided to the Committees show that there was ample evidence that the attack was planned and intentional. **The coordinated, complex, and deadly attack on the Annex – that included sophisticated weapons – is perhaps the strongest evidence that the attacks were not spontaneous. The question of why a deliberately misleading and incomplete narrative to the contrary was initially perpetuated by the Administration despite the existence of this information has not yet been fully answered and must be addressed as oversight efforts continue.**

Timeline of the Administration's Narrative

In the days after the events, the White House and senior Administration officials sought to portray the attacks as provoked by a YouTube video.[44] The President, Secretary Clinton, White House Press Secretary Jay Carney, and United States Ambassador to the United Nations Susan Rice each made statements denouncing the video and condemning those who purportedly used it to justify their behavior.[45] The President and Secretary Clinton also appeared in a $70,000 advertisement campaign in Pakistan to disavow the video.[46]

---

[41] Email from State Department Operations Center to various recipients, September 11, 2012, 4:05 p.m. Eastern.
[42] Email from State Department Operations Center to various recipients, September 11, 2012, 6:08 p.m. Eastern.
[43] The ARB also concluded that "there was no protest prior to the attacks, which were unanticipated in their scale and intensity."
[44] "Administration Statements on the Attack in Benghazi," *The New York Times*, September 27, 2012. See also, Remarks by the President to the UN General Assembly, United Nation Headquarters, New York, New York, September 25, 2012, 10:22 a.m.
[45] *Id.*
[46] Found at: http://www.youtube.com/watch?v=6akGlF6g-Zw.

APPENDIX

On Sunday, September 16, 2012, Ambassador Rice appeared on five morning television programs to discuss the Administration's account of the attack. In nearly identical statements, she stated that the attack was a spontaneous protest in response to a "hateful video," similar to what transpired in Cairo, Egypt, earlier that day.[47] Rice asserted that "we do not have information at present that leads us to conclude that this was premeditated or preplanned."[48] Her interviews stand in sharp contrast to interviews given on the same morning talk shows by the President of the Libyan National Congress, Mohamad Magarif, who characterized the attack as criminal and preplanned.[49] Further, on that same day and prior to Ambassador Rice's scheduled appearances on the Sunday morning programs, a senior official on the ground in Libya informed senior leaders at the State Department that there was no demonstration prior to the attack.[50]

The Administration echoed Ambassador Rice's statements until September 19 when National Counterterrorism Center (NCTC) Director Matt Olsen testified before the Senate Homeland Security and Government Affairs Committee that our diplomats died "in the course of a terrorist attack on our embassy."[51]

Director Olsen's testimony marked a significant shift in the Administration's rhetoric. Immediately afterward, Administration officials began referring to the event as a terrorist attack. On September 20, 2012, Mr. Carney stated that, "it is, I think, self-evident that what happened in Benghazi was a terrorist attack."[52] Similarly, on September 21, Secretary Clinton stated, "What happened in Benghazi was a terrorist attack, and we will not rest until we have tracked down and brought to justice the terrorists who murdered four Americans."[53] On October 9, the State Department held a conference call briefing for reporters in which Department officials publicly acknowledged that there had been no protest outside the Benghazi diplomatic facility prior to the assault. Members should note that the following day, senior State Department officials were scheduled to appear before the House Oversight and Government Reform Committee.

Analysis of the Evolving Drafts of the Talking Points

To protect the State Department, the Administration deliberately removed references to al-Qa'ida-linked groups and previous attacks in Benghazi in the talking points used by Ambassador Rice, thereby perpetuating the deliberately misleading and incomplete narrative that the attacks evolved from a demonstration caused by a YouTube video.

---

[47] "Timeline: How Benghazi attack, probe unfolded," CBS News, November 2, 2012.
[48] *Id.*
[49] Transcript of *Meet the Press* interview found at: http://www.cbsnews.com/8301-3460_162-57513819/face-the-nation-transcripts-september-16-2012-libyan-pres-magariaf-amb-rice-and-sen-mccain/.
[50] Email from William V. Roebuck to Beth Jones, "Update: 9-16-12," (Sept. 16, 2012 8:38 AM).
[51] Testimony of National Counterterrorism Center Director Matt Olsen before the Senate Committee on Homeland Security and Governmental Affairs, September 19, 2012.
[52] "Timeline: How Benghazi attack, probe unfolded," CBS News, November 2, 2012.
[53] *Id.*

APPENDIX

The Administration's talking points were developed in an interagency process that focused more on protecting the reputation and credibility of the State Department than on explaining to the American people the facts surrounding the fatal attacks on U.S. diplomatic facilities and personnel in Libya. Congressional investigators were given access to email exchanges, in which White House and senior Department officials discussed and edited the talking points. Those emails clearly reveal that Administration officials intentionally removed references in the talking points to the likely participation by Islamic extremists, to the known threat of extremists linked to al-Qa'ida in Benghazi and eastern Libya, and to other recent attacks against foreign interests in Benghazi.

The talking points in question were initially created for the House Intelligence Committee, after a briefing by then-Director of the CIA, David Petraeus.[54] Members of the Committee sought guidance on how to discuss the attacks publicly and in an unclassified manner. The CIA generated the initial drafts of the unclassified talking points and provided them to other officials within the Executive Branch for clearance. The initial CIA draft circulated to the interagency group included references to:

1. previous notifications provided to Embassy Cairo of social media reporting encouraging jihadists to break into the Embassy;
2. indications that Islamic extremists participated in the events in Benghazi;
3. potential links to Ansar al-Sharia;
4. information about CIA-produced assessments of the threat from extremists linked to al-Qa'ida in Benghazi and eastern Libya; and
5. information about five previous attacks against foreign interests in Benghazi since April 2012.[55]

When draft talking points were sent to officials throughout the Executive Branch, senior State Department officials requested the talking points be changed to avoid criticism for ignoring the threat environment in Benghazi. Specifically, State Department emails reveal senior officials had "serious concerns" about the talking points, because Members of Congress might attack the State Department for "not paying attention to Agency warnings" about the growing threat in Benghazi.[56] This process to alter the talking points can only be construed as a deliberate effort to mislead Congress and the American people.

After slight modifications were made on Friday, September 14, a senior State Department official again responded that the edits did not "resolve all my issues or those of my building leadership," and that the Department's leadership was "consulting with [National Security Staff]."[57] Several minutes later, White House officials responded by stating that the State

---

[54] House Intelligence Committee classified briefing with Director Petraeus, September 14, 2012.
[55] Draft talking points circulated via email within interagency at 6:52 p.m., September 14, 2012.
[56] Email from Senior State Department official to interagency team at 7:39 p.m., Friday, September 14, 2012.
[57] Email from Senior State Department official to interagency team at 9:24 p.m., Friday, September 14, 2012.

Department's concerns would have to be taken into account and asserted further discussion would occur the following morning at a Deputies Committee Meeting.[58]

After the Deputies Committee Meeting on Saturday, September 15, 2012, at which any interagency disagreement would be resolved by the White House,[59] a small group of officials from both the State Department and the CIA worked to modify the talking points to their final form to reflect the decision reached in the Deputies meeting.[60] The actual edits were made by a current high-ranking CIA official.[61] **Those edits struck any and all suggestions that the State Department had been previously warned of threats in the region, that there had been previous attacks in Benghazi by al-Qa'ida-linked groups in Benghazi and eastern Libya, and that extremists linked to al-Qa'ida may have participated in the attack on the Benghazi Mission.**[62] The talking points also excluded details about the wide availability of weapons and experienced fighters in Libya, an exacerbating factor that contributed to the lethality of the attacks.[63]

Administration officials have said that modification of **the talking points was an attempt to protect classified information and an investigation by the FBI**,[64] but the evidence refutes these assertions. Administration officials transmitted and reviewed different drafts of the talking points—many of which included reference to al-Qa'ida-associated groups, including Ansar al-Sharia—over unsecure email systems. Also, **there were no concerns about protecting classified information in the email traffic**. Finally, the FBI approved a version of the talking points with significantly more information about the attacks and previous threats than the version requested by the State Department. Claims that the edits were made to protect the FBI investigation are not credible.[65]

---

[58] A Deputies meeting is an interagency gathering – often done in person or over a secure video conferencing system (SVTC)—at which deputies of all relevant departments advocate for their departments' positions. Deputies typically reach a consensus, or the White House will provide a decision if there is continued dispute. In this case, the Deputies met by (SVTC) on the morning of Saturday, September 15, 2012. While Congress has not yet been given minutes of that meeting, it appears to have included representatives of the State Department, the CIA, DOD, the FBI/DOJ, and the White House, represented by National Security Staff.

[59] This appears to directly contradict White House Spokesman Jay Carney's comments at the Daily Press Briefing on November 28, 2012: "The White House and the State Department have made clear that the single adjustment that was made to those talking points by either of those two—of these two institutions were changing the word 'consulate' to 'diplomatic facility,' because 'consulate' was inaccurate. Those talking points originated from the intelligence community. They reflect the IC's best assessments of what they thought had happened."

[60] Email to Ambassador Rice, Saturday, September 15, 2012, discussing the results of the Deputies meeting.

[61] Final version of talking points circulated at 9:52 a.m., September 15, 2012.

[62] Id.

[63] Id.

[64] CIA Acting Director Michael Morrell suggested at a hearing before the Senate Select Committee on Intelligence that the talking points were changed to protect an ongoing FBI investigation. See, e.g., http://www.cbsnews.com/9301-250_162-57555984/who-changed-the-benghazi-talking-points/

[65] Email from Senior State Department Official to second Senior State Department Official explaining that the FBI "did not have major concerns" with the talking points and "offered only a couple minor suggestions." 8:59 p.m., September 14, 2012.

Appendix

Key Quotes

"The White House and the State Department have made clear that the single adjustment that was made to those talking points by either of those two—of these two institutions were changing the word 'consulate' to 'diplomatic facility,' because 'consulate' was inaccurate. Those talking points originated from the intelligence community. They reflect the IC's best assessments of what they thought had happened." – *White House Spokesman Jay Carney, White House Daily Press Briefing, November 28, 2012*

"Secondly, because the process was one of declassifying classified information, and in that process the talking points that were provided to Ambassador Rice to members of Congress and to others, including myself in the executive branch, were written in the way that was presented by Ambassador Rice." – *White House Spokesman Jay Carney, White House Daily Press Briefing, January 8, 2013*

Ambassador Rice received the approved talking points in advance of her appearances on Sunday, September 16, 2012 on various television programs.[66] **She was informed that the talking points were created for Congressional members, and modified to protect State Department equities and the FBI investigation**.[67] Ambassador Rice then appeared the next morning on five Sunday morning talk shows, during which she focused on the attacks being provoked by the Cairo events and the "hateful video."

The Administration made a conscious decision to focus on the deliberately misleading and incomplete narrative that demonstrations protesting a YouTube video evolved into attacks on the Benghazi Mission. This decision resulted in a senior Administration official appearing on major national news programs to discuss a terrorist attack against the United States without mentioning the known threat to the region by al Qa'ida affiliates, the likely participation by Ansar al-Sharia in the incident, and the previous attacks on Western interests in Benghazi.

---

[66] Email to Ambassador Rice, Saturday, September 15, 2012.
[67] *Id.*

APPENDIX

IV. **The Administration's investigations and reviews of the Benghazi attacks highlight its failed security policies leading to the attacks while undermining the ability of the United States government to bring the perpetrators to justice.**

A Compromised FBI Criminal Investigation

The Administration responded to the Benghazi attacks with an FBI investigation, as opposed to a more thorough military or intelligence response. Regrettably, the FBI simply did not have the ability to access the location of the attacks with sufficient speed to ensure that all evidence was accumulated as quickly as possible. Due to security concerns and bureaucratic entanglements among the Departments of Justice, State, and Defense,[68] the FBI team investigating the terrorist attacks did not access the crime scene until more than three weeks later, on October 4, 2012. During this time, the site was not secured, and curious locals and international media were able to pick through the burned-out remains of the U.S. facility. The FBI spent less than one day collecting evidence at the Benghazi Mission. FBI officials indicated that the security situation delayed and deterred a more thorough investigation of the site.

The FBI has interviewed all U.S. Government personnel on the ground during the attacks, but has encountered difficulty accessing other witnesses or suspects. For example, one suspect jailed in connection with the attacks, Ali Harzi, was released for lack of evidence on January 7, 2013, by Tunisian authorities. FBI agents questioned Mr. Harzi in December 2012, but the questioning did not result in sufficient information for the FBI to stop his release. Media reports also indicate that the FBI has recently been given access to question an individual of interest, Faraj al-Shibli, in Libya. The scope of that questioning is currently unconfirmed, and it remains unclear whether the access is sufficient enough to yield evidence that could be used to prosecute Shibli or other individuals.

FBI Director Robert Mueller testified before the Senate Select Committee on Intelligence (SSCI) that the investigation is complicated by the lack of security in eastern Libya.[69] Without significant progress in finding and questioning suspects, it appears that the decision to proceed with an FBI investigation – presumably with the intention of obtaining a criminal indictment in U.S. courts – was ill-advised. For instance, the United States responded to the attacks against U.S. embassies in Africa in the 1990s and against the U.S.S. *Cole* in 2000 with criminal investigations. On their own, those investigations failed to bring many of those responsible to justice and likely encouraged further terrorist activity. This approach is not the most effective method of responding to terrorist attacks against U.S. interests in foreign countries.

It was only after the September 11, 2001, attacks, when the United States responded to terrorism with military force, that the government successfully brought some of the perpetrators of those attacks and the previous attacks to justice. Terrorists who successfully attack U.S.

---

[68] The Department of Defense offered to provide a U.S. military security team to accompany the FBI team. This option was not pursued.

[69] Senate Select Committee on Intelligence, World Wide Threats Hearing, March 13, 2013.

interests are not deterred by criminal investigations. Because members of terrorist organizations that attack U.S. interests around the world are conducting more than a crime, they must be responded to accordingly to be thwarted.

The Administration's decision to respond to the terrorist attacks with an FBI criminal investigation did a public disservice in two ways. First, it prevented the American public from fully understanding the motivation of the terrorist attacks and the ongoing nature of the threat against U.S. interests in the region. Second, by using a compromised criminal investigation as a justification to initially withhold significant information, it skewed the public's perception and understanding of the events before, during, and after the terrorist attacks, thereby eroding public trust and confidence in the information the Administration did eventually share and release in the aftermath.

An Inadequate State Department Accountability Review Board Process

The State Department's Accountability Review Board (ARB) highlights the "systemic failures" of Washington, D.C.-based decision-makers that left the Benghazi Mission with significant security shortfalls. Yet, the Board also failed to conduct an appropriately thorough and independent review of which officials bear responsibility for those decisions.

After Secretary Clinton determined that the attacks that led to the deaths of Ambassador Stevens, Information Officer Sean Smith, and U.S. security personnel, and former U.S. Navy SEALs, Glen Doherty and Tyrone Woods on September 11, 2012, involved loss of life at or related to a U.S. mission abroad,[70] she convened an Accountability Review Board, headed by Thomas Pickering, a retired U.S. ambassador, to examine the facts and circumstances of the attacks and to report findings and recommendations.[71]

The ARB made several findings that are consistent with facts uncovered in the Committees' ongoing investigations:

1. there was no protest prior to the attack, which was "unanticipated" in "scale and intensity";
2. there was a "pervasive realization among personnel who served in Benghazi that the Special Mission was not a high priority for Washington when it came to security-related requests"; and
3. regarding the Special Mission's security posture, there was an inadequate number of DS staff in Benghazi on the day of the attack. [do we mean "was" or "was not"?]

---

[70] "Convening of an Accountability Review Board To Examine the Circumstances Surrounding the Deaths of Personnel Assigned in Support of the U.S. Government Mission to Libya in Benghazi, Libya on September 11, 2012," Notice by the Department of State, Federal Register, October 4, 2012, available at https://www.federalregister.gov/articles/2012/10/04/2012-24504/convening-of-an-accountability-review-board-to-examine-the-circumstances-surrounding-the-deaths-of.
[71] *Id.*

Appendix

A number of the ARB findings, however, are inconsistent with facts uncovered by the Committees and appear to incorrectly place or imply blame for the attacks:

- The Board determined "systemic failures" in Washington, D.C. led to decisions that left the Benghazi Mission with significant security shortfalls. Specifically, the Board found key leadership failures in the Diplomatic Security (DS) Bureau as well as in the Bureau of Near Eastern Affairs (NEA) which led to confusion over decision-making in relation to security and policy in Benghazi. These factors likely contributed to the insufficient priority given to the Benghazi Mission's security-related requests. The Board's finding regarding the security decisions in Benghazi, however, was limited to Diplomatic Security professionals and the Bureau of Near Eastern Affairs. **The Committees' review shows that the leadership failure in relation to security and policy in Benghazi extended to the highest levels of the State Department, including Secretary Clinton.**

- The Board attempted to shift blame to Congress, asserting Congress "must do its part ... and provide necessary resources to the State Department to address security risks and meet mission imperatives." This finding implies that a lack of appropriations from Congress led to the security decisions in Benghazi. **Under direct questioning from Members of Congress, State Department personnel have testified that funding was not a reason for the drawdown of security levels in Benghazi.**[72]

- The **Board determined there was no breach of duty by any single U.S. Government employee,** citing legal limits on the definition of breach of duty. The Committees find the Board's determination in the area of disciplinary action especially unsatisfactory, as the Board ascertained the gross mismanagement among senior leadership at the State Department contributed to the inadequate security for the Benghazi Mission.[73] **The House Foreign Affairs Committee expects to consider anticipated legislation to provide future Accountability Review Boards with the authority to recommend disciplinary action against a State Department employee when misconduct or unsatisfactory performance leads to a security incident.**

- The Board also determined the security systems and procedures in place were implemented properly. The Committees are deeply concerned with this determination as extensive oversight work uncovered repeated failures by senior State Department officials to support the U.S. Mission in Libya's security requests, even in the face of overwhelming evidence that such security was needed.

---

[72] Testimony of Deputy Assistant Secretary of State for Diplomatic Security Charlene Lamb before the House Committee on Oversight and Government Reform, October 10, 2012; email exchange between Assistant Secretary Eric Boswell and Diplomatic Security Chief Financial Officer Robert Baldre, September 28, 2012 ("I do not feel that we have ever been at a point where we sacrificed security due to a lack of funding...Typically Congress has provided sufficient funding.")

[73] Department of State, Accountability Review Board for Benghazi Attack of September 2012, Dec. 19, 2012, p. 4.

Appendix

- The Board echoed other Administration attempts to lay blame for the Benghazi attacks at the feet of the Intelligence Community (IC) by highlighting that U.S. intelligence provided no immediate and specific warning of the attack. A Congressional review of the facts reveals that, while the IC had no awareness of an imminent attack on the TMF in Benghazi, the **IC provided State Department officials and others countless reports on the deteriorating security situation in Benghazi and the risks faced by U.S. diplomatic personnel**.

Analysis of the Accountability Review Board

While the work of the ARB provides some insight into the decisions leading up to the attacks, its report fundamentally fails to satisfy its legislative mandate to conduct a thorough review of accountability within the State Department.

While Secretary Hillary Clinton claimed she accepted "responsibility" for Benghazi, the Committees remain concerned that the ARB neglected to directly examine the role that she and her Deputy Secretaries played in overseeing the gross mismanagement or the "systemic failures" within the Department. The Committees note the Board has failed to provide a satisfactory explanation as to why it did not interview Secretary Clinton or her Deputies. In a similar vein, it is unclear why the ARB report made no reference to Under Secretary Patrick Kennedy's decision to withdraw a SST from Libya, despite multiple warnings from Ambassador Stevens of a deteriorating security environment. The ARB's complete omission of the roles played by these individuals undermines the credibility of its findings and recommendations.

The Committees have determined that this Accountability Review Board was staffed by current and former State Department employees. The Board's reluctance to undertake a more comprehensive investigation, and to make more forceful recommendations, may have stemmed from the fact that the State Department's decisions and actions were investigated internally, undermining public confidence that the review was objective and conducted by individuals free from institutional bias. The current "in-house orientation" of an ARB may have provided a built-in motivation or prejudice, even for the best-intentioned investigators, to deflect blame and to avoid holding specific individuals accountable, especially superiors. The House Foreign Affairs Committee will soon introduce legislation to increase the ARB's independence and objectivity. Although the report did provide some helpful recommendations regarding various State Department procedures, the Committees conclude it stopped well short of a full review of the policymakers, policies, and decisions that created the inadequate security situation that existed at the Benghazi Mission on September 11, 2012.

310

Appendix

V. The Benghazi attacks revealed fundamental flaws in the Administration's approach to securing U.S. interests and personnel around the world.

U.S. personnel on the ground in Benghazi on September 11, 2012, responded bravely and honorably, using all resources available to defend themselves and their colleagues against dozens of armed militants. The Committees' review of the attacks against U.S. interests revealed several policy failures that deserve attention and remediation if the United States hopes to avoid further catastrophes like that day.

First, the attacks revealed the United States' poor defensive posture in North Africa and the Near East. The Committees are concerned that the Administration positioned the nation's military assets in the region and established force protection requirements for U.S. personnel in Libya based, in large part, on the absence of specific, tactical intelligence warnings of an imminent attack on U.S. facilities in Benghazi. This decision did not properly account for the generalized threat posed by al-Qa'ida-affiliated groups and other extremists, the many attacks that had already occurred in and around Benghazi, or the dynamic and evolving nature of these groups.

The attack also demonstrated the limitations of the U.S. military capability and capacity to respond to "Benghazi-style" attacks in the region. The strategic posture of U.S. AFRICOM requires continued focus and oversight. While the Defense Department contends that a dedicated AFRICOM special operations force could not have arrived in time to assist the efforts on the ground in Benghazi, the force's response time would have been dependent on the precise position of those assets and whether enablers were immediately available to such a force. There is a critical link between U.S. forward presence in Europe and the military's ability to respond to contingencies in Northern Africa in particular, and the broader Middle East, in general. Additional cuts to U.S. force posture within EUCOM will likely undermine AFRICOM's ability to conduct operations on the continent.[74]

Second, the Administration failed to acknowledge a deteriorating security environment and respond to the extensive body of intelligence reporting that did exist. The IC collected considerable information about the threats in the region, and disseminated regular assessments warning of the deteriorating security environment in Benghazi, evidenced by previous events targeting American interests, facilities, and personnel. Despite ample warning, the Administration simply failed to provide adequate security arrangements to reflect the level of known risk and threats faced by U.S. personnel in the region. Moreover, in response to the intelligence available and in anticipation that a terrorist attack could occur on the anniversary of the terrorist attacks of September 11, 2001, the military apparently raised its force protection levels at regional military installations. But the military did not increase its readiness or posture

---

[74] Testimony from EUCOM Commander, Admiral Stavridis, March 15, 2013, before the Armed Services Committee, "They [bases in Europe] are the forward operating bases for 21st century security. They allow us to support Carter Ham in Africa. They allow us to support Jim Mattis in the Levant, in the near Middle East, and indeed in Central Asia. So geography matters as well."

assets to respond to unforeseen events. The Administration's lack of sufficient consideration of the broader security and political context continues to lend doubt to the U.S. Government's ability to respond to, or prevent, the next attack on U.S. assets and interests in Libya and the region.

Third, the attacks highlight the failure of the Administration to properly plan for the post-Gadhafi environment. After the U.S.-backed Libyan revolution resulted in the end of the Gadhafi regime, the Administration failed to provide sufficient U.S. security elements to protect U.S. interests on the ground. Despite repeated requests for further security by U.S. officials working in the high-risk, high-threat environment, requests were denied by senior leadership at the State Department. Moreover, the Administration does not have a clear policy that defines U.S. interests or a strategy designed to comprehensively secure U.S. interests in the region and achieve U.S. policy goals. Thus, the Administration was willing to provide necessary force to expel Gadhafi in support of the Libyan opposition, yet it simply failed to provide sufficient protection for the U.S. personnel and interests that remained.

Fourth, the events after the attacks present similar concerns. The FBI was seriously hamstrung in its ability to quickly access the Benghazi site, and its investigation and interview of key witnesses were too slow. The Administration did not ensure adequate security for a swift, thorough, and accurate FBI investigation. It should have considered deploying other non-civilian agencies to perform the mission. A civilian investigative team is not the most effective resource to investigate a national security attack in an unstable region with inadequate security.

Fifth, the Administration perpetuated a deliberately misleading and incomplete narrative that the attacks evolved from a political demonstration by minimizing the role played by al-Qa'ida-affiliated entities and other groups. White House officials directed that talking points be changed to protect the reputation of the State Department, highlighting the overall desire to dismiss the continued threat posed by al-Qa'ida-affiliated and other extremist groups in the region. Specifically, the facts reveal that the talking points were modified to remove references to likely participation by Islamic extremists. They were also altered to remove references to the threat of extremists linked to al-Qa'ida in Benghazi and eastern Libya, including information about at least five other attacks against foreign interests in Benghazi by unidentified assailants, including a June 2012 attack against the British Ambassador's convoy. It is clear that the State Department expressed concerns – and was backed by the White House – that the information be removed to avoid criticism for ignoring the general threat environment in Benghazi.

In sum, the events in Benghazi thus reflect this Administration's lack of a comprehensive national security strategy or effective defense posture in the region. **This singular event will be repeated unless the United States recognizes and responds to the threats faced around the world, and properly positions resources and security assets to reflect those threats.** Until that time, the United States will remain in a reactionary mode and should expect many more situations like Benghazi, where those on the ground act bravely, but the United States simply fails to provide the resources for an adequate response. Ultimately, those opposed to U.S. interests will continue to take advantage of perceived U.S. weakness, the United States will continue to lose credibility with our allies, and we will face the worst of all possible outcomes in strategically important locations around the world.

Congress must maintain pressure on the Administration to ensure that the United States takes all necessary steps to find the Benghazi attackers. Congress will also articulate to the American people the true nature of the threats faced around the world, and advocate for a more robust and proper defense posture for the United States. The Committees expect the Administration to fully comply with all current and future document requests about the attacks, and the Committees will continue reviewing several outstanding questions detailed below.

In light of the facts and unanswered questions documented in this progress report, the House Armed Services Committee will continue to review:

- The U.S. government's assumptions and risk analysis – as reflected in the U.S. military and State Department posture in Libya and the region – given the historic importance and activities of extremists and al-Qa'ida-associated groups in Libya;

- The precise nature of the intelligence, if any, that was lost by the failure of U.S. officials to gain quick access to the U.S. facilities in Benghazi after the attacks;

- U.S. policymakers' assumptions about al-Qa'ida, the global jihad, and the use of applying U.S. military resources to weak states, ungoverned spaces, and insecure contexts;

- The 1) operational capability, 2) resourcing, 3) readiness, and 4) intelligence collection and analysis of our forces in light of the Benghazi attacks;

- The implications of the events in Benghazi for conventional forces', the Fleet Anti-Terrorism Forces' (FAST), and special operations forces' training, readiness, resourcing, and posture;

- The U.S. Africa Command's Commander in-Extremis Force (CIF) for fully operational capability and posture; and

- The intelligence, surveillance, and reconnaissance (ISR) capability, capacity, and requirements analysis of our forces in light of the Benghazi attacks.

The House Foreign Affairs Committee will continue to review:

- The ARB process and the need to create a more independent review body with greater ability to make disciplinary recommendations;

- The responsibility of senior State Department officials for the failure to provide proper security prior to the Benghazi attacks;

- Needed improvements in embassy security; and

- The State Department's alertness to the overall political climate and resultant terrorist threats in high-risk environments.

The House Judiciary Committee will continue to review:

- The Administration's decision to respond to the attacks with an FBI investigation;

- The U.S. government's access to specific detainees and potential suspects; and

- The status of the FBI investigation.

The House Oversight and Government Reform Committee will continue to review:

- Interagency coordination, information sharing, and decision making leading up to, during, and after the attacks in Benghazi, particularly with a view toward both preventing and improving the response to similar attacks in the future;

- The Administration's lack of transparency and accountability, including providing misleading information to the public and Congress;

- The inadequacy of the Administration's investigation of the attacks, including the decision to treat the attacks as a law enforcement matter and the shortcomings of the Accountability Review Board;

- The Administration's treatment of personnel and whistleblowers following the attack on Benghazi; and

- Any new or outstanding issues raised by whistleblowers.

- The Committee will also amplify and support the efforts of other Committees, as requested.

The House Permanent Select Committee on Intelligence will continue to review:

- The IC's success at identifying and tracking the attackers;

- The IC's information sharing among agencies and the incorporation of on-the-ground information into formal intelligence channels to better allow analysts to review such information in a timely fashion; and

- The value of on-the-ground reporting versus other intelligence reporting in a crisis.

APPENDIX

Appendix I: Oversight Activities by Committee

The Committees have thus far reviewed tens of thousands of documents, including agency and White House emails, intelligence reporting, summaries of FBI interviews, classified and unclassified cables, and the various versions of the talking points created for HPSCI and used by Ambassador Susan Rice. They have also spoken with dozens of government officials in both interviews and open testimony. As the Committees' reviews are ongoing, they expect full cooperation and compliance by the Administration with all past and future document and interview requests.

House Armed Services Committee:

- Systematic monitoring of intelligence traffic and multiple secure calls with DoD.

- HASC staff briefings and discussions with outside experts.

- HASC Chairman formal letters of inquiry to:
  o President Barack Obama
  o General Martin Dempsey, Chairman of the Joint Chiefs of Staff
  o Vice Admiral Kurt Tidd, Director of Operations, The Joint Staff
  o Lieutenant General Flynn, Director of the Defense Intelligence Agency
  o General Carter Ham, Commander of U.S. Africa Command (AFRICOM)
  o Admiral William McRaven, Commander of U.S. Special Operations Command (SOCOM)

- September 12, 2012: Staff classified briefing on Weapons of Mass Destruction (WMD) in Libya.

- September 19, 2012: Full Committee hearing on the attack in Benghazi.

- October 18, 2012: Staff classified briefing on intelligence and operations related to the attack in Benghazi.

- October 29, 2012: Chairman letter to the President.

- November 20, 2012: Staff classified briefing on intelligence and operations related to the attack in Benghazi.

- November 16, 2012: Staff participated in DoD briefing to House Members.

- November 29, 2012: Full Committee, Members only, briefing on the attack in Benghazi.

- February 6, 2013: Full Committee briefing on intelligence and operations related to North and East Africa.

APPENDIX

- March 15, 2013: Full Committee hearing on the posture of U.S. EUCOM and U.S. AFRICOM.

House Foreign Affairs Committee:

- HFAC sent six letters – individually and collaboratively with sister Committees – requesting documents and information from the State Department. Obtained a public commitment by Secretary Kerry to reassess the restricted manner by which documents have been provided to the Committee.

- Reviewed thousands of pages of documents and information produced by the State Department pursuant to this investigation. It has interviewed State Department and DoD personnel.

- Approached a DS agent who was on the scene in a not-yet-successful effort to obtain additional information. This individual wishes to remain anonymous.

- Building on its Benghazi investigation, the Committee is taking a broader look at embassy security to determine whether the State Department is adequately protecting its personnel at other diplomatic facilities. Improving embassy security is a Committee legislative priority. The Committee is particularly concerned about, and is currently investigating, the security situation at the U.S. Embassy in Afghanistan.

- November 14, 2012: Classified briefing for Committee Members and cleared staff.

- November 15, 2012: Full Committee hearing with private experts entitled, "Benghazi and Beyond: What Went Wrong on September 11, 2012, and How to Prevent it from Happening at other Frontline Posts, Part I."

- December 19, 2012: Classified briefing for Committee Members and cleared staff with Ambassador Pickering and Admiral Mullen, Chair and Vice Chair of the Accountability Review Board.

- December 20, 2012: Full Committee hearing with State Department Deputy Secretaries Burns and Nides entitled, "Benghazi Attack, Part II: The Accountability Review Board Report."

- January 23, 2013: Full Committee hearing with Secretary of State Hillary Clinton entitled, "Terrorist Attack in Benghazi: The Secretary of State's View." (Committee Members submitted more than 100 Questions For the Record and have received responses to nearly all.)

Appendix

House Judiciary Committee:

- Following the September 11, 2012, Benghazi, Libya, terrorist attack, House Judiciary Committee staff and members received classified briefings from IC components, including the FBI.

House Committee on Government and Oversight Reform

- September 20, 2012: Letter from National Security Subcommittee Chairman Jason Chaffetz to Secretary of State Hillary Clinton requesting documents and information related to the Benghazi attacks and Libya-related security decisions.

- September 27, 2012: Staff interview of Lieutenant Colonel Andrew Wood, former commander of the Site Security Team at Embassy Tripoli.

- October 1, 2012: House Oversight and Government Reform Committee Chairman Darrell Issa and Chairman Chaffetz interview Eric Nordstrom, former Regional Security Officer at Embassy Tripoli.

- October 2, 2012: Letter from Chairmen Issa and Chaffetz to Secretary Clinton requesting information about the State Department's awareness of the deteriorating security environment in Libya.

- October 6, 2012: Chairman Chaffetz travels to Stuttgart, Germany, to meet with General Carter Ham, Commanding Officer, U.S. Africa Command.

- October 7, 2012: Chairman Chaffetz travels to Tripoli, Libya, to meet with Embassy leadership.

- October 9, 2012: Transcribed interview of David Oliveira, former Assistant Regional Security Officer at the Benghazi Special Mission Compound.

- October 9, 2012: Transcribed interview of Charlene Lamb, Deputy Assistant Secretary of State for International Programs, Bureau of Diplomatic Security.

- October 10, 2012: Full Committee hearing entitled "The Security Failures of Benghazi."

- October 19, 2012: Letter from Chairmen Issa and Chaffetz to President Obama requesting information about White House involvement in Libya-related security decisions.

- October 25, 2012: Transcribed interview of Erfana Dar, former Special Assistant to Under Secretary of State for Management Patrick Kennedy.

Appendix

- October 29, 2012: Letter from Chairmen Issa and Chaffetz to Secretary Clinton requesting information about any investigations conducted by the Department or the Government of Libya in response to the April 6, 2012, and June 6, 2012, bombings of the Benghazi Special Mission Compound.

- November 1, 2012: Letter from Chairmen Issa and Chaffetz to Secretary Clinton requesting documents and information related to media reports about pre-attack surveillance of the Benghazi Special Mission Compound.

- November 16, 2012: Letter from Chairmen Issa and Chaffetz to Secretary Clinton reiterating the Committee's unfulfilled request for documents and information related to the Benghazi attacks.

- November 20, 2012: Letter from Chairmen Issa and Chaffetz to Acting CIA Director Michael Morrell requesting an official, unclassified timeline of CIA actions in response to the Benghazi attacks.

- November 26, 2012: Letter from Chairmen Issa and Chaffetz to Secretary of Defense Leon Panetta requesting information about the U.S. military response to the Benghazi attacks.

- December 13, 2012: Classified briefing by the Defense Department on actions taken in response to the Benghazi attacks.

- January 12, 2013: Chairman Issa travels to Rota, Spain, to meet with military personnel sent to reinforce security at Embassy Tripoli immediately following the attacks in Benghazi.

- January 28, 2013: Joint letter from House Foreign Affairs Committee Chairman Ed Royce and Chairmen Issa and Chaffetz to Secretary Clinton requesting access to all documents reviewed by, and the names of all individuals interviewed by, the Accountability Review Board.

- March 15, 2013: Members of the Committee receive a classified briefing from General Ham.

- The Committee has reviewed over 25,000 pages of classified and unclassified documents made available by the State Department.

- The Committee has heard from, and continues to hear from, multiple individuals with direct and/or indirect information about events surrounding the attacks in Benghazi.

Appendix

House Permanent Select Committee on Intelligence:

- Requested, received, and reviewed thousands of pages of documents, including emails, cables, and classified intelligence assessments. These documents contain various drafts of the talking points created for HPSCI and used by Ambassador Rice, and emails from Administration officials, including those from White House officials, related to the creation of those talking points. The Committee continues to submit questions for the record and receive documents from the IC on an ongoing basis.

- September 13, 2012: Full Committee classified roundtable discussion with NCTC Director Olsen.

- September 14, 2012: Full Committee classified roundtable discussion with Director of CIA, David H. Petraeus.

- November 15, 2012: Full Committee classified hearing on Benghazi attacks with officials from the Office of the Director of National Intelligence (ODNI), CIA, NCTC, DoD, FBI, and State.

- November 16, 2012: Full Committee classified hearing on Benghazi Attacks with former Director of CIA Petraeus.

- December 13, 2012: Full Committee classified hearing on efforts to find the Benghazi terrorists.

- March 19, 2013: Full Committee classified briefing led by ODNI General Counsel Bob Litt to discuss Benghazi talking points.

- The Committee staff conducted numerous staff meetings and maintains a running list of questions for the record.

- HPSCI Chairman Rogers sent a letter to Acting CIA Director Morell raising his concerns about information sharing and analytic issues uncovered to date.

Appendix

Appendix II: Consolidated Timeline of Events

March-October 2011

The Libyan revolution was supported by the United States most directly in the form of NATO air operations, which lasted from March through October of 2011.

Tuesday, December 27, 2011

A State Department memorandum circulated at the end of 2011 recommended that U.S. personnel remain in Benghazi. It explained that many Libyans were "strongly" in favor of a U.S. outpost in Benghazi, in part because they believed a U.S. presence in eastern Libya would ensure that the new Tripoli-based government fairly considered eastern interests.

Wednesday, March 28, 2012

Ambassador Cretz sent a cable to Secretary Clinton requesting additional security assets. Specifically, he asked for the continued deployment of both Mobile Security Detachment (MSD) teams, or at least additional DS agents to replace them, as well as the full five DS agents which the December 2011 memorandum claimed would be stationed in Benghazi.

Friday, April 6, 2012

The Temporary Mission Facility (TMF) in Benghazi came under attack when disgruntled Libyan contract guards allegedly threw a small improvised explosive device (IED) over the perimeter wall. No casualties were reported.

Thursday, April 19, 2012

State responded to Ambassador Cretz's request for additional security assets. The cable response to Tripoli bears Secretary Clinton's signature, and specifically acknowledges Ambassador Cretz's March 28 request for additional security. Despite the Ambassador's March request, the April cable from Clinton stipulates that the plan to drawdown security assets will proceed as planned. The cable further recommends that State's Bureau of Diplomatic Security and the U.S Mission in Libya conduct a "joint re-assessment of the number of DS agents requested for Benghazi."

Wednesday, June 6, 2012

The TMF was attacked again by unknown assailants who used an IED powerful enough to blow a hole in the perimeter wall. Again, no casualties were reported.

Thursday, June 7, 2012

Ambassador Stevens made a personal plea for an increase in security. In a June 2012 email, he told a Department official that with national elections in July and August, the Mission "would feel much safer if we could keep two MSD teams with us through this period [to support] our staff and [personal detail] for me and the [Deputy Chief of Mission] and any VIP visitors." The

Department official replied that due to other commitments and limited resources, "unfortunately, MSD cannot support the request."

Monday, July 9, 2012
A July 2012 cable from Ambassador Stevens stressed that security conditions in Libya had not met the requisite benchmarks established by the Department and the U.S. Mission in Libya to initiate a security drawdown, and requested that security personnel, including the MSD teams, be permitted to stay. After being apprised of this pending request, Deputy Assistant Secretary Charlene Lamb exclaimed: "NO I do not [I repeat] not want them to ask for the MSD team to stay!" The MSD team was withdrawn, though it is unclear whether the Department ever formally rejected the Ambassador's July request.

Monday, June 11, 2012
Britain's ambassador to Libya was in a convoy of cars attacked in the eastern city of Benghazi. The convoy was hit by a rocket-propelled grenade (RPG). Two protection officers were injured.

Monday, August 27, 2012
U.S. officials were aware that Libya remained volatile. They were particularly concerned with the numerous armed militias that operated freely throughout the country. In August 2011, the State Department warned U.S. citizens against traveling to Libya, explaining that "inter-militia conflict can erupt at any time or any place."

- The security environment in Benghazi was similarly deteriorating throughout 2012. From June 2011 to July 2012, then-Regional Security Officer (RSO) for Libya Eric Nordstrom, the principal security adviser to the U.S. Ambassador to Libya, compiled a list of over 200 security incidents in Libya, 50 of which took place in Benghazi. These included violent acts directed against diplomats and diplomatic facilities, international organizations, and third-country nationals, as well as large-scale militia clashes.
- In spite of these mounting security concerns, for most of 2012 the Benghazi Mission was forced to rely on fewer than the approved number of DS agents. Specifically, while the State Department memorandum signed by Under Secretary Kennedy claimed that five agents would be provided, this was only the case for 23 days in 2012. Reports indicate the Benghazi Mission was typically staffed with only three agents, and sometimes as few as one or two.

Monday, September 10, 2012
Ambassador Stevens travelled to Benghazi on September 10, 2012, both to fill staffing gaps between principal officers in Benghazi, and to allow the Ambassador to reconnect with local contacts. There were also plans for him to attend the establishment of a new American Corner at a local Benghazi school.

Appendix

SEPTEMBER 11 ATTACK TIMELINE

Tuesday, September 11, 2012

All times are Eastern European Time (EET, Benghazi)

~9:42 p.m.   The attack begins at the TMF in Benghazi. Dozens of lightly armed men approached the TMF, quickly and deliberately breached the front gate, and set fire to the guard house and main diplomatic building. The attackers included members of Libya-based Ansar al-Sharia (AAS) and al-Qa'ida in the Lands of the Islamic Maghreb (AQIM), among other groups. A State Department officer in the TMF's Tactical Operations Center immediately put out calls for help to the TMF Annex — another facility for U.S. officials — the U.S. Embassy in Tripoli, and State Department Headquarters in Washington, DC. At the time of the attack, Ambassador Stevens, Sean Smith, the information management officer, and one of the five Diplomatic Security (DS) officers were located in Villa C, the main building of the TMF. (DoD timeline/pg. 11)

9:59 p.m.   An unarmed, unmanned, surveillance aircraft is directed to reposition overhead the Benghazi facility. (DoD timeline)

~10:02 p.m.   Within 20 minutes of the attack, Stevens, Smith, and the DS officer suffered effects from smoke inhalation inside the main diplomatic building and tried to escape by crawling along the floor towards a window. The DS officer unknowingly lost touch with Ambassador Stevens and Mr. Smith somewhere along the smoke-filled escape route. After crawling out of a window and realizing that Ambassador Stevens and Mr. Smith were not with him, the DS officer, under gunfire, repeatedly re-entered the burning building to search for them. The DS officer used his radio to call for help. Security officers from other parts of the TMF complex responded and supported the DS officer's search for the missing individuals. (pg. 11)

10:05 p.m.   In an "Ops Alert" issued shortly after the attack began, the State Department Operations Center notified senior Department Officials, the White House Situation Room, and others, that the Benghazi compound was under attack and that "approximately 20 armed people fired shots; explosions have been heard as well."

~10:07 p.m.   A U.S. security team departed the Annex for the TMF. The security team tried to secure heavy weapons from militia members encountered along the route, and faced some resistance in getting to the TMF. Even in the face of those obstacles, the Annex security team arrived, under enemy fire, within 25 minutes of the beginning of the initial assault. Over the course of the following hour, the Annex security team joined the TMF security officers in searching for Ambassador Stevens and Mr. Smith. Together, they repelled sporadic gunfire and RPG fire and assembled all other U.S. personnel at the facility. Officers retrieved the body of Mr. Smith, but did not find Ambassador Stevens.

10:32 p.m. The National Military Command Center at the Pentagon, after receiving initial reports of the incident from the State Department, notifies the Office of the Secretary of Defense and the Joint Staff. The information is quickly passed to Secretary Panetta and General Dempsey. (DoD timeline)

11:00 p.m. Secretary Panetta and General Dempsey attend a previously scheduled meeting with the President at the White House. The leaders discuss potential responses to the emerging situation. (DoD timeline)

11:10 p.m. The diverted surveillance aircraft arrives on station over the Benghazi facility. (DoD timeline)

~11:15 p.m. After about 90 minutes of repeated attempts to go into the burning building to search for the Ambassador, the Annex security team assessed that the security situation was deteriorating and they could not continue their search. The Annex security team loaded all U.S. personnel into two vehicles and departed the TMF for the Annex. The exiting vehicles left under heavy gunfire and faced at least one roadblock in their route to the Annex. The first vehicle left around 11:15 p.m. and the second vehicle departed at about 11:30 p.m. All surviving American personnel departed the facility by 11:30 p.m.

Wednesday, September 12, 2012

12:06 p.m. In a second "Ops Alert" the State Department Operations Center reported that al-Qaeda linked Ansar al-Sharia claimed responsibility for the attack and had called for an attack on Embassy Tripoli

12:00-2:00 a.m. Secretary Panetta convenes a series of meetings in the Pentagon with senior officials including General Dempsey and General Ham. They discuss additional response options for Benghazi and for the potential outbreak of further violence throughout the region, particularly in Tunis, Tripoli, Cairo, and Sana'a. During these meetings, Secretary Panetta authorizes:

Appendix

- A Fleet Antiterrorism Security Team (FAST) platoon, stationed in Rota, Spain, to prepare to deploy to Benghazi, and a second FAST platoon, also stationed in Rota, Spain, to prepare to deploy to the Embassy in Tripoli.
- A EUCOM special operations force, which is training in Central Europe, to prepare to deploy to an intermediate staging base in southern Europe.
- A special operations force based in the United States to prepare to deploy to an intermediate staging base in southern Europe.

During this period, actions are verbally conveyed from the Pentagon to the affected Combatant Commands in order to expedite movement of forces upon receipt of formal authorization.

12:30 a.m.	A seven-man security team from U.S. Embassy Tripoli, including two DoD personnel, departs for Benghazi.
~1:15 a.m.	The American security team from Tripoli lands in Benghazi. (DoD timeline)
2:30 a.m.	The National Military Command Center conducts a Benghazi Conference Call with representatives from AFRICOM, EUCOM, CENTCOM, TRANSCOM, SOCOM, and the four services.
2:39 a.m.	As ordered by Secretary Panetta, the National Military Command Center transmits formal authorization for the two FAST platoons, and associated equipment, to prepare to deploy and for the EUCOM special operations force, and associated equipment, to move to an intermediate staging base in southern Europe.
2:53 a.m.	As ordered by Secretary Panetta, the National Military Command Center transmits formal authorization to deploy a special operations force, and associated equipment, from the United States to an intermediate staging base in southern Europe.
5:00 a.m.	A second, unmanned, unarmed surveillance aircraft is directed to relieve the initial asset still over Benghazi.
5:15 a.m.	At around 5:15 a.m., within 15 minutes of the Tripoli team's arrival at the Annex from the airport, a short but deadly coordinated terrorist attack began at the Annex. The attack, which included small arms, rocket-propelled grenade (RPG),

and well-aimed mortar fire, killed two American security officers, and severely wounded two others.

6:05 a.m.   AFRICOM orders a C-17 aircraft in Germany to prepare to deploy to Libya to evacuate Americans.

7:40 a.m.   The first wave of American personnel depart Benghazi for Tripoli via airplane. (DoD timeline)

10:00 a.m.   The second wave of Americans, including the fallen, depart Benghazi for Tripoli via airplane.

2:15 p.m.   The C-17 departs Germany en route to Tripoli to evacuate Americans.

7:17 p.m.   The C-17 departs Tripoli en route Ramstein, Germany, with the American personnel and the remains of Mr. Sean Smith, Mr. Tyrone Woods, and Mr. Glen Doherty.

7:57 p.m.   The EUCOM special operations force, and associated equipment, arrives at an intermediate staging base in southern Europe.

8:56 p.m.   The FAST platoon, and associated equipment, arrives in Tripoli.

9:28 p.m.   The special operations force deployed from the United States, and associated equipment, arrives at an intermediate staging base in southern Europe.

10:19 p.m.   The C-17 arrives in Ramstein, Germany.

END OF SEPTEMBER 11 ATTACK TIMELINE

<u>Wednesday, September 12, 2012</u>
- FBI formally opens an investigation into the deaths of Ambassador Sevens and the three other Americans killed in the attack.
- Relying on analytical intuition with limited reporting on September 12, 2012, IC analysts correctly evaluated soon after the attacks that the event was a terrorist attack against a U.S. facility, likely conducted by Islamic extremists.

<u>Thursday, September 13, 2012</u>
Beginning on September 13, 2012, analysts began receiving and relying on a larger volume of diverse intelligence reporting that referenced protests and demonstrations in Benghazi. Analysts

revised their assessments again to determine finally that the attack was deliberate and that a protest was not occurring at the time of the attack. The IC's modification of its assessments reflects the reasonable evolution of tactical intelligence analysis.

Saturday, September 15, 2012
HPSCI staff received the IC talking points on the Benghazi attack.

Sunday, September 16, 2012
On Sunday, September 16, 2012, U.S. Ambassador to the United Nations Susan Rice appeared on five morning talk shows to discuss the Administration's account of the attack. In nearly identical statements, she stated that the attack was a spontaneous protest in response to a "hateful video."

Wednesday, September 19, 2012
The National Counterterrorism Center Director testified before the Senate Homeland Security and Government Affairs Committee that our diplomats died "in the course of a terrorist attack on our embassy." This testimony marked a significant shift in the Administration's rhetoric.

Thursday, September 20, 2012
After Director of NCTC's testimony, Administration officials began referring to the event as a terrorist attack. On September 20, 2012, Jay Carney stated that, "it is, I think, self-evident that what happened in Benghazi was a terrorist attack."

Friday, September 21, 2012
Secretary Clinton stated that, "What happened in Benghazi was a terrorist attack, and we will not rest until we have tracked down and brought to justice the terrorists who murdered four Americans."

Thursday, October 4, 2012
- Due to security concerns and bureaucratic entanglements among the Departments of Justice, State, and Defense, the FBI team investigating the terrorist attack did not access the crime scene until more than three weeks later, on October 4, 2012. The FBI spent less than one day collecting evidence at the TMF. FBI officials indicated that the security situation delayed and undermined a more thorough investigation of the site.
- Secretary Clinton convened an Accountability Review Board (ARB), headed by Thomas Pickering, a retired U.S. ambassador, to examine the facts and circumstances of the attacks and to report findings and recommendations.

Appendix

Tuesday, October, 9, 2012

The State Department held a conference call briefing for reporters in which the Department publicly acknowledged that there had been no protest outside the Benghazi diplomatic facility prior to the assault. State Department officials would testify before the House Oversight and Government Reform Committee the next day.

Tuesday, November 27, 2012

Administration officials have blamed their initial statements on "evolving" intelligence reports. To that end, Ambassador Rice stated on November 27, 2012, that Acting CIA Director Michael Morell "explained that the talking points provided by the intelligence community, and the initial assessment upon which they were based, were incorrect in a key respect: there was no protest or demonstration in Benghazi."

Notes

Introduction

1. Dennis Chalker with Kevin Dockery, *One Perfect Op: An Insider's Account of the Navy SEAL Special Warfare Teams* (New York: Harper Paperbacks, 2011), page 34.

Chapter 1: The Froggy Origins of the Navy SEALs

1. Bill Sizemore, "Medal of Honor Recipient Shares Story in Beach," *Virginian Pilot*, May 19, 2010.

Chapter 2: The Violent Birth of SEAL Team Six

1. T. L. Bosiljevac, *SEALs: UDT/SEAL Operations in Vietnam* (Boulder, CO: Paladin Press, 1990).

2. Thomas H. Keith, and J. Terry Riebling, *SEAL Warrior: The Only Easy Day Was Yesterday* (New York, NY: Thomas Dunne Books/St. Martin's Griffin, 2010).

3. "Man of the Year: The Mystic Who Lit the Fires of Hatred," *Time*, January 7, 1980, www.content.time.com/time/magazine/article/ 0,9171,923854,00.html.

4. Fereydoun Hoveyda, *The Shah and the Ayatollah: Iranian Mythology and Islamic Revolution* (Westport, CT: Praeger, 2003).

5. Richard A. Radvanyi, *Operation Eagle Claw—Lessons Learned* (Quantico, VA: United States Marine Corps Command and Staff College, 2002).

6. The full account comes from Tim Wells, *444 Days: The Hostages Remember* (San Diego: Harcourt Brace Jovanovich, 1985): "Fortunately, we were sequestered from the press. They were kept down at the front gate of the hospital where they couldn't get to us. We were free to wander down there and talk to them if we wanted to, but we didn't have to. I remember Bruce German walked by the gate, and one of the reporters asked him if he'd ever go back to Iran. Bruce said, 'Yeah, in a B-52.'" (page 438)

Chapter 4: Drago's War

1. Based on an author interview with Drago in April 2013.
2. Ibid.

Chapter 6: Fallujah: The Perfect Op That Led to Prosecutions

1. Jeremy Scahill, *Blackwater: The Rise of the World's Most Powerful Mercenary Army* (New York, NY: Nation Books, 2007), page 88.

2. Jeffrey Gettleman, "Enraged Mob in Falluja Kills 4 American Contractors," *New York Times*, March 31, 2004, www.nytimes.com/2004/03/31/international/worldspecial/31CND-IRAQ.html?pagewanted=all.

Chapter 7: Benghazi, Libya: SEALs Alone

1. U.S. State Department, daily press briefing, April 5, 2011, http://www.state.gov/r/pa/prs/dpb/2011/04/160022.htm#LIBYA.

2. Joby Warrick and Liz Sly, "U.S. Envoy Arrives in Libya To Seek Ways to Help Rebels," *Washington Post*, April 6, 2011.

3. U.S. State Department, daily press briefing, April 7, 2011, http://www.state.gov/r/pa/prs/dpb/2011/04/160298.htm#LIBYA.

4. Juliane von Mittelstaedt and Volkhard Windfuhr, "The Benghazi Mission," *Der Spiegel*, June 21, 2011.

5. "Security Incidents Since June 2011," compiled by the Regional Security Office, U.S. embassy, Tripoli, Libya, November 2012, page 1. This document was obtained by ABC News and posted on its website (abcnews.go.com/images/Politics/7.19.12%20Libya%20Security .pdf). We are reporting only the incidents in Benghazi detailed in this document.

6. U.S. State Department, "On the Record Briefing: U.S. Representative to the Transitional National Council Chris Stevens on Libya," August 2, 2011, www.state.gov/r/pa/prs/ps/2011/08/169486.htm.

7. U.S. State Department, "Background Briefing on Libya," October 9, 2012, www.state.gov/r/pa/prs/ps/2012/10/198791.htm.

8. "Security Incidents Since June 2011," page 1.

9. Ibid.

10. Tabassum Zakaria, Susan Cornwell, and Hadeel al-Shalchi, "For Benghazi Diplomatic Security, U.S. Relied on Small British Firm," Reuters, October 17, 2012, www.reuters.com/article/2012/10/18/us -libya-usa-bluemountain-idUSBRE89G1TI20121018.

11. "Security Incidents Since June 2011," page 10.

12. Ibid., page 12.

13. Ibid., page 13.

14. Ibid., page 15.

15. Ibid., page 16.

16. Ibid., page 18.

17. Sheryl Attkisson and Margaret Brennan, "Security Dwindled before Deadly Libyan Consulate Attack," CBS News, October 8, 2012, www.cbsnews.com/8301-18563_162-57528335/security-dwindled -before-deadly-libyan-consulate-attack/.

18. "Security Incidents Since June 2011," page 23.

19. U.S. Senate, Committee on Homeland Security and Governmental Affairs, *Flashing Red: A Special Report on the Terrorist Attack at Benghazi*, by Joseph I. Lieberman and Susan M. Collins, December 30, 2012, page 17.

20. "Security Incidents Since June 2011," page 24.

21. Ibid., pages 24–25.

22. Ibid., page 25.

23. Ibid.

24. Cable from U.S. embassy in Tripoli, Libya, to Secretary of State in Washington, D.C., dated March 28, 2012.

25. "Security Incidents Since June 2011," page 28.

26. Ibid., page 29.

27. Ibid., page 30.

28. Chris Stephen, "US Diplomatic Mission Bombed in Libya," *Guardian* (London), June 6, 2012, www.theguardian.com/world/2012/jun/06/us-embassy-attack-libya.

29. "Security Incidents Since June 2011," page 33.

30. Ibid., pages 33–34.

31. Ibid., page 39.

32. Ibid., pages 39–40.

33. Ibid., page 40.

34. Ibid., page 41.

35. Ibid., page 44.

36. "Libyan Jihadis Claims US Consulate Attack," Agence France Presse, June 11, 2012.

37. U.S. Library of Congress, Federal Research Division, *Al Qaeda in Libya: A Profile*, August 2012, page 3, available at www.fas.org/irp/world/para/aq-libya-loc.pdf.

38. "Supporters of Shariah Call for Implementation of Islamic Law in Libya," BBC Monitoring Middle East, June 16, 2012.

39. Steve Inskeep, "In the New Libya, Lots of Guns and Calls for Shariah," *NPR Morning Edition*, June 13, 2012, www.npr.org/2012/06/13/154839952/in-the-new-libya-lots-of-guns-and-calls-for-shariah.

40. Tara Bahrampour, "As Libya Holds Post-Gaddafi Election, Islamists' Strength to Be Tested," *Washington Post*, July 4, 2012, articles.washingtonpost.com/2012-07-03/world/35487400_1_islamist-group-libyan-voters-secular-parties.

41. George Grant, "British Ambassador Escapes Missile Attack on Car," *Times* (London), June 12, 2012, www.thetimes.co.uk/tto/news/world/middleeast/article3442776.ece. Ibrahim Majbari, "RPG Hits British Diplomatic Convoy in Libya, 2 Hurt," Agence France Presse, June 11, 2012.

42. "British Guns Accounted For after Benghazi Consulate Attack," *Tripoli Post*, October 12, 2012, www.tripolipost.com/articledetail.asp?c=1&i=9292. But the article says the guns were unaccounted for!

43. Mohamed Al-Tommy and Hadeel al-Shalchi, "Gunmen Attack Tunisian Consulate in Benghazi," Reuters, June 18, 2012, http://www.reuters.com/article/2012/06/18/us-libya-gunmen-tunisia-idUSBRE85H1V620120618. "Gunmen storm Tunisian Consulate in Libya's Benghazi," Agence France Presse, June 18, 2012.

44. Chris Stephen, "Libyan Military Prosecutor Shot Dead in Benghazi," *Guardian* (London), June 22, 2012, www.theguardian.com/world/2012/jun/22/libyan-military-prosecutor-shot-benghazi.

45. As quoted in *Flashing Red*, page 7.

46. "Security Incidents Since June 2011," page 47.

47. Cable from U.S. embassy in Tripoli, Libya, to Washington, D.C., July 9, 2012.

48. Nancy A. Youssef, "Ambassador Stevens Twice Said No to Military Offers of More Security, U.S. Officials Say," McClatchyDC,

May 14, 2013, www.mcclatchydc.com/2013/05/14/191235/amb-stevens
-twice-said-no-to-military.html.

49. *Flashing Red*, page 11.

50. Testimony of Eric Nordstrom before the House Oversight
and Government Reform Committee, October 14, 2012.

Chapter 8: Benghazi 911: When SEALs Answer the Call

1. Jack Murphy and Brandon Webb, "Breaking: The Benghazi
Diary, a Hero Ambassador's Final Thoughts," June 26, 2013; sofrep.
com/22460/ambassador-chris-stevens-benghazi-diary/.

2. U.S. State Department, Accountability Review Board (ARB)
Report (unclassified), December 2012, page 19, www.state.gov/
documents/organization/202446.pdf.

3. Cable from U.S. embassy in Tripoli, Libya, to State Department, Washington, D.C.

4. Accountability Review Board Report, page 20.

5. Ibid.

6. Abd-al-Sattar Hatitah, "Al-Sharq al-Awsat Obtains the Story
of the Guards Who Talked to the Culprits of the Attack on the US
Consulate from Benghazi," *Al-Sharq al-Awsat,* October 11, 2012
(translated FBIS).

7. Nancy A. Youssef and Suliman Ali Zway, "No Protest before
Benghazi Attack, Wounded Libyan Guard Says," McClatchyDC,
September 13, 2012, www.mcclatchydc.com/2012/09/13/168415/no
-protest-before-benghazi-attack.html.

8. Hatitah, "Al-Sharq Al-Awsat Obtains the Story."

9. U.S. House of Representatives, *Interim Progress Report for the
Members of the House Republican Conference on the Events Surrounding
the September 11, 2012 Terrorist Attacks in Benghazi, Libya*, April 23,

2013, page 38, oversight.house.gov/wp-content/uploads/2013/04/Libya-Progress-Report-Final-1.pdf.

10. Siobhan Hughes and Adam Entous, "Diplomat Airs Benghazi Attack Details," *Wall Street Journal,* May 8, 2013, online.wsj.com/news/articles/SB10001424127887324244304578470880723398290.

11. *Interim Progress Report,* page 38, quoting Defense Department timeline.

12. Ibid., quoting Defense Department timeline. Accountability Review Board Report, page 2.

13. *Interim Progress Report,* page 38, quoting Defense Department timeline.

14. Ibid., page 39.

15. Ibid.

16. Ibid.

17. Hughes and Entous, "Diplomat Airs Benghazi Attack Details."

18. *Interim Progress Report,* page 39.

19. Ibid.

20. Ibid., pages 39–40. "Benghazi Timeline: How the Attack Unfolded," CBS News, November 2, 2012, www.cbsnews.com/8301-202_162-57544719/.

21. Adam Housley, "Special Forces Could've Responded to Benghazi Attack, Whistle-Blower Tells Fox News," Fox News, April 30, 2013, www.foxnews.com/politics/2013/04/30/special-ops-benghazi-whistleblower-tells-fox-news-government-could-have/.

22. Lee Ferran, "American Killed in Libya Was on Intel Mission to Track Weapons," ABC News, September 13, 2012, www.abcnews.go.com/Blotter/glen-doherty-navy-seal-killed-libya-intel-mission/story?id=17229037.

23. Jack Murphy and Brandon Webb, *Benghazi: The Definitive Report* (New York: HarperCollins, 2013).

24. Hughes and Entous, "Diplomat Airs Benghazi Attack Details."

25. *Interim Progress Report*, page 40.

26. Ibid., pages 40–41.

27. Ibid., page 41.

28. Ibid.

29. Ibid.

30. Ibid.

Chapter 9: The Rescue That Wasn't

1. Lucy Madison, "Panetta on Benghazi: We Did 'Everything We Could,'" CBS News, February 7, 2013, www.cbsnews.com/8301 -250_162-57568199/panetta-on-benghazi-we-did-everything-we -could/.

2. Julian Pecquet, "White House Defends Obama's 'Bump in the Road' Comment," *Hill*; September 24, 2012, www.thehill.com/ blogs/global-affairs/middle-east-north-africa/251265-carney-defends -obamas-bump-in-the-road-comment-on-middle-east-violence.

3. Rod Powers, "Installation Overview—Aviano Air Base, Italy," About.com, undated, usmilitary.about.com/od/airforcebaseprofiles/ ss/Aviano.htm.

4. U.S. Air Force, Aviano Air Base, "31st Operations Group," fact sheet, April 24, 2009, http://www.aviano.af.mil/library/factsheets/ factsheet.asp?id=4354.

5. James Rosen, "Sen. Graham Challenges Joint Chiefs Chairman on Benghazi Testimony," Fox News, May 10, 2013, www.foxnews.com/ politics/2013/05/09/sen-graham-challenges-joint-chiefs-chairman-on -benghazi-testimony/

6. Franklin Fisher, "Osan Airmen Practice 'Hot Pit Refueling,'" *Stars and Stripes*, March 26, 2004, www.stripes.com/news/osan -airmen-practice-hot-pit-refueling-1.18050.

7. Jake Tapper and Dana Bash, "Former Dep. Chief of Mission in Libya: U.S. Military Assets Told to Stand Down during Benghazi Attack," Fortuna's Corner, May 6, 2013, www.fortunascorner.wordpress .com/2013/05/06/former-dep-chief-of-mission-in-libya-u-s-military -assets-told-to-stand-down-during-benghazi-attack/.

8. Mark Townsend, "Benghazi Attack by Gaddafi's Forces Was 'Ploy to Negate Air Strikes,'" *Guardian* (London), March 19, 2011, www.theguardian.com/world/2011/mar/19/benghazi-gaddafi-military -air-strikes.

9. Josh Bennett, "USS *Mount Whitney* Remembers 9/11," America's Navy, press release, September 11, 2012, www.navy.mil/submit/ display.asp?story_id=69492.

10. Micah Zenko and Emma Welch, "Where the Drones Are: Mapping the Launch Pads for Obama's Secret Wars," *Foreign Policy*, May 29, 2012, www.foreignpolicy.com/articles/2012/05/29/where_the _drones_are.

11. Sharyl Attkisson, "Diplomat: U.S. Special Forces Told 'You Can't Go' to Benghazi during Attacks," CBS News, May 6, 2013, www.cbsnews.com/8301-250_162-57583014/diplomat-u.s-special -forces-told-you-cant-go-to-benghazi-during-attacks/.

12. Norman Friedman, *The Naval Institute Guide to World Naval Weapon Systems*, (Annapolis: Naval Institute Press, 2004).

Chapter 10: Benghazi Timeline

1. U.S. State Department, daily press briefing, April 5, 2011, www.state.gov/r/pa/prs/dpb/2011/04/160022.htm#LIBYA.

2. Joby Warrick and Liz Sly, "U.S. Envoy Arrives in Libya To Seek Ways to Help Rebels," *Washington Post*, April 6, 2011.

3. U.S. State Department, daily press briefing, April 7, 2011, www.state.gov/r/pa/prs/dpb/2011/04/160298.htm#LIBYA.

4. U.S. State Department, "Briefing on Recent Developments in the Middle East and Other Issues," with Jake Sullivan, April 26, 2011, www.state.gov/p/nea/rls/rm/161818.htm.

5. "Security Incidents Since June 2011," compiled by the Regional Security Office, U.S. Embassy, Tripoli, Libya, November 2012, page 1, www.abcnews.go.com/images/Politics/7.19.12%20Libya%20Security .pdf.

6. U.S. State Department, "On the Record Briefing: U.S. Representative to the Transitional National Council Chris Stevens on Libya," August 2, 2011, www.state.gov/r/pa/prs/ps/2011/08/169486 .htm.

7. U.S. State Department, "Background Briefing on Libya," October 9, 2012, http://www.state.gov/r/pa/prs/ps/2012/10/198791.htm. The person speaking is identified in the transcript as "Senior State Department Official Number One."

8. "Security Incidents Since June 2011," page 1.

9. Ibid.

10. Tabassum Zakaria, Susan Cornwell, and Hadeel al-Shalchi, "For Benghazi Diplomatic Security, U.S. Relied on Small British Firm," Reuters, October 17, 2012, www.reuters.com/article/2012/10/18/us -libya-usa-bluemountain-idUSBRE89G1TI20121018.

11. "Security Incidents Since June 2011," page 8.

12. Ibid., page 10.

13. Ibid., page 12.

14. Ibid., page 13.

15. Ibid., page 15.

16. Ibid., page 16.

17. Ibid., page 18.

18. Sheryl Attkisson and Margaret Brennan, "Security Dwindled before Deadly Libyan Consulate Attack," CBS News, October 8, 2012,

www.cbsnews.com/8301-18563_162-57528335/security-dwindled
-before-deadly-libyan-consulate-attack/.

19. "Security Incidents Since June 2011," page 23.

20. U.S. Senate, Committee on Homeland Security and Governmental Affairs, *Flashing Red: A Special Report on the Terrorist Attack at Benghazi*, by Joseph I. Lieberman and Susan M. Collins, December 30, 2012, page 17.

21. "Security Incidents Since June 2011," page 24.

22. Ibid., pages 24–25.

23. Ibid., page 25.

24. Ibid.

25. Cable from U.S. embassy in Tripoli, Libya, to Secretary of State in Washington, D.C., dated March 28, 2012.

26. "Security Incidents Since June 2011," page 28.

27. Ibid., page 29.

28. Ibid., page 30.

29. Ibid.

30. Chris Stephen, "US Diplomatic Mission Bombed in Libya," *Guardian* (London), June 6, 2012, www.theguardian.com/world/2012/jun/06/us-embassy-attack-libya.

31. "Security Incidents Since June 2011," page 31.

32. Ibid., page 32.

33. Ibid., page 33.

34. Ibid.

35. Ibid., pages 33–34.

36. Ibid., page 34.

37. Ibid., page 39.

38. Ibid., pages 39–40.

39. Ibid., page 40.

40. Ibid., page 41.

41. Ibid., page 44.

42. "Libyan Jihadis Claims US Consulate Attack," Agence France Presse, June 11, 2012.

43. U.S. Library of Congress, Federal Research Division, *Al Qaeda in Libya: A Profile*, August 2012, page 3, available at www.fas.org/irp/world/para/aq-libya-loc.pdf.

44. "Supporters of Shariah Call for Implementation of Islamic Law in Libya," BBC Monitoring Middle East, June 16, 2012.

45. Steve Inskeep, "In the New Libya, Lots of Guns and Calls for Shariah," *NPR Morning Edition*, June 13, 2012, www.npr.org/2012/06/13/154839952/in-the-new-libya-lots-of-guns-and-calls-for-shariah.

46. Tara Bahrampour, "As Libya Holds Post-Gaddafi Election, Islamists' Strength to Be Tested," *Washington Post*, July 4, 2012, www.articles.washingtonpost.com/2012-07-03/world/35487400_1_islamist-group-libyan-voters-secular-parties.

47. George Grant, "British Ambassador Escapes Missile Attack on Car," *Times* (London), June 12, 2012, www.thetimes.co.uk/tto/news/world/middleeast/article3442776.ece. Ibrahim Majbari, "RPG Hits British Diplomatic Convoy in Libya, 2 Hurt," Agence France Presse, June 11, 2012.

48. "British Guns Accounted For after Benghazi Consulate Attack," *Tripoli Post*, October 12, 2012, www.tripolipost.com/articledetail.asp?c=1&i=9292.

49. Mohamed Al-Tommy and Hadeel al-Shalchi, "Gunmen Attack Tunisian Consulate in Benghazi," Reuters, June 18, 2012, www.reuters.com/article/2012/06/18/us-libya-gunmen-tunisia-idUSBRE85H1V620120618. "Gunmen Storm Tunisian Consulate in Libya's Benghazi," Agence France Presse, June 18, 2012.

50. Chris Stephen, "Libyan Military Prosecutor Shot Dead in Benghazi," *Guardian* (London), June 22, 2012, www.theguardian.com/world/2012/jun/22/libyan-military-prosecutor-shot-benghazi.

51. As quoted in *Flashing Red*, page 7.

52. "Security Incidents Since June 2011," page 47.

53. Cable from U.S. embassy in Tripoli, Libya, to Washington, D.C., July 9, 2012.

54. Cable from U.S. embassy in Tripoli, Libya, to State Department in Washington, D.C., August 2, 2012.

55. Nancy A. Youssef, "Ambassador Stevens Twice Said No to Military Offers of More Security, U.S. Officials Say," McClatchyDC, May 14, 2013, www.mcclatchydc.com/2013/05/14/191235/amb-stevens-twice-said-no-to-military.html.

56. *Flashing Red*, 11.

57. Testimony of Eric Nordstrom before the House Oversight and Government Reform Committee, October 14, 2012.

58. U.S. State Department, Accountability Review Board (ARB) Report (unclassified), December 2012, page 19, www.state.gov/documents/organization/202446.pdf.

59. Cable from U.S. embassy in Tripoli, Libya, to Washington, D.C.

60. Accountability Review Board Report, page 20.

61. Ibid.

62. Abd-al-Sattar Hatitah, "Al-Sharq al-Awsat Obtains the Story of the Guards Who Talked to the Culprits of the Attack on the US Consulate from Benghazi," *Al-Sharq al-Awsat*, October 11, 2012 (translated FBIS).

63. Nancy A. Youssef and Suliman Ali Zway, "No Protest before Benghazi Attack, Wounded Libyan Guard Says," McClatchyDC,

September 13, 2012, www.mcclatchydc.com/2012/09/13/168415/no -protest-before-benghazi-attack.html.

64. Hatitah, "Al-Sharq Al-Awsat Obtains the Story."

65. U.S. House of Representatives, *Interim Progress Report for the Members of the House Republican Conference on the Events Surrounding the September 11, 2012 Terrorist Attacks in Benghazi, Libya*, April 23, 2013, page 38, oversight.house.gov/wp-content/uploads/2013/04/Libya -Progress-Report-Final-1.pdf.

66. Siobhan Hughes and Adam Entous, "Diplomat Airs Benghazi Attack Details," *Wall Street Journal*, May 8, 2013, online.wsj.com/news/ articles/SB10001424127887324244304578470880723398290.

67. *Interim Progress Report*, page 38, quoting Defense Department timeline.

68. Ibid., page 38. Accountability Review Board Report, page 22.

69. *Interim Progress Report*, page 38.

70. Ibid., page 39.

71. Ibid.

72. Ibid.

73. Hughes and Entous, "Diplomat Airs Benghazi Attack Details."

74. *Interim Progress Report*, page 39.

75. Ibid.

76. Ibid. "Benghazi Timeline: How the Attack Unfolded," CBS News, November 2, 2012, www.cbsnews.com/8301-202_162 -57544719/.

77. Adam Housley, "Special Forces Could've Responded to Benghazi Attack, Whistle-Blower Tells Fox News," Fox News, April 30, 2013, www.foxnews.com/politics/2013/04/30/special-ops-benghazi -whistleblower-tells-fox-news-government-could-have/.

78. *Interim Progress Report*, page 40. Hughes and Entous, "Diplomat Airs Benghazi Attack Details."

79. Hughes and Entous, "Diplomat Airs Benghazi Attack Details."

80. *Interim Progress Report*, page 40.

81. Ibid., pages 40–41.

82. Ibid., page 41.

83. Ibid.

84. Ibid.

85. Ibid.

86. Ibid.

Chapter 11: The Teams: Why the Unique Culture of the SEALs Matters

1. "Parents of Slain Navy SEAL: Obama Admin Put a Target on Our Son's Back," Fox News Insider, May 10, 2013, www.foxnewsinsider.com/2013/05/10/parents-navy-seal-aaron-vaughn-blast-biden-2011-helicopter-crash-killed-their-son.

Glossary

AFRICOM: United States Africa Command

BALACLAVA: a knitted hood commonly used by counterterrorism operators to conceal facial features

BDU: Battle Dress Uniform

BEARCAT: radio-frequency scanner

BLACK: synonym for any covert or clandestine activity

BLACK HAWK: H-60 Army chopper (troop transport)

BLOWOUT KIT: medical pouch

BOOT (BOOTLEGGER) TURN: a 180-degree turn done in a vehicle while it is moving forward. The parking or emergency brake is used in conjunction with the wheel to execute the turn. Called a bootleg because of its earliest uses by moonshiners and bootleg liquor runners.

BTR-60PB: Soviet eight-wheeled (8×8) armored personnel carrier armed with 14.5 mm KPVT heavy machine gun (500 rounds), and PKT coaxial 7.62 mm machine gun (3,000 rounds). It was replaced by the BTR-70.

C-3: a yellowish, solid plastic explosive of pre–Vietnam War vintage, used in Mk-135 satchel charges

C-4: a white plastic explosive

C-5A: the U.S. Air Force's largest transport plane

C-130: Hercules turboprop transport aircraft, originally made by Lockheed in 1951 and still flying all over the world

C-141: a jet transport with a range of up to five thousand miles

CCT: Combat Control Team—a team of Air Force personnel organized, trained, and equipped to locate, identify, and mark drop/landing zones; provide limited weather observations; install and operate navigational aids and air traffic control communications necessary to guide aircraft to drop/landing zones; and control air traffic at these zones

CINC: Commander IN Chief. The commander in chief of a Navy unit, or the president of the United States. A Navy CINC is usually of flag rank (admiral) and is in charge of a large area, command, or fleet.

CINCLANT: Commander IN Chief, AtLANTic

CINCLANTFLT: Commander IN Chief, AtLANTic FLeeT

CINCPAC: Commander IN Chief, PACific

CINCPACFLT: Commander IN Chief, PACfic FLeeT

CNO: Chief of Naval Operations

CQC: close quarters combat

CUTVEE: a cut-down Humvee without a top, doors, or windows; also known as M-988 cargo/troop carrier

CVIC: Aircraft Carrier Intelligence Center

DSS: Diplomatic Security Service. As federal agents, all DSS special agents have the power to arrest, carry firearms, and serve arrest warrants.

EC-130: a C-130 configured by the Navy (or Air Force) as a command/control/communications (C^3) aircraft

EOD: Explosives Ordinance Disposal

ESCAPE AND EVASION (E & E): the procedures and operations which downed pilots and SEAL snipers use to avoid hostile forces and return to base

FOB: forward operating base

FOUR-STRIPER: U.S. Navy captain (equal in rank to a colonel)

GRS: Global Response Staff (CIA)

HAHO: High Altitude, High Opening. Refers to parachute jumping.

HALO: High Altitude, Low Opening. Refers to parachute jumping.

HK: Heckler and Koch, make of firearm commonly used by Special Operations forces in various makes, including 9 mm submachine gun

HRT: Hostage Rescue Team

HUMINT: HUMan INTelligence, information gathered on a subject by people on the ground, either trained intelligence specialists or locals

IBL: Inflatable Boat, Large

IBS: Inflatable Boat, Small

IED: Improvised Explosive Devices

JSOC: Joint Special Operations Command; it commands Special Mission Units that include SEAL Team Six, Delta Force, and the air force's Twenty-Fourth Special Tactics Squadron.

JTF: Joint Task Force

KIA: Killed In Action

KNOT: one knot equals roughly 1.15 miles per hour

LAW: Light Antitank Weapon that fires one 66 mm unguided rocket. Replaced by the AT-4.

LITTLE BIRD: special operations light helicopters. Armament includes guns, rockets, and missiles.

LOADOUT: the equipment, munitions, and materials for an operation or exercise. A loadout can include all the weapons, ammunition, and equipment used by a single man or by an entire unit.

LST: Lightweight Satellite Terminal; an encrypted radio that can send burst packets to a satellite for fast relay

Glossary

LZ: Landing Zone

M60: a machine gun that fires 7.62 mm ammunition

MI6: a basic .223-caliber weapon, used in Vietnam

MC-130: USAF special operations aircraft

MNF: MultiNational Force

MOB-6: Mobility-6; SEAL Two's counterterror unit, a precursor of SEAL Team Six

MP5: an HK submachine gun favored by CT units including SEAL Team Six and GSG-9

NAVY PLATFORMS: ships and other assets of the U.S. Navy used to launch or go to during an operation

NCO: NonCommissioned Officer

NVDS: Night Vision Devices. Also NVGs: Night Vision Goggles. Electro-optical devices that are handheld, weapons mounted, or worn over the eyes to magnify or convert available light and allow vision at night.

OPSEC: OPerational SECurity. Very important in black ops.

P-3 ORION: Navy spy plane

PEARY, CAMP: CIA training facility near Williamsburg, Virginia, also known as the Farm

PLASTIQUE: plastic explosive (see **C-4**)

RH-53D: Pave Low special operations chopper

RPG: Rocket-Propelled Grenade (Soviet-made)

SAS: British Special Air Service. Motto: "Who dares, wins."

SATCOM: SATellite COMmunications

SCIF: Special Classified Intelligence Facility. A secure room that cannot be eavesdropped on using electronic or human means

SDV: Swimmer Delivery Vehicle

SEALS: the Navy's Sea-Air-Land units

SECDEF: SECretary of DEFense

SECNAV: SECretary of the NAVy

SFOD-D: Special Forces Operational Detachment–Delta (Delta Force).

SIGINT: SIGnals INTelligence. Intelligence gathered by intercepting signals between people and intercepting electronic signals

SNARE: horse-collar loop used for snatching SEALs from the water into an IBL

SOF: Special Operations Force

SPECWAR: Special Warfare

STAB: SEAL Tactical Assault Boat

TAD: Temporary Additional Duty (in SEAL slang: Traveling Around Drunk)

TASK FORCE 160: nicknamed the "Night Stalkers," this army helicopter unit usually operates at night, flying fast and low, to avoid radar detection

TAT: Terrorist Action Team

TECHINT: TECHnical INTelligence

TRIDENT: the common name for the naval special warfare insignia. It is a large, gold, uniform device made up of four parts: the anchor, which symbolizes the Navy; Neptune's three-pronged trident, which symbolizes the underwater world; a cocked flintlock pistol that shows the Team's constant preparedness for war; and behind it all is the bald eagle, symbol of the United States of America.

UDT: Underwater Demolition Team. The frogmen, ancestors of the SEALs.

WARCOM (also **SPECWARCOM** and **NAVSPECWARCOM**): the Navy Special Warfare Command, the overall command structure for the Navy SEAL Teams and all their attached units

WIA: Wounded In Action

WMD: Weapons of Mass Destruction. Nuclear, chemical, or biological weapons that will affect an area or population far out of proportion to the physical size of the weapon

WPS (also **WILLY PETERS**): White Phosphorous grenades

XO: Executive Officer

ZULU: Greenwich Mean Time (GMT) designator, used in all formal military communications

Bibliography

Bahmanyar, Mir. (2004). *Afghanistan Cave Complexes 1979–2004.* Oxford, UK: Osprey.

———. (2003). *U.S. Army Ranger 1983–2002.* New York, NY: Osprey.

———. (2005). *U.S. Navy SEALs.* New York, NY: Osprey.

Bergen, Peter L. (2006). *The Osama bin Laden I Know: An Oral History of al Qaeda's Leader.* New York, NY: Free Press.

Berntsen, Gary, and Ralph Pezzullo. (2005). *Jawbreaker: The Attack on bin Laden and Al-Qaeda.* New York, NY: Crown.

Bishop, Chris. (2003). *Bell UH-1 Huey "Slicks" 1962–75.* Oxford, UK: Osprey.

———. (2006). *Huey Cobra Gunships.* New York, NY: Osprey.

Blehm, Eric. (2012). *Fearless: The Undaunted Courage and Ultimate Sacrifice of Navy SEAL Team Six Operator Adam Brown.* Colorado Springs, CO: WaterBrook Press.

Bodansky, Yossef. (1993). *Target America: Terrorism in the U.S. Today.* New York, NY: S.P.I. Books.

Bonner, Carolyn, and Kit Bonner. (2002). *U.S. Navy SEALs: The Quiet Professionals.* Atglen, PA: Schiffer.

Bowden, Mark. (2006). *Guests of the Ayatollah: The Iran Hostage Crisis.* New York, NY: Grove Press.

BIBLIOGRAPHY

Brisard, Jean-Charles, and Damien Martinez. (2005). *Zarqawi: The New Face of al-Qaeda*. New York, NY: Other Press.

Chalker, Dennis, with Kevin Dockery. (2011). *One Perfect Op: An Insider's Account of the Navy SEAL Special Warfare Teams*. New York, NY: Harper Paperbacks.

Cole, Roger, and Richard Belfield. (2011). *SAS Operation Storm: Nine Men Against Four Hundred in Britain's Secret War*. London, UK: Hodder and Stoughton.

Coll, Steve. (2004). *Ghost Wars: The Secret History of the CIA, Afghanistan, and bin Laden, from the Soviet Invasion to September 10, 2001*. New York, NY: Penguin Press.

Couch, Dick. (2005). *Down Range: Navy SEALs in the War on Terrorism*. New York, NY: Crown.

———. (2003). *The Warrior Elite: The Forging of SEAL Class 228*. New York, NY: Three Rivers Press.

Crile, George. (2003). *Charlie Wilson's War*. New York, NY: Atlantic Monthly Press.

Denver, Rorke, and Ellis Henican. (2013) *Damn Few: Making the Modern SEAL Warrior*. New York, NY: Hyperion.

Dockery, Kevin. (2004). *Weapons of the Navy SEALs*. New York, NY: Berkley.

Exum, Andrew. (2004). *This Man's Army: A Soldier's Story from the Front Lines of the War on Terrorism*. New York, NY: Gotham Books.

Fawcett, Bill, ed. (1996). *Hunters and Shooters: An Oral History of the U.S. Navy SEALs in Vietnam*. New York, NY: Avon Books.

Feith, Douglas J. (2008). *War and Decision: Inside the Pentagon at the Dawn of the War on Terrorism*. New York, NY: HarperCollins.

Fury, Dalton. (2009). *Kill bin Laden: A Delta Force Commander's Account of the Hunt for the World's Most Wanted Man*. New York, NY: St. Martin's Griffin.

Grau, Lester W., and Michael A. Gress, trans. and ed. (2002). *The Soviet-Afghan War: How a Superpower Fought and Lost*. Lawrence, KS: University Press of Kansas.

Grossman, Dave. (1996). *On Killing: The Psychological Cost of Learning to Kill in War and Society*. New York, NY: Back Bay Books.

Halberstadt, Hans. (2006). *U.S. Navy SEALs*. St. Paul, MN: Zenith Press.

Hollenbeck, Cliff, and Dick Couch. (2003). *To Be a U.S. Navy SEAL*. Minneapolis, MN: Zenith Press.

Hull, Edmund J. (2011). *High-Value Target: Countering al Qaeda in Yemen*. Washington, DC: Potomac Books.

Isaacson, Walter, and Evan Thomas. (1986). *The Wise Men: Six Friends and the World They Made*. New York, NY: Simon & Schuster.

Kaplan, Fred. (2013). *The Insurgents: David Petraeus and the Plot to Change the American Way of War*. New York, NY: Simon & Schuster.

Kelly, Orr. (1996). *Never Fight Fair!: Inside the Legendary U.S. Navy SEALs*. New York, NY: Pocket Books.

Kyle, Chris, Scott McEwen, and Jim DeFelice. (2012). *American Sniper: The Autobiography of the Most Lethal Sniper in U.S. Military History*. New York, NY: William Morrow.

Kyle, James H., and John Robert Eidson. (2002). *The Guts to Try: The Untold Story of the Iran Hostage Rescue Mission by the On-Scene Desert Commander*. New York, NY: Ballantine Books.

Landau, Alan M., and Frieda W. Landau. (1999). *U.S. Special Forces*. Osceola, WI: MBI.

Larson, Chuck, ed. (2008). *Heroes Among Us: Firsthand Accounts of Combat from America's Most Decorated Warriors in Iraq and Afghanistan*. New York, NY: NAL Caliber.

Lawrence, Richard Russell, ed. (2006). *The Mammoth Book of Special Ops: The 40 Most Dangerous Special Operations of Modern Times.* New York, NY: Carroll and Graf.

Luttrell, Marcus, and Patrick Robinson. (2007). *Lone Survivor: The Eyewitness Account of Operation Redwing and the Lost Heroes of Seal Team 10.* New York, NY: Little, Brown.

Marcinko, Richard, and John Weisman. (1993). *Rogue Warrior: The Explosive Autobiography of the Controversial Death-Defying Founder of the U.S. Navy's Top Secret Counterterrorist Unit—Seal Team Six.* New York, NY: Pocket Books.

Miller, David. (2002). *The Illustrated Directory of Special Forces.* St. Paul, MN: MBI.

Moore, Robin. (2004). *Hunting Down Saddam: The Inside Story of the Search and Capture.* New York, NY: St. Martin's Press.

Murphy, Jack, and Brandon Webb. (2013). *Benghazi, The Definitive Report.* New York, NY: HarperCollins.

Naylor, Sean. (2005). *Not a Good Day to Die: The Untold Story of Operation Anaconda.* New York, NY: Berkley.

Omrani, Bijan, and Matthew Leeming, eds. (2005). *Afghanistan: A Companion and Guide.* New York, NY: Odyssey Books and Guides.

Peters, Rudolph. (1996). *Jihad in Classical and Modern Islam.* Princeton, NJ: Markus Wiener.

Pfarrer, Chuck. (2011). *SEAL Target Geronimo: The Inside Story of the Mission to Kill Osama bin Laden.* New York, NY: St. Martin's Press.

———. (2004) *Warrior Soul: The Memoir of a Navy SEAL.* Toronto, Ontario: Random House.

Pushies, Fred J. (2005). *Night Stalkers: 160th Special Operations Aviation Regiment (Airborne).* St. Paul, MN: Zenith Press.

Rashid, Ahmed. (2000). *Taliban: Militant Islam, Oil, and Fundamentalism in Central Asia*. New Haven, CT: Yale University Press.

Rottman, G. (2006). *Viet Cong and NVA Tunnels and Fortifications of the Vietnam War*. New York, NY: Osprey.

Schroen, Gary C. (2005). *First In: An Insider's Account of How the CIA Spearheaded the War on Terror in Afghanistan*. New York, NY: Presidio Press/Ballantine Books.

Smucker, Philip. (2004). *Al Qaeda's Great Escape: The Military and the Media on Terror's Trail*. Dulles, VA: Brassey's.

Temple-Raston, Dina. (2007). *The Jihad Next Door: The Lackawanna Six and Rough Justice in an Age of Terror*. New York, NY: PublicAffairs.

Tenet, George. (2007). *At the Center of the Storm: My Years at the CIA*. New York, NY: HarperCollins.

Waller, Douglas C. (1995). *The Commandos: The Inside Story of America's Secret Soldiers*. New York, NY: Dell.

Wasdin, Howard E., and Stephen Templin. (2012). *SEAL Team Six: Memoirs of an Elite Navy SEAL Sniper*. New York, NY: St. Martin's Griffin.

Weisman, John. (2011). *KBL: Kill bin Laden: A Novel Based on True Events*. New York, NY: William Morrow.

Wells, Tim. (1985). *444 Days: The Hostages Remember*. San Diego, CA: Harcourt Brace Jovanovich.

Wright, Lawrence. (2006). *The Looming Tower: Al-Qaeda and the Road to 9/11*. New York, NY: Alfred A. Knopf.

Zaloga, Steven J. (2006). *Scud Ballistic Missile and Launch Systems 1955–2005*. New York, NY: Osprey.

Acknowledgments

We would like to thank our researchers and assistants, Martin Moorse Wooster, Lisa Merriam (of Merriam Associates, LLC.), Rhiannon Burruss, Tonya Johnson, and Anastassiya Ravdugina.

We'd also like to thank our literary agent, Ian Kleinert, at Objective Entertainment.

We'd like to thank our editor Kate Hartson.

Additional thanks are due to: David Martosko of the *Daily Mail* (U.K.), John Tamny at Forbes, John Fund, and James Taranto of the *Wall Street Journal*.

We also thank Nathaniel C. Moffat of American Media Institute.

We would also like to thank all current and former members of the United States Navy SEAL Teams that agreed to be interviewed for this work. One Team—One fight!